MORALITY AND CULTURAL DIFFERENCES

MORALITY AND
CULTURAL DIFFERENCES

John W. Cook

New York   Oxford

OXFORD UNIVERSITY PRESS

1999

Oxford University Press

Oxford New York
Athens Auckland Bangkok Bogotá Buenos Aires Calcutta
Cape Town Chennai Dar es Salaam Delhi Florence Hong Kong Istanbul
Karachi Kuala Lumpur Madrid Melbourne Mexico City Mumbai
Nairobi Paris São Paulo Singapore Taipei Tokyo Toronto Warsaw

and associated companies in
Berlin Ibadan

Copyright © 1999 by John W. Cook

Published by Oxford University Press, Inc.
198 Madison Avenue, New York, New York 10016

Oxford is a registered trademark of Oxford University Press

Library of Congress Cataloging-in-Publication Data
Cook, John W. (John Webber), 1930–
Morality and cultural differences / John W. Cook.
p.   cm.
ISBN 0-19-512679-3
1. Ethics.   2. Anthropology.   3. Ethical relativism.
I. Title
BJ52.C66   1999
171'.7—dc21   98-27685

1 2 3 4 5 6 7 8 9

Printed in the United States of America
on acid-free paper

For Annie

Preface

This book grew out of the years I spent thinking about moral philosophy while teaching at the University of Oregon. I had the good fortune to have colleagues there who shared my view that this area of philosophy was in need of a complete overhaul. Our discussions, spanning a dozen years, yielded many new points of departure, some of which will be found in part III of this book. Looking back on those discussions, I find it difficult to sort out which ideas were originally mine and which I owe, in part at least, to the others. Accordingly, I hereby give my thanks to those colleagues who in some degree shaped—or stimulated—my thinking about moral philosophy: Robert Paul, Joe Stephens, Peter Kushner, and William Davie. I hope they will find this book original in its entirety, but I will happily concede whatever insights they may regard as their own.

I wish to thank also my wife, Annie, who prodded me into publishing this material. She not only helped with the typing but wielded her red pencil with authority and precision throughout several drafts. Without her considerable assistance, I might never have completed this project.

Parts of several chapters of this book, or the ideas contained therein, I have previously published. The articles drawn from are the following: "Moral Relativism: An Ethnocentric Notion," in *The Philosophy of Society*, ed. Rodger Beehler and Alan Drengson (Methuen, 1978), pp. 289–315; and "Is There Evidence for Moral Relativism?" in *Philosophy and Science*, ed. Frederick Mosedale (Prentice-Hall, 1979), pp. 306–14.

Captiva, Florida   J.W.C
July 1996

Contents

The problems [of philosophy] are solved, not by giving new information, but by arranging what we have always known.
—Ludwig Wittgenstein, *Philosophical Investigations*

And the end of all our exploring
Will be to arrive where we started
And know the place for the first time.
—T. S. Eliot, "Little Gidding"

MORALITY AND CULTURAL DIFFERENCES

Introduction

Moral relativism, sometimes called "cultural relativism," is a philosophical doctrine about the nature of morality. Yet the principal proponents of this doctrine have been anthropologists rather than philosophers. They claim that their studies of various cultures have enabled them to show that morality is relative to each culture, which implies, among other things, that we cannot rightly pass moral judgment on members of other cultures except by their own cultural standards, which may differ from ours.

For many years this doctrine was regarded as an arcane academic subject, and the general public took little notice of it. This is no longer the case. With the increased influence of Christian fundamentalism in politics, the debate over moral relativism has created nearly as much public controversy as did the debate over Darwin's theory of evolution during the 1920s.

The reason for such controversy becomes evident when relativists make explicit the implications of their doctrine. Here, for example, is the way one anthropologist, John R. Cole, states the matter:

> Cultural relativism . . . is the idea that one culture is not superior to and should not judge others. It may be the single most influential anthropological precept. . . . To relativists, Western society, American politics and capitalism, and Judaeo-Christian ideas of morality are not absolute or perfect any more than is New Guinea tribal life. To people committed to absolute standards defined by the will of God (*or* nature), relativism is a humbling, subversive doctrine. It removes an individual's group from the pinnacle of culture, just as evolution's demonstration that people are simply one more variety of animal removes humans from the center of life.[1]

Cole is unquestionably right in declaring that many people regard moral relativism as a "subversive doctrine." This was the reaction of, for example, Congressman William Dannemeyer of California in remarks he made several years ago in the U.S. House of Representatives. He had risen to demand

3

that a congressman from Massachusetts be expelled from the House because he had permitted certain homosexual activities to go on in his home. Mr. Dannemeyer spoke, in part, as follows:

> When matters of this nature come up . . . we must stand and affirm the existence of [the] standards of our society, because to put the issue in perspective, what is going on in America is a cultural war. It has reached an increasing intensity in the last twenty-five years, because we have two conflicting philosophies struggling for dominance in our society. The Judeo-Christian ethic on which this Nation was founded says very clearly that there are fixed standards which God gave to man to govern people in any society. The philosophy of moral relativism, on the other hand, says that there are no standards, that man himself is capable of establishing any rule at any time, . . . do anything you want so long as the perception is that you are not harming anybody else.[2]

Mr. Dannemeyer went on to say that moral relativism and the Judeo-Christian ethic are "two philosophies in conflict."

The academic debate over moral relativism, carried on by both philosophers and anthropologists, has a long history, and one might think that the matter would have been settled by now. It has not, and one reason for this is that those engaged in the debate have concerned themselves with either the philosophical or the anthropological aspect of the doctrine. This division of labor has produced nothing but misunderstandings, and it is clear that if we are to arrive at a definitive appraisal of moral relativism, we must examine both the philosophical and anthropological issues involved. Accordingly, in part II of this book we will consider the claims made by anthropologists and will take up in part III the philosophical issues involved.

One thing we will quickly discover is that moral relativism is an elusive doctrine, in the sense that it cannot be easily formulated and is readily misunderstood. (For example, Mr. Dannemeyer declares that a relativistic view of morality implies that "there are no standards" so that you may "do anything you want" provided you do others no harm, but proponents of moral relativism insist that this is not so.) We must therefore proceed patiently with this subject. By resisting the impulse to rush in either to attack or defend moral relativism, we may hope to understand the issues better than either the critics or the proponents of this doctrine have. Only then will we have the right to make up our minds about it.

THE CLAIMS OF MORAL RELATIVISM

1

Moral Relativism versus Moral Absolutism

When we try to think about philosophical issues, it often happens that we end in confusion and frustration or become embroiled in futile partisan debates. The best way to avoid such unhappy endings is to make sure that we are free of misconceptions at the beginning of our inquiries. So before asking whether moral relativism is true, we will do well to begin with two preliminary questions whose answers will help us avoid some misunderstandings: (i) What reasons do moral relativists claim to have for embracing their view of morality? and (ii) What exactly does it mean to say that morality is relative to a culture? I will take up the first of these questions in this chapter and the second in chapter 2.

To address the first question, we may begin with an observation no one will dispute—that proponents of moral relativism recommend their doctrine as an alternative to moral absolutism and that they do so because they believe moral absolutism to be fatally flawed. So our first question can be answered by discovering what problem relativists claim to find in moral absolutism. But, first, what is moral absolutism?

The absolutist is one who holds that there are moral principles (or rules or standards) that apply to all people everywhere, even to those who do not acknowledge these particular principles but conduct themselves, instead, according to other (false) principles. Moreover, the absolutist is not content to say: "It's certain that there *are* moral principles that apply to everyone, regardless of their culture, but we don't know what they are." On the contrary, his concern is a practical one: He holds that people can recognize or discover these true universal principles and be guided by them both in deciding what their own conduct should be and in judging the conduct of others. Moreover, the absolutist (or at least the absolutist of concern to the relativist) is confident that he is already cognizant of such principles, so that he is equipped to pass judgment on anyone.[1]

It is the absolutist's confidence in this matter that distresses the relativist, for the relativist insists that it is a mistake for anyone to think that he knows what is right and wrong for everyone everywhere, including the people of cultures very different from his own. This alleged mistake has been given the name "ethnocentrism." Thus we find Alfred Kroeber, an anthropologist, explaining that ethnocentrism is the "tendency . . . to see one's in-group as always right and all out-groups as wrong wherever they differ."[2] This cannot be entirely accurate, for there are, of course, differences among cultures that are not going to elicit condemnation. People whose custom it is to greet one another with a bow are surely not going to think that those who shake hands, instead, are doing something morally wrong. So Kroeber's explanation needs some qualification. The cases he had in mind, presumably, are those in which there is some actual moral disagreement regarding a given sort of conduct. We will be accused of ethnocentrism, then, if we condemn as wrong not only those actions that occur in and violate the moral principles of our culture but also those *same* actions when they occur in another culture, even if no one in that culture regards these actions as violating a moral principle. So relativists would say that Europeans were guilty of ethnocentrism when they condemned as immoral the "wife-swapping" practiced by the Greenland Eskimos, who regarded the practice as perfectly natural.

It is this attitude of moral superiority, this sort of criticism across cultural lines, that relativists aim to combat. As Kroeber puts it, moral relativism leads to "tolerance and . . . diminution of ethnocentrism."[3] And it allegedly achieves this result by showing that absolutists are mistaken in thinking one can know which (universal) moral principles are the right or true ones. So the question we want answered is this: How, according to relativists, has it been shown that this *is* a mistake?

Melville Herskovits, an anthropologist and staunch defender of relativism, answers this question as follows: "The principle of cultural relativism derives from a vast array of factual data gained from the application of techniques in field study that have permitted us to penetrate the underlying value-systems of societies having diverse customs."[4] Similarly, Kroeber and Kluckhohn tell us that "sincere comparison of cultures leads quickly to recognition of their 'relativity.' "[5] The claim, then, is that the relativity of morals has been demonstrated by the fieldwork of cultural anthropologists. But what facts have been turned up in this way, and what bearing, if any, do they have on a philosophical theory of morality?

Relativists often explain this matter by saying simply that anthropological studies have shown that there are different moralities among the world's various cultures. This is not, however, an adequate formulation of their claim, for it does not make explicit the way in which these allegedly different moralities differ. A more adequate formulation was given by Edward Westermarck, who explained that cultures have different moralities if "a mode of conduct which among one people is condemned as wrong is among other people viewed with indifference or enjoined as a duty."[6] We may find that this definition requires further examination, but for the moment we may take it that this is the sort of difference relativists have in mind when they claim that there are "different moralities."

The sort of evidence put forth to demonstrate that there are different moralities can be illustrated by the following passage from Christoph von Fürer-Haimendorf's book *Morals and Merit*:

> Students of German drama and connoisseurs of Italian opera are familiar with the scenes in which Don Carlos confesses to the horrified Marquess of Posa his love for the queen, the young wife of his father Philip II. To a Western audience the situation of a son passionately in love with his step-mother appears fraught with tragedy, and it seems inevitable that the drama should end with the hero's doom. A Tibetan audience would not understand what all the excitement is about, for Tibetans see no harm in the sharing of one wife by father and son. An arrangement which one society considers the height of immorality, is thought natural and innocuous by another. Similarly, a European peasant, beheading a woman from a neighboring village whom he happened to encounter on her way home from the fields, would be locked up as a criminal lunatic; whereas in a Naga village a youth returning with a human head captured under similar circumstances earns the insignia of a successful headhunter. Examples of such extreme differences in the moral assessment of conduct could easily be multiplied.[7]

Fürer-Haimendorf goes on to remark that philosophers, in constructing their moral theories,

> did not pay much attention to the fact that two persons of different cultural background may react to identical circumstances in a totally different manner, even though each may be convinced of the righteousness of his conduct. . . . Most moral philosophers had little knowledge of ethnographic data relating to the conduct and beliefs of pre-literate populations, and in their analyses of moral concepts there was hence only limited scope for any transcultural comparisons.[8]

Herskovits agrees with this assessment, saying that relativism is "a scientific, inductive attack on an age-old philosophical problem, using fresh, cross-cultural data, hitherto not available to scholars."[9]

What science, in the form of cross-cultural comparisons, is supposed to have established is that there are cultures having different moralities. But it still needs to be shown how this supposed fact proves that moral absolutism is false. I have quoted Kroeber and Kluckhohn as saying that "sincere comparison of cultures leads quickly to recognition of their relativity." But what is this "quick recognition"? They seem to be saying that the discovery that there are different moralities is *by itself* sufficient to show that morality is relative. But is this true?

If moral absolutists held that there is but one set of moral standards to be found in all of the world's cultures, then absolutism might be quickly disposed of by the following argument: "It has been discovered that there are different moralities in the world, so absolutism, which denies this, is false." In fact, however, absolutists do not hold a view that can be disposed of so easily. What they hold is not that the same set of moral standards is accepted in all cultures, but rather that morality consists of a single set of *true* moral standards that apply to people of every culture—even if some fail to accept these standards and conduct themselves, instead, according to other, false standards (or none at all). This, then, is the view that relativists must somehow dispose of, and it is obvious that they cannot do so by simply claiming that different moralities have been found among the world's cultures, for that is not something the absolutist denies. This being so, some additional argument is needed, and the recognition of relativity cannot be as "quick" as some have supposed.

Just what the relativist's additional argument could be is not at all obvious, and one rarely finds relativists stating the argument explicitly. Herskovits is one of the rare exceptions. He states the additional argument as follows:

> Cultural relativism developed because the facts of differences . . . in moral systems, plus our knowledge of the mechanisms of cultural learning, forced the realization of the problem of finding valid cross-cultural norms. In every case where criteria to evaluate the ways of different peoples have been proposed, the question has at once posed itself: "Whose standards?" The force of the enculturative experience channels all judgments. In fact, the need for a cultural relativistic point of view has become apparent because of the realization that there is no way to play this game of making judgments across cultures except with loaded dice.[10]

In this passage the relativist's additional argument is first hinted at in the phrase "plus our knowledge of the mechanisms of cultural learning" and is then made explicit in the remark: "The force of the enculturative experience channels all judgments." Herskovits is saying, in part, that we acquire our morality from the culture in which we grow up. For example, a Naga tribesman is taught that it is honorable to engage in head-hunting, while Europeans are taught that killing innocent people is wrong. But how is this relevant to a refutation of moral absolutism?

Notice, first of all, that absolutists would be missing the point if they were to reply to Herskovits: "The fact that people acquire their morality from the culture in which they grow up does not even begin to disprove our claim that the moral principles taught in some cultures are true while those taught in others are false." Such a reply would miss the point because Herskovits's argument is aimed, not simply at the claim that there *are* true universal moral principles, but at the absolutist's claim to *know* which principles are the true ones. What needs explaining, then, is this: If Herskovits is right about how we acquire morality, how does this undermine the absolutist's claim to have knowledge of (universal) moral principles?

Herskovits is addressing this question when he explains that relativism is "an epistemology that derives from a recognition of the force of enculturative conditioning in shaping thought and behavior."[11] His characterization of relativism as "an epistemology"—a theory of knowledge—is essential to the argument. For this makes it clear that the relativist's argument, when stated fully, runs as follows:

> *If* we had acquired our moral views in the way we acquire scientific views, namely, by means of a rational fact-finding procedure, then we could criticize other cultures wherever their morality differs from ours, just as we criticize, for example, the idea that illness is caused by witchcraft. But we do *not* acquire our moral views by discovering objective moral facts. (This becomes obvious when we realize that moral principles differ from culture to culture, for this state of affairs would not exist if there were a realm of objective moral facts *everyone* can discern—as everyone can discern that the sky is blue.) Moral principles are acquired, not by any *rational* process, but by the *causal* process of "enculturative conditioning," that is, they are impressed upon us in subtle ways by the culture in which we are raised. We do not, therefore, have any grounds—any good *reasons*—for holding the moral views that we do hold. And that being so, it is a mistake to think that our moral views are both (a) *known* by us to be true and (b) apply to people of other cultures who don't share our moral views.

This, then, is the relativists' argument (I will refer to it henceforth as their "Fully Developed Argument"), and in it we can see the role played by the claim that empirical research has shown that there are different moralities among the world's cultures. This claim is alleged to support the further claim that we acquire our morality, not in any rational way, but by a causal process of "enculturative conditioning."[12]

This claim about how we acquire morality is the key to the relativists' Fully Developed Argument, and when Herskovits addresses that argument to the absolutist, he states it as follows: "Eternal verities only seem so because we have been taught to regard them as such; . . . every people, whether it expresses them or not, lives in devotion to verities whose eternal nature is as real to them as are those of Euroamerican culture to Euroamericans."[13] Stated somewhat more fully, the argument is this:

> You believe that there are universal moral truths, but you believe this only because you imagine yourself to *know* that certain principles are indeed true. And yet you are in exactly the same position as the people of other cultures who imagine that they, too, know that their principles (which conflict with yours) are true. But since you regard their "knowledge" as illusory, you must admit that yours is too, for your certitude has the same source as theirs, that is, you, like they, learned your morality from your own culture. You must agree, then, that there is no knowledge whatsoever of universal moral principles and hence must also agree (unless you hold the absurd view that universal moral principles exist but are never known to anyone) that such principles do not exist. So the most you can claim to know is that in *your* culture certain conduct—stealing, for example— is condemned as wrong.

This piece of reasoning constitutes the answer to the first of the questions posed at the beginning of this chapter: What reasons do moral relativists claim to have for embracing their view of morality? Whether this reasoning is sound is a matter we will take up in later chapters, but let us now turn to the second of our preliminary questions: What exactly does it mean to say that morality is relative to a culture?

2

Moral Relativism:

A Statement of the Doctrine

We must now try to formulate a positive account of the relativists' version of morality, for we have thus far been concerned only to understand their reasons for opposing absolutism and have made no attempt to say what account relativists would put in its place. Relativists, as we have seen, reject the absolutists' view that the moral judgments we make about people ("You shouldn't have lied to him") are grounded in universal principles (e.g. "Lying is wrong") which we *know* to be true. But which part, or parts, of this absolutist version do relativists reject? Do they want to say that we have no knowledge of moral principles or do they want to say that we have knowledge of moral principles but that these principles are not universal, that is, not applicable to everyone regardless of their cultural affiliation?

Because relativists seldom give an explicit answer to this question, they are often misunderstood. Critics of moral relativism often claim that it is a form of moral *skepticism,* that relativism denies that we have *knowledge* of moral principles. But such an interpretation is surely mistaken. After all, relativists claim that anthropologists, by studying various cultures, have discovered that these cultures have different moral principles (or values), and in making this claim they are implying that moral principles *are* knowable— at least to anthropologists. But if they can be known to anthropologists, they are surely known also to the members of the cultures studied by anthropologists. So relativists, rather than saying that we have *no knowledge* of moral principles, are saying that while each of us *knows* what is right and what is wrong, moral principles are not universal but pertain only to members of a particular culture. What Euro-Americans *know* is that, for example, it is wrong for members of *their culture* to steal or commit murder and that in *their culture* honesty is counted a virtue. This is not, of course, any sort of skepticism.[1]

On the relativists' view, then, moral principles are—in some respects, anyway—like certain rules we follow in driving a car. In England the rules of the road prescribe that one drive on the left, rather than on the right, as in the United States. Drivers typically know what these rules prescribe, and when an Englishman says of someone in his own country, "He was driving on the wrong side," he is drawing on his knowledge of these rules. Moreover, what he *means* in saying "He was driving on the wrong side" is that the man was driving on the side that is wrong *in England*. This rule is, of course, entirely arbitrary, in the sense that it would be absurd to think that we could discover which country has the correct rule and absurd also for an American to say that Englishmen, by driving on the left, are regularly driving on the wrong side of the road.

In that sense, according to relativists, moral principles, too, are arbitrary. When we say, for example, that a neighbor of ours did something wrong, because he cheated someone, all that we can *rightly* mean by this is that he violated a precept of *our* culture. It would, therefore, be just as absurd for us to think that the Eskimos' wife-swapping is immoral as it would be for an Englishman to think that Americans, when driving in their own country, regularly drive on the wrong side of the road. And it would be absurd for the same reason: one can do something wrong or immoral only by violating the rules or principles of *one's own* culture. As William Graham Sumner put it: " 'Immoral' never means anything but contrary to the mores of the time and place."[2]

What distinguishes relativists from absolutists, then, is the following. Proponents of absolutism will say, for example, "Head-hunting is wrong," and mean by this that people who engage in head-hunting are acting immorally even if their culture condones or requires head-hunting. The relativist, on the other hand, maintains that saying such a thing is perfectly absurd; it makes no sense to say, without reference to a particular culture, that the taking of heads is wrong. Head-hunting is not wrong in and of itself; rather, someone has done wrong in taking human heads only in case his culture prohibits it. If I think to myself, "Head-hunting is wrong; it's just *wrong*!" then I am thinking as confusedly as an Englishman who thought, "Driving on the right, as Americans do, is wrong; it's absolutely wrong!"

What, then, is the appropriate way of stating the relativist's positive account of morality? The most accurate statement of it, I think, would be the following:

> Because no action can rightly be thought of as (or said to be) wrong in and of itself, that is, absolutely wrong, a moral principle cannot be properly formulated in an entirely general way (e.g., "Head-hunting is wrong"); rather, a moral principle is properly formulated only when a "relativizing clause" is attached to it, so that you would have something like "*For Americans* headhunting is wrong" or "*Americans* are morally obligated to do such and such."

This explication of moral relativism, then, provides the answer to the second of our preliminary questions: What does it *mean* to say that moral principles (or values) are relative? So if relativism is true, a person's conduct can rightly be judged according to a given moral principle only if he or she is covered by its relativizing clause, as all Americans are in the two examples just given.

This definition of moral relativity speaks of the *proper* formulation of moral principles, and that raises the following question. Are relativists saying: "The proper formulation makes explicit a relativizing clause that was already inherent in the moral principle"? Or are they saying: "In a properly formulated principle something new—the relativizing clause—has been added to a principle which, as it stood, was not relativized"? Some critics assume that the former alternative is meant, and they then argue that, because of this, relativism is false. Bernard Williams, for example, writes:

> Relational relativism in ethics is excluded altogether. . . . [I]t is implausible to suppose that ethical conceptions of right or wrong have a logically inherent relativity to a given society. . . . When [a traditional] society is first exposed to another culture and invited to reflect, it cannot suddenly discover that there is an implicit relativization hidden in its language. . . . [W]hen they have never reflected or thought of an alternative to "us" . . . how could [relativizing clauses] have come into their language?[3]

Clearly, Williams believes that the first alternative provides the correct interpretation of relativism. What do relativists say? Herskovits, for example, was clearly embracing the other alternative when he spoke of "the ethnocentrism implicit in the particular value-systems of [any] society."[4] By this, I take it, he meant the following. When we make a moral judgment about the conduct of someone in our own community, as when we say to a man who is guilty of bigamy, "It was wrong of you to marry Ellen when you already had a wife," we are implying that it is wrong for *any* man to have more than one wife, *even where polygamy is the cultural norm*. If Herskovits were asked *how* we imply this, he would presumably answer: When we say that someone in our culture did something wrong, we are deriving this particular judgment from a general (nonrelativized) principle, such as "It is wrong to have more than one wife." So Herskovits, in speaking of the *ethnocentrism* implicit in a "value-system," was saying that our moral principles, in their original form, are *not* relativized. In Herskovits, then, we have a relativist who plainly rejects Williams's interpretation. He rejects the idea that there is "an implicit relativization" hidden in our language.

How, then, can Herskovits claim that morality is relative? Clearly, he must not be understood to be *describing* our moral principles, for if they are, as he says, implicitly ethnocentric, he can't mean that they are relative *as they stand*. What sort of claim, then, is he making? Presumably he would say that he is specifying how we *ought* to formulate moral principles if we are going to formulate them in accordance with what anthropologists have discovered.[5]

Now that we know what it means to say that moral principles are relative, we can see that certain common formulations of moral relativism are mistaken. One formulation attempts to explain the relativity of a moral principle in terms of the extent of its applicability, as when the disagreement between relativists and absolutists is explained as a disagreement about whether *all* people can be judged according to certain moral principles. Such an explanation is given by Elvin Hatch when he writes:

> Ethical relativism is generally conceived as standing at the opposite pole from absolutism, which is the position that there is a set of moral principles that are *universally* valid as standards of judgment. One absolutist ethical theory is the traditional Christian view that right and wrong are God-given, and that *all people* may be judged according to Christian values.[6]

To see what is wrong with this explanation, consider the following. Suppose that there are exactly two cultures in the world, X and Y, and that the people of X, but not the people of Y, hold the principle P. Absolutists maintain that if P is a moral principle it can be stated in an entirely general way: "It is wrong to do so-and-so." Relativists insist that the principle should be qualified by a relativizing clause that specifies the scope of its applicability, and they would say that in the circumstances I've described the relativizing clause would include the people of X but not those of Y. But let us suppose now that the people of Y come to adopt P. (Perhaps zealous missionaries from X are responsible for this.) So now *all* cultures espouse P, and *everyone's* conduct can now be judged according to P. But would the fact that P now applies to everyone make it an absolute (nonrelative) principle? No, for relativists would insist that it is still a mistake to state the principle in an entirely general way. They would insist that even in the circumstance in which P applies to every living person, the principle itself, to be correctly stated, must be qualified by a clause that restricts it to the culture *or cultures* involved. So the relativity of a principle has nothing to do with whether or not it applies to everyone. Hatch's mistake was to think that the disagreement between relativists and absolutists can be explained by using such phrases as "some people" and "all people."[7]

What Hatch meant to say, perhaps, is that relativists take the position that (a) there are, at present, people who are not Christians and (b) for *this* reason it's not true that *all* people may be judged according to Christian values. But even this would not be a correct formulation, for the relativist does not want the truth of his doctrine to depend on the happenstance that some people are not Christians or even on the happenstance that there is *no* set of moral principles that everyone accepts. Relativists would not, that is, want to allow that their doctrine would be false—and absolutism true—if there existed but one worldwide culture, so that the same set of moral rules applied to every living person. On the contrary, relativists would say that if we lived in a culturally homogeneous world, moral principles would still be relative because (i) they would prescribe conduct for only this existing (worldwide) culture, and (ii) it would be absurd to think that if some distinct culture later evolved, its principles would be defective insofar as they differed from ours.

There is another misleading phrase in the passage I quoted from Hatch, for he speaks of principles that are "universally valid as standards of judgment." This phrase—or simply the phrase "universally valid principles"—could mean "principles that are *universally accepted* (and are, for that reason, universally applicable)" or it could mean "principles that are *universally applicable* (even if they are not universally accepted)." So when relativism is said to reject the idea that *there are universally valid moral principles,* this is ambiguous because it might be understood in either of these ways. If fact, however, only the second meaning is appropriate: When Hatch says that relativists deny that "there is a set of moral principles that are *universally valid,*" this will not be true unless he means that relativists deny that there are principles that are *universally applicable* (even if they are not universally accepted). If the first meaning were appropriate, Hatch would be saying that relativists are claiming: There is no moral principle (or set of principles) that is accepted in all cultures, so there is none that applies to everyone. Such a claim would be false in a world with but one homogeneous culture, so relativists wouldn't care to make the claim. Nor would absolutists care to deny it.

One reason it is important to avoid ambiguity on this point is that if one fails to do so, one may make the mistake of thinking that relativism could be effectively challenged if it were discovered that some moral principles are "cultural universals," that is, accepted in all cultures. Some anthropologists have attempted to challenge moral relativism in just this way. There are, say these critics, at least *some* "cultural universals," such as a prohibition against incest. But this attempt at criticism is plainly misguided. For the relativist will reply as follows: A principle that is found to be accepted in all cultures is just as relative as a principle that is accepted in some but not all cultures, for (i) those that are universally accepted still prescribe conduct for only the members of presently existing cultures, and (ii) it would be absurd to think that if a new culture evolved tomorrow, it would be morally inferior if it did not incorporate those principles that are now universally accepted.

The alleged *relativity* of moral principles (or values) is not, then, the same thing as the absence of universal acceptance. So moral relativism has been misunderstood by everyone—including anthropologists—who thinks that limits could be placed on relativism by the discovery of "cultural universals." Let there be found as many cultural universals as you please, this discovery would not oblige relativists to modify their doctrine. The failure to realize this has evidently occurred because relativists undertake to support their doctrine by insisting that there are different moralities among the world's cultures. Someone who fails to follow the rest of the relativist's argument (the part about "enculturative conditioning") might then think that the relativist's doctrine amounts simply to the idea that there are different moralities and that the relativity of a moral principle comes to the same as its not being universally accepted. This, as we have seen, is a mistaken interpretation, but someone who failed to realize this could easily make the further mistake of thinking that the discovery of cultural universals would render relativism innocuous by showing that at least *some* sorts of conduct are absolutely wrong.

But wouldn't the discovery of cultural universals at least undermine the argument by which relativists support their conclusion? It might seem so, for relativists argue as follows:

> Moral principles are arbitrary because we acquire our moral views, not by means of any truth-finding procedure, but by the process of enculturative conditioning. That this is so is shown by the fact that peoples have different moralities, a fact impossible to account for on the view that there is a realm of objective moral truths that everyone can discern.

To this argument an absolutist might reply:

> If it were found that there are cultural universals—for example, that all cultures prohibit incest—this universal acceptance, even by the most isolated cultures, would have to be explained either as the result of an enormous coincidence or as the result of humans having a universal capacity for discovering moral truths, such as that incest is wrong. But of these two explanations, the first can be dismissed on the grounds that one simply cannot believe that a coincidence of that magnitude has occurred. We are obliged, then, to accept the second explanation: The existence of a universally held moral principle is the result of humans having a shared capacity for intuiting moral truths. And in that case, morality is not arbitrary, for if humans have indeed *discovered* that incest is wrong, then although some tribe might, through moral depravity, condone and engage in incest, we could say that those people are immoral, that they are (knowingly) doing something wrong.

Such an argument would, I think, leave the relativist unmoved, for he would most likely reply as follows:

> Let us suppose that in all cultures incest is regarded as wrong. We would then have to consider how people acquire this idea. But do people really think that they *discovered* that incest is wrong and that they can explain how they discovered this? Surely not! For when we observe people, we find that they are *taught* that incest is wrong: They are either told not to engage in it or they pick up the idea from seeing that no one does engage in incest or from seeing that those who do so are ostracized or punished. (That morality is acquired in this fashion is something anthropologists *could* have discovered even if all living people shared the same morality. So the fact that anthropologists, instead, inferred it from observations of how cultures differ in their moral principles is but an accident of history, not the essence of our argument.) In short, people learn that incest is wrong by the *same* process of enculturative conditioning that leads them to regard other forms of conduct as wrong, including conduct that is not everywhere judged according to the same moral principles. Therefore, whatever the explanation may be of the fact that incest is universally prohibited, we already know that it will not refute the argument for relativism.

We can explore this matter further by considering the other side of the coin: What would someone have to show in order to maintain with plausibility that some principle is absolute, rather than relative? Would it suffice to show that it is universally accepted? No, for the relativist will say that the principle, despite its universal acceptance, is relative to the culture or cultures which accept it. Would it suffice, then, to show in regard to a particular moral principle that it is not qualified by a relativizing clause specifying the scope of its application? Could a Christian, for example, show that "Adultery is wrong [or immoral]" is an absolute principle simply by pointing out that it is entirely *general* in its formulation? No, but this is a step in the right direction, for showing that its proper formulation is, in this sense, entirely general would be *part* of what is required for demonstrating that a principle is a moral absolute.

To see what more is required, let us consider the following. Suppose that someone (perhaps the ruler of some tribe) simply *invented* a generally worded principle, such as "It is immoral for people over the age of seventy to have sexual relations." Would moral absolutists allow that *this* principle is a moral absolute? They would not if they thought that it had merely been *invented* by someone. But now suppose that this principle came to be *accepted* by the members of this tribe—perhaps because the king tells his people that the gods have ordained it. In that case absolutists would say: "The mere fact that it has come to be *accepted* doesn't change things; it is still not an absolute moral truth." But consider what absolutists would say about the members of this tribe. Not only have these people accepted a principle which is *formulated* in an entirely general way, but they also *apply* it in an entirely general way, that is, they go about morally condemning *all* septuagenarians who engage in sex, and they are not dissuaded from this by the knowledge that people from other cultures protest that such conduct is *not* wrong (or immoral). So if absolutists are asked to characterize this, they will say that the members of this tribe *believe* that their principle is a moral absolute—even though it is not.

What this shows is that absolutists distinguish between principles that someone may *believe* to be moral absolutes and others which *are* moral absolutes. And from this we can infer that absolutists will say that a principle, in order to be a *genuine* moral absolute, must satisfy both of the following requirements: (i) it must be formulated in an entirely general way, so that *if* it is genuine (true) it is applicable to everyone, including any who may themselves accept the principle, and (ii) it must be shown that the principle is *known* (not merely believed) to be applicable, that is, that whoever violates the principle is a *genuine* wrongdoer and not merely deemed (arbitrarily) to be a wrongdoer. So if the absolutist is to present us with a bona fide example of an absolute moral truth, he has the burden of showing that his example fulfills both of these requirements.

It is, of course, the second requirement that presents a difficulty, for it means that someone who wants to produce a bona fide example of an absolute moral principle will have to show that it is *known* to be true. Suppose, for instance, that, when asked to give an example, an absolutist says, "Homosexual conduct is immoral." He must then be able to answer the question: How do you *know* it's immoral? This, of course, is very different from the question: Why do you *believe* it's immoral? He may believe that homosexual conduct is immoral because he "feels it in his gut" or because he was *taught* that such conduct is immoral or because he believes that God forbids it. But in this respect he does not differ from the people of our imaginary tribe who believe that it's immoral for septuagenarians to have sexual relations. And yet he would insist that theirs is *not* a genuine moral principle, and he would do so, presumably, on the grounds that if it were genuine, the king wouldn't have had to invent it because its truth would already have been discerned and could now be discerned by others. How, then, is he to distinguish his own example from the one he dismisses as a fake, that is, how is he to satisfy the second of the aforementioned requirements?

This, of course, is the question posed by the moral relativist, who insists that the absolutist *cannot* satisfy that requirement and that therefore someone like Congressman Dannemeyer, who *believes* that certain principles or standards are absolute, is no different from the people in our imaginary tribe who believe it is wrong—absolutely wrong—for septuagenarians to have sexual relations.

Moral absolutists, it should be said, have not been willing to cave in at this point and concede victory to the relativists. Some of them, at least, remain confident that a way can be found to satisfy the second requirement, that is, to show that we do have knowledge of moral truths that apply to everyone, regardless of their cultural circumstances. (They often state this by saying that moral truths have a rational basis or foundation.) A contemporary effort along these lines is provided by James Q. Wilson, who, in his recent book, *The Moral Sense*,[8] has undertaken to join in the debate I have outlined in this chapter and to do so as a defender of moral absolutism.

Wilson's mission, he tells us, is to "defend morality" against what he calls "modern skepticism." Such a defense is called for, he thinks, because "modern philosophy asserts that no rational foundation can be given for any [moral] judgment,"[9] and anthropologists maintain that "moral standards are arbitrary."[10] These two claims—that moral judgments have no rational foundation and that moral standards are arbitrary—constitute what Wilson calls "modern skepticism," which he also describes as the view that "morality has no basis in science or logic."[11] Accordingly, he promises to defend morality by showing that "scientific findings provide substantial support for its existence and power."[12]

Although Wilson does not make the structure of his argument very explicit, it eventually becomes clear that he assumes that the dispute over how we acquire moral principles presents us with a legitimate issue, one that deserves a straightforward answer. It also becomes clear that in order to find the point at which Wilson intends to engage relativists, we must bear in mind that their argument, when fully set out, runs in part as follows:

If we acquired our moral views in the way we acquire scientific views, namely, by means of a rational truth-finding procedure, then we could morally criticize other cultures wherever they differ from ours, just as we criticize, for example, the belief that illness is caused by witchcraft. But we do *not* acquire our moral views by means of any truth-finding procedure.

Wilson accepts this challenge and undertakes to demonstrate that, contrary to the theories of the relativist, we do acquire our moral views in a way that yields truth and knowledge.

Central to his demonstration is his claim that "there are many ways of knowing; the teachings of the heart deserve to be taken as seriously as the lessons of the mind."[13] He does not say which "lessons of the mind" he is alluding to, but it is clear that he means to say that "the teachings of the heart" deserve to be taken seriously *as sources of knowledge*. And by this he means that "the teachings of the heart" (which he also calls "sentiments") yield truths, *moral* truths. Thus, he speaks of there being "deeply held sentiments whose *truth* we find self-evident."[14] Intending to provide an example of such a heartfelt truth, he writes: "Suppose your heart tells you that it is wrong to torture babies to death for fun."[15]

The passages I have quoted thus far show that Wilson means to satisfy what I have called "the second requirement"; he means to show that we have *knowledge* of universally applicable moral truths. And Wilson aims to meet this requirement by saying that we have knowledge of moral truths because our hearts, that is, our *sentiments,* reveal such truths to us. In explaining what such revelations are like, he says: "When we think about it, we realize that the aversion we feel to baby torturing . . . springs from deeply held sentiments whose truth we find self-evident."[16] Presumably he means: The aversion we feel is so great that we find it self-evidently true that baby torturing is wrong.

At this point we must ask: What leads Wilson to think that, in his battle with philosophical skepticism, he is entitled to count "teachings of the heart"—such as an aversion to baby torturing—as being a source of *knowledge, of truth*? His answer is that our aversion to baby torturing is not peculiar to us, for it has been found to exist in people of many and diverse cultures. It has, in short, been found to be a cultural universal. Wilson, it turns out, is one of those thinkers who has made the mistake (see above) of thinking that the issue between relativists and absolutists turns on whether a moral principle is accepted in all cultures or only in some.[17] Accordingly, he undertakes a search for cultural universals, and his discovery of them constitutes, he assures us, a "scientific finding" that establishes the "existence" of morality.

This, then, is Wilson's attempted refutation of the philosophical skeptic. The trouble is that in order to find any merit in his "refutation," one would need to accept his pronouncement that "teachings of the heart," that is, certain *sentiments,* deserve to be taken seriously *as sources of knowledge—*

provided that they are common to all mankind. But why do they "deserve" this special status? Wilson does not explain, and it looks as though he has simply invented his own criterion for what is to count as knowledge. Stated more explicitly his criterion is this: "If *all* humans are disposed by their sentiments to condemn a certain action as morally wrong (or to approve a certain action as morally right), the universality of this sentiment confers on such moral judgments the status of being *known* to be true." But why should the *universality* of a sentiment be regarded as a sure sign of truth and knowledge? It is clear that Wilson cannot answer by saying: Whenever I have found a sentiment to be universal, I have *also* found that the moral judgments it gives rise to are *true*. Were he to say *this,* he would be obliged to explain how he determines that those judgments *are* true, and since he cannot now appeal to the universality of a sentiment, he will have accomplished nothing. What he is obliged to say, rather, is that it is a *necessary* truth that if a sentiment is universal, it will give rise only to true moral judgments. But what makes this a necessary truth, that is, why *couldn't* a false judgment result from a universal sentiment? And how is one to discern that it *is* a necessary truth? (It is certainly not true by definition!) Wilson says nothing about this, and one can only surmise that he simply hasn't thought through the implications of his position.

It is not surprising that Wilson has no idea of what it takes to effectively address the philosophical skeptic, for he is not a philosopher but a political scientist. As Alan Ryan, a more philosophically sophisticated political scientist, remarks in his review of Wilson's book: "Philosophers have learned not to insult social science by pretending that they knew all along what it takes painstaking empirical research to discover; Professor Wilson has not yet learned the converse lesson—that moral philosophy can't be set to rights by a few insights from social science."[18]

I might add that in declaring Wilson's project a failure, I do not mean to give comfort to his opponents. For we may find that Wilson's mistake was to assume that the long-standing dispute between moral relativists and absolutists presents us with a legitimate issue. If it turns out that the parties to this dispute have made the same false assumption, then of course neither side can emerge victorious.

One indication that there is trouble all around is this. Behind Wilson's reasoning lies the assumption that the philosophical skeptic has presented us with a genuine problem, that is, a problem that deserves an answer—if not Wilson's, then some other. But by conceding this much to the skeptic, Wilson is implicitly telling us that no one really knows the difference between right and wrong until someone does the research that will put a scientific foundation under morality. This is a very odd thing for Wilson to be telling us. As H. L. A. Hart, writing in another context, has observed: "The moral monster who thinks there is nothing morally wrong in torturing a child except that God has forbidden it, has a parallel in the moralist who will not treat the fact that the child will suffer agony as *in itself* a moral reason enough."[19] Wilson is just such a "moralist," for in his eagerness to answer the skeptic, he has put himself in the odd position of implying that our ordinary moral resources are not, in themselves, sufficient—that they need the backing of science. Normally, we would think we had given a reason that is adequate in itself if, in explaining why we can't vouch for a man's moral character, we say, "Because he sells drugs to children." Wilson, oddly, agrees with the skeptic that this reason hangs in the air unless we can provide scientific justification for thinking that it's wrong to ruin children's lives. Wilson's readiness to concede this is a difficulty he cannot shed by supplying what he deems to be the needed scientific backing. He is inescapably saddled with the difficulty Hart calls attention to once he assumes that the skeptic has posed a genuine problem, one we might hope to answer. His plight, then, is not simply that his answer is, as we have seen, unacceptable, for he was already in trouble the moment he took the skeptic's bait.

Further Misconceptions about Moral Relativism

In recent decades discussions of moral relativism have tended to ignore the concerns that led anthropologists in the early years of this century to attach great importance to this doctrine. Recent discussions have focused, instead, on what relativism purports to tell us about the nature of morality. Such discussions are of general philosophical interest, but by ignoring the special concerns of anthropologists they have given rise to some misguided criticisms of moral relativism. In this chapter I will first show that these criticisms miss the mark and will then explain why anthropologists have defended relativism so vigorously.

The principal aim of moral relativists is to combat what they call "ethnocentrism." In recent discussions, unfortunately, this aim has been explained as that of advocating tolerance—"tolerance of the alien." This makes it sound as though relativists are intent upon combating *in*tolerance, which suggests that they are embarked on a moral crusade. Accordingly, we find Elvin Hatch saying that

> ethical relativism . . . does not assert that there is no general standard of value. Rather, it supplies such a standard, one that should be adhered to in all societies. Presumably, the Navajo, Trobrianders, and Samoans should be just as tolerant of others as should middle-class Americans; conversely, they, like Americans, can be judged for their intolerance.[1]

He goes on to say that "the [relativists'] call for tolerance is a value judgment"[2] and speaks of the relativists' "ethical principle . . . of tolerance."[3] Hatch obviously thinks that relativists are advancing an *ethical* principle, namely, that everyone is *morally* obliged to be tolerant of whatever conduct other people exhibit if their culture deems it acceptable. Hatch adds that anyone who fails to abide by this principle can, according to relativists, "be judged for their intolerance," meaning that relativists regard such intolerance, or ethnocentrism, as a *moral* failing, akin to bigotry. I will call this "the moralistic interpretation" of relativism.

When moral relativism is interpreted moralistically, it appears to be vulnerable to a variety of criticisms. For example, it is said that the doctrine is logically inconsistent, for it declares that all values are relative while at the same time declaring, in absolutist fashion, that it is wrong—always and everywhere—to be intolerant of alien ways. In other words, relativists are accused of arguing for the thesis that *all* values are relative but then sliding into absolutism when it comes to one value, tolerance.[4]

To evaluate this criticism, we must first decide whether relativism should be interpreted moralistically. So let us ask: What makes that interpretation seem plausible? I have already given part of the answer: Relativism is sometimes described by using the words "tolerance" and "intolerance," where intolerance is understood to be a form of bigotry or something *like* bigotry.[5] Bigotry, of course, is a *moral* failing, a sign of bad character, and conduct that betokens bigotry is reprehensible. So when relativism is described by means of the words *tolerance* and *intolerance,* this immediately suggests that relativists are saying it is *wrong* to pass judgment on other cultures, and this, of course, is the moralistic interpretation. But should moral relativism be described by means of the words *tolerance* and *intolerance?*

As we saw in the preceding chapter, moral relativism is best described as an account of the proper way to formulate moral principles: These principles need a relativizing clause that specifies the scope of their application. This is what it *means* to say that morality is relative. So relativism says that we are making a mistake if we invoke our own moral principles to criticize members of other cultures, unless, of course, they too subscribe to those principles. But are relativists obliged to say that someone who makes this mistake is being *intolerant*? They are obliged, of course, to say that such a person is guilty of ethnocentrism, for the term "ethnocentrism" was invented for precisely this purpose. But being ethnocentric is not at all the same thing as being intolerant. The ethnocentrism that relativists may accuse us of is not a *moral* failing; it is said to result from a failure—a very common and understandable failure—to realize what is proved by the relativists' Fully Developed Argument (see chapter 1), namely, that moral principles, to be properly formulated, must include a clause that specifies the scope of their applicability. But a person's failure to comprehend a piece of intellectual reasoning is not at all like being a bigot. Ethnocentrism, then, is to be thought of as an *intellectual,* not a *moral,* failing. And when relativists chide us for judging others ethnocentrically, they aren't saying we have violated a moral principle.

It is a mistake, then, to interpret moral relativism moralistically. It does not make (or warrant) a *moral* criticism, so it also does not make (or warrant) an *absolute* moral criticism. So those critics are mistaken who say that relativists are logically inconsistent. It is simply not true that relativists argue for the general thesis that values are relative but then slide into moral absolutism when it comes to one value, tolerance.

To avoid a misunderstanding, I should point out here that the aforementioned critics are not as far wrong as it might appear. They say: "When it comes to intolerance, relativists are moral absolutists." To turn this false statement into a true one, we need to make only two changes: change "intolerance" to "ethnocentrism" and drop the word *moral*. We then get: "When it comes to ethnocentrism, relativists are absolutists." They are absolutists in the sense that they maintain that *anyone* who exhibits ethnocentrism is thereby making a mistake, regardless of his or her culture. No exception is made for a theocratic culture, which operates on the belief that its own morality is God given and that those who won't submit to it are wicked. Relativists would say that even these people should embrace relativism. But there is no inconsistency in this, for when they admonish people of all cultures to shed their ethnocentrism, they are not making a moral demand on anyone. They think their doctrine should be found acceptable by people of any culture because they believe that the argument they put forth as proof of their doctrine—their Fully Developed Argument—relies on objective *intellectual* grounds, grounds whose truth can be recognized by anyone, regardless of his or her culture. In other words, people who shed their ethnocentrism by accepting relativism are to have intellectual, not moral, grounds for doing so: They will see that ethnocentrism is the product of defective or ill-informed thinking. It is therefore unjust to accuse relativists of slipping, inconsistently, into *moral* absolutism.

Since the moralistic interpretation of moral relativism is wrong, another common criticism of it can be dismissed. Critics who interpret relativism moralistically have said that when relativists attempt to support their doctrine with empirical data, they commit the fallacy of trying to derive an "ought" from an "is."[6] These critics take for granted an idea expressed by Hatch as follows: "According to [the relativist's] argument, the ethical principle . . . of tolerance follows from the empirical fact that cultures have different values." The criticism, then, is that (in Hatch's words) "it is logically impossible to derive the one [i.e., the ethical principle] from . . . the fact of moral diversity."[7] But relativists, as we have seen, do *not* intend to argue for an ethical principle, so it is a mistake to accuse them of fallaciously reasoning from an "is" to an "ought," that is, from a factual claim to an ethical principle.

Hatch's criticism is misguided in another way as well, for he represents relativists as holding that their doctrine "follows from the empirical fact that cultures have different values." While it is true that this alleged empirical fact plays a role in the relativists' reasoning, this is not the whole of their reasoning. As we saw in chapter 1, the role assigned to this alleged empirical fact is that of proving that morality is acquired by "enculturative conditioning." While there may be something amiss in this reasoning, relativists are not guilty of the fallacious reasoning Hatch attributes to them.

Why have the critics of moral relativism so often misunderstood it? A partial explanation may be that even some relativists have failed to appreciate the difference between ethnocentrism and intolerance and have, as a result, made the mistake of depicting relativism moralistically, as a moral crusade against intolerance wherever it occurs, even in authoritarian cultures, such as Spain under Franco.[8] This misrepresentation occurs most often in the way relativists advertise their doctrine, for they frequently seek to drum up enthusiasm for it by saying that relativism promotes tolerance. Thus we find Herskovits saying that "cultural relativism is a philosophy which . . . lays stress on . . . the need for tolerance of conventions though they may differ from one's own."[9] He also speaks of "the humility reflected in the tolerance of the cultural relativistic position."[10] This sounds very high minded, of course, because tolerance is generally regarded as a moral virtue. The truth, however, is that what moral relativism aims for cannot properly be called "tolerance." To see that this is so, we need some reminders about both tolerance and moral relativism.

The "alien ways" of concern to relativists are those we normally regard as morally objectionable, so if moral relativism is to promote tolerance of such conduct, it must overcome our moral objections. Moreover, it must do this in a particular way. (One does not become tolerant of something by becoming *inured* to it.) To see what sort of change of mind is required for securing our tolerance, consider an example. Suppose that a woman says: "Before I got divorced I thought divorce was morally indefensible, that no decent person would break their marriage vows, etc., etc. But then I discovered in my own marriage that there can be reasons for divorce which I hadn't thought of." Someone who explains her change of mind in this way, by claiming a moral justification for the previously deplored conduct, can say: "At one time I was very intolerant of divorce, but I am not any longer," or "I have become much more tolerant of people who get divorced. I don't automatically assume that they aren't decent people."

In cases like the foregoing, then, becoming tolerant involves overcoming one's moral objection to something in a quite particular way: by finding a morally acceptable excuse or justification for the conduct in question. But is this what moral relativism does? Does one, by embracing relativism, acquire a new set of justifications for conduct one previously deplored?

The answer will become clear if we describe with some care the way a relativist must think. Notice first that when a relativist sets about studying another culture, his thoughts and actions will be indistinguishable from those of a nonrelativist until he comes upon conduct which, although it satisfies the norms of that culture, he would deplore in his neighbors at home. Let us suppose that he is in Thailand and finds that parents regularly sell their young daughters into prostitution. How must our relativist think about this? In what way will his thought be distinctively relativistic? We can imagine him thinking somewhat as follows: "I used to have moral objections to the child prostitution condoned in some cultures, but now that I've embraced moral relativism my previous moral convictions have been circumscribed in such a way that they now apply only within my own culture. So when I find cultures condoning conduct that I would deplore at home, I must not even *think about it* as I once did. I must take my previous moral convictions out of play altogether and merely report what members of those cultures do." This is certainly a distinctively relativistic way of thinking. But it is also a completely novel way of thinking, and deserves a name other than "tolerance." Perhaps we should call it "moral recusal."

So whatever moral relativism may do, there is one thing it does not do: It does not show us that the conduct in question deserves our tolerance. What we call "tolerance" is not something that can be extended to every sort of conduct. Tolerance can, of course, be extended beyond our cultural borders to ways that are quite alien to us, but only if, as in the case of the woman who became tolerant of divorce in certain cases, we can find a moral justification for the "alien ways" we had formerly deplored. The word *tolerance* would no longer mean what it does if it became permissible to say that a man exhibited his "great tolerance" by claiming to see nothing wrong with selling children into prostitution. It is not tolerance if it is to be extended, indiscriminately, to *whatever* sort of conduct we might encounter elsewhere. And yet that is precisely what moral relativism requires. David Bidney once remarked: "The cultural relativist is so afraid of ethnocentrism and possible intolerance that he is prepared, in theory at least, to tolerate any violation of his cultural standards by members of another society, on the assumption that . . . they would still be in accord with the principle of the relativity of values."[11] Could a relativist reply: "This is a caricature of relativism, for our profession of tolerance is meant to extend only to quaint and harmless folkways"? Plainly not. If they were promoting only that, they would not be relativists. And folkways that have a rightful claim on our tolerance need no protection from moral relativism.

What makes a person a relativist has nothing to do with being tolerant—even of other cultures. So when Herskovits and other relativists declare that their doctrine promotes tolerance, they not only misrepresent it but needlessly invite their critics to charge them with being inconsistent.

There may be another reason why people have imagined that this doctrine is to be interpreted moralistically. Moral relativism found its most fertile soil in our own culture, which has not, since the eighteenth century, been conducive to theocracies. Freedom of conscience is very important to us, and in the United States we have a long tradition (think of Mark Twain) of debunking moral busybodies. It is our policy, for the most part, to "live and let live." (A justice of the U.S. Supreme Court once remarked that the U.S. Constitution gives people "the right to be let alone.") This constitutes a large part of our tradition of political liberalism.[12] That being so, it might be thought that embracing moral relativism and embracing political liberalism would have the same result: People would not impose their values on those who don't share them. And this, in turn, might lead someone to equate a relativistic view of morality with political liberalism. This seems to be what Hatch was thinking when he wrote:

> The [relativists'] call for tolerance was an appeal to the liberal philosophy regarding human rights and self-determinism [sic]. It expressed the prin-

ciple that others ought to be able to conduct their affairs as they see fit, which includes living their lives according to the cultural values and beliefs of their society. Put simply, what was at issue [for relativists] was human freedom.[13]

This being so, says Hatch, relativism contains "an element that is hard to fault. This is the value of freedom: People ought to be free to live as they choose, to be free from the coercion of others more powerful than they."[14]

It is a mistake, however, to think that in practice relativism and political liberalism amount to the same thing. Relativism requires one to adopt a new way of thinking of one's moral convictions: one is to think of their scope as being limited by a relativizing clause. Political liberalism does no such thing. It requires citizens to keep their religious beliefs out of the political arena, but it does not tell people to *abandon* those beliefs whenever, as in the case of the Ten Commandments, they are meant to have unrestricted applicability. Whereas moral relativism requires people to *replace* such moral teachings with relativized versions, political liberalism requires only that citizens not try to enact such teachings into laws of the land. In this respect, then, relativism and political liberalism are utterly different. So a champion of political liberalism can perfectly well reject moral relativism.

Let us turn, finally, to an altogether different respect in which moral relativism has been misunderstood. I began this chapter by remarking that recent discussions of relativism have focused exclusively on what it says about the nature of morality, thereby ignoring what led anthropologists to attach great importance to this doctrine. This has fostered the impression that moral relativism, if it were shown to be unsatisfactory, could be simply abandoned by anthropologists. Philosophers, I suspect, have always thought of the matter in this way, but in doing so they were failing to realize that many anthropologists have regarded relativism as an important methodological precept of modern anthropology. As Kroeber remarks, anthropologists "take the principle [of relativism] for granted as underlying their work."[15] Similarly, Herskovits declares that "the relativistic point of view regarding cultures that differ from one's own . . . is essential to the ethnographer who is to carry on field research successfully."[16] "The present-day field worker," he says, "accepts the relativistic principle as a basic postulate."[17]

Why do anthropologists attach such significance to relativism? Kroeber explains the matter as follows: "Ethnocentricity is implied in the elevation of any one actual standard as absolute. . . . That the first condition to the scientific study of culture is the barring of ethnocentrism has been a basic canon of anthropology for three-quarters of a century."[18] Stated more explicitly, Kroeber's reasoning is as follows: Moral absolutists are guilty of ethnocentrism, which is incompatible with the scientific—the *objective*—study of cultures, and therefore relativism, which is the only means of eliminating absolutism (and hence ethnocentrism), is indispensable to the science of anthropology.

When relativists declare ethnocentrism to be incompatible with sound anthropology, they do not think of themselves as warning against some merely imagined threat to their discipline. They have in mind an actual—and much deplored—chapter in the history of anthropology. During the nineteenth century there arose theories about "primitive man" that today are regarded as inherently ethnocentric, that is, theories that depict preliterate people as being not only technologically inferior but also artistically and morally inferior to the people of nineteenth-century Europe. These were the evolutionist theories of culture advanced by E. B. Tylor and others (of which more will be said later), and what relativists now say about these theories is that their plausibility depended on a defective methodology—defective because the authors of these theories, instead of making objective comparisons of various cultures, imposed their Victorian morality upon their findings and consequently ranked as "inferior" to their own any culture found to conduct itself according to different standards.

Theories of humankind that involve such rankings cannot be scientific, say these critics, because a theory, to be truly scientific, must be one whose truth can be discovered by everyone who has the same data available. Yet obviously if someone from a non-European culture were asked to rank cultures as higher and lower, his ranking, if he took his own moral convictions as the standard of comparison, would be very different from that of the Victorian evolutionists. Such rankings are, therefore, unscientific, and for this reason, say the relativists, it is essential that such rankings be avoided by anthropologists. But such rankings will seem entirely appropriate to moral absolutists, for they claim to know that their own moral principles are true. That is why moral absolutism is pernicious: It leads to the development of theories that, while they purport to be unbiased and objective, are not. And the recommended corrective is that anthropologists should eradicate from their thinking all traces of absolutism by embracing moral relativism.

It is for this reason, then, that anthropologists—or a great many of them—have been unwilling to allow that they could simply abandon moral relativism. Whether their reasoning on this point is entirely sound is a matter we will have to look into in later chapters.

It should now be evident that to make a thorough investigation of moral relativism, we must pursue several quite different lines of inquiry. First, we must examine evolutionary theories of culture to discover what error, if any, they are guilty of and whether anthropologists are right in thinking that moral relativism supplies the needed corrective. This will be the topic of chapters 5 though 8. Another line of inquiry, taken up in chapters 9 to 12, is the question whether there are, in truth, different (i.e., conflicting) moralities. And finally, in chapters 13 to 19 we will go to the heart of the relativists' Fully Developed Argument by investigating the claim that morality is acquired by a process of "enculturative conditioning."

Before we turn to these matters there is one more item of business to attend to. Very little reflection is needed to discover that moral relativism has some rather peculiar implications. The question arises, therefore, whether the very peculiarity of these implications provides us with a good and sufficient reason for dismissing this doctrine. In the next chapter I will discuss these implications and try to decide whether they are by themselves enough to render relativism unacceptable.

4

The Paradoxes of Relativism

Moral relativism, as we have seen, is regarded by its proponents as both an enlightened doctrine (because it has the facts on its side) and as an essential methodological precept of anthropology. For these reasons, relativists are likely to regard anyone who challenges their doctrine as being both ignorant and a threat to the proper conduct of anthropology. This presents a rather daunting prospect to anyone setting out to reconsider the whole matter. And yet moral relativism has a number of paradoxical implications, generally overlooked by its proponents, which make the doctrine less attractive and less plausible than it is generally thought to be. In this chapter I will call attention to several of these paradoxes. It may be, of course, that pointing out to a relativist the paradoxical aspects of his doctrine will not force him, logically, to abandon it. Even so, an awareness of these paradoxes may lead impartial inquirers to realize that if, later on, we find good reasons for abandoning relativism, we need not regret its passing.

(1) One of the principal merits claimed for relativism is that it will, if adopted, put an end to transcultural moral criticisms. But is this really a good thing? Proponents of the doctrine make it seem so, but they achieve this by the sort of illustrations they offer. They pick examples such as the following. During the nineteenth century an English missionary in the Pacific wrote of the Tahitians that "notwithstanding the apparent mildness of their disposition, and the cheerful vivacity of their conversation, no portion of the human race was ever, perhaps, sunk lower in brutal licentiousness and moral degradation."[1] This missionary was condemning the Tahitians' un-inhibited sex life. And when relativists parade before us examples of this sort, we may be inclined to nod with appreciation, for we may be happy enough to see them erecting a barrier against the contemptuous attitudes that members of "our" culture exhibit toward foreigners.

It is highly misleading, however, to explain moral relativism by means of such examples. For it is the relativist's contention that *any* moral criticism made across some cultural divide is inappropriate, and therefore any example of such criticism should serve as well as any other to illustrate the merits of relativism. Let us set aside, then, examples in which Tahitians or Eskimos are the object of "our" criticisms and consider instead cases in which "we" are criticized from without. If the relativist is right, it should be apparent from such examples just how high-minded it is to invoke the relativist's doctrine as a barrier to "ethnocentrism."

Consider the case of Abba Thulle, ruler of the Pelew Islands in the last decade of the eighteenth century. We are privileged to know what Abba Thulle thought of "us" because in 1791 Amasa Delano sailed with the East India Company to Micronesia, where he met Abba Thulle and recorded their conversation as follows:

> I told [Abba Thulle], that Christian nations considered it as within the acknowledged system of lawful and honorable warfare, to use stratagems against enemies, and to fall upon them whenever it was possible, and take them by surprise. He replied, that war was horrid enough when pursued in the most open and magnanimous manner; and that although he thought very highly of the English, still . . . in this respect [they] did not obtain his approbation, and he believed his own mode of warfare more politic as well as more just. He said, that if he were to destroy his enemies when they were asleep, others would have a good reason to retaliate the same base conduct upon his subjects, and thus multiply evils, where regular and open warfare might be the means of a speedy peace without barbarity. Should he subdue his rebellious subjects by stratagem and surprise, they would hate both him and his measures, and would never be faithful and happy, although they might fear his power and unwillingly obey his law.[2]

Abba Thulle, plainly enough, had strong moral views about the use of ambush and other such treacherous stratagems of warfare. He not only counseled against them as being impolitic, but denounced them as immoral. (Although the English words *evil, base,* and *barbarous* are no doubt Delano's, he chose them, presumably, to capture the moral tenor of Abba Thulle's condemnation.) Moreover, it is obvious that, in voicing these criticisms, he was not merely reporting that *in his culture* such stratagems are forbidden. On the contrary, Abba Thulle was denouncing anyone's use of ambush and was criticizing the British in particular.

Here, then, is precisely the sort of case that should illustrate the great virtue of moral relativism. For if any case can be regarded as an example of blatant ethnocentrism, this one can. We may therefore conclude that, had a relativist been present at the conversation reported above, he would have vigorously objected to Abba Thulle's criticism of the British. Perhaps he would have spoken as follows: "As you were told, the British regard ambush and similar stratagems as appropriate means of warfare. It is therefore perfectly absurd to think that their use of these stratagems is immoral. If you think that you can denounce ambush as being wrong in and of itself, you are deluded, for there is no transcultural standard of right and wrong." This, according to the relativist, is what we, too, should think of Abba Thulle:

He was an ignorant and deluded man, who was trying to impose his own local values on others whose moral principles differed from his.

As I said above, it should be a matter of indifference to the relativist what sort of example we choose for illustrating the merits of his doctrine, provided only that the example falls under his definition of "ethnocentrism." What merit, then, can we find in the application of moral relativism to Abba Thulle? So far as I can see, only this: It frees us from the misguided way in which we would otherwise think of Abba Thulle. Were it not for relativism we would think of him as a wise and morally concerned person. (Delano himself remarked that the British "might learn from Abba Thulle.") But according to the relativist's doctrine, none of this makes any sense. Moral relativism tells us that there is nothing we can learn from people of another culture; we cannot be the wiser for listening to a man such as Abba Thulle, nor should what he says make us contrite about our ways. The lesson, more generally, is that whenever our ways are morally criticized by someone of another culture, we can shut our ears and dismiss such critics as ignorant folk who are guilty of "ethnocentrism." You can see, then, what a marvelous thing it is to have the relativist's doctrine as a shield. It is just what one needs if one wants to ignore inconvenient moral criticism by outsiders.

Is this, however, the lesson that relativists meant to teach us? I think not. Yet this is where their doctrine leads us. If they haven't realized this, that can only be because they have never thought about cases like that of Abba Thulle. But they cannot now disavow the foregoing implication of their doctrine by saying that, because of Abba Thulle's thoughtfulness and wisdom, his criticism of the British was not really a instance of ethnocentrism. For if they were to qualify the meaning of "ethnocentrism" in this way, they would be abandoning their entire doctrine, which holds that no distinction can be made between a man like Abba Thulle and a prudish Victorian missionary expressing his disgust at the sex life of the Tahitians. To be a relativist means dumping both sorts of examples into the same basket.

It is only to be expected, of course, that a relativist in love with his theory will continue to dismiss Abba Thulle as a man who needs to learn the lessons of moral relativism. I do not, therefore, pretend to have refuted the relativist by pointing out this peculiar implication of his doctrine. What I hope to have shown is only that relativism is very far from being a high-minded defense of misunderstood peoples suffering unwarranted abuse from smug Victorians. To think of relativism in that way is to misunderstand it completely.

(2) The central thesis of moral relativism is that morality is nothing but the stock of moral attitudes and practices of the world's various cultures. As Sumner put it in a remark quoted above, "immoral" never means anything but "contrary to the mores of the time and place." Or as Ruth Benedict has put it, "Morality . . . is a convenient term for socially approved habits."[3] What this comes to is that anyone who goes against the grain of his culture is doing wrong, is immoral. That, according to the relativist, is what the words *wrong* and *immoral* mean.

It may be worth pointing out here that relativism does not rule out our making (what the relativist regards as) moral criticisms of people in other cultures. It only requires that when we say that someone in another culture did wrong or acted immorally, we judge him by the standards of his own culture, not by ours. (Compare: an American can perfectly well say that an Englishman who is driving on the right in London is driving on the wrong side of the road, e.g., "He was driving on the wrong side of the road and caused an accident.") It is the relativist's view, in other words, that there are perfectly objective moral standards, so long as "right," "wrong," "good," and "bad" are used relatively. And the standards are the mores of each culture: A person is doing the right thing if he abides by those mores and is doing wrong if he does otherwise.

Let us consider what this amounts to in an actual case. It should not, of course, matter to the relativist just what the mores are in the case we choose for illustration, and therefore the following case should serve as well as any.

Some years ago an Associated Press dispatch from Alcamo, Sicily, carried a story about a twenty-year-old woman, Franca Viola, who "broke a thousand years of Sicilian tradition." The dispatch reported that "Franca refused to wed the rich man's son who kidnapped and raped her. Since the Middle Ages, kidnap and rape have been the sure road to the altar for a rejected Sicilian suitor. If the girl didn't say yes after that, she was dishonored and no one else would marry her."

Franca's flouting of tradition did not end with her refusal to marry this wealthy suitor; she went a step further and took him to court on a charge of rape. The community's reaction, we are told, was vehement: "Franca and her family were threatened with vengeance for her violation of the ancient code." (The "code" in this case, obviously, was that women were expected to submit to such manipulation.) Despite such threats, Franca eventually married another man, who, on the day of their wedding, carried a gun for protection.

Consider, now, what relativism teaches us to think and say of the principals in this account. The rapist, since he was merely following a thousand years of Sicilian tradition, was doing nothing wrong. Franca, on the other hand, because she both refused to submit to this man and then married another, was doing wrong. We can properly think of her—indeed, can *only* think of her—as an immoral woman. This is the lesson that relativism teaches. It teaches us to measure the morality of a person's actions by their conformity to local mores. What the mores themselves happen to be in a given case is, of course, irrelevant, for the relativist's contention is that we cannot make any moral assessment of mores themselves: They are all on a par with one another. We cannot think of Franca Viola as refusing to be manipulated in a degrading way, for that would imply that the Sicilian mores deserve our contempt, and this implication is what relativism is designed to preclude. Such contempt would be blatantly "ethnocentric."

Is this, however, the lesson that relativists have meant to teach us? I think not. But they cannot now withdraw this lesson by saying that I have chosen my example unfairly, that I should have chosen a case in which the mores themselves were admirable. So relativists will have to live with the foregoing lesson and declare us guilty of ethnocentrism if we refuse to think that the man who raped Franca Viola was beyond reproach.

Again, I do not present this case with the idea that it refutes moral relativism. The dedicated theorist follows his argument where it leads, and if it leads to something wholly counterintuitive, he merely declares our intuitions misguided.

(3) Another way to express the central tenet of relativism is to say that what a culture condones, what it views with indifference, or even expects of its members, cannot be thought to be wrong, and if someone undertakes to oppose and morally criticize the accepted ways of his own culture, he can only be regarded as a kind of lunatic, or at least as seriously confused. He is to be compared (if there could be such a case) to an Englishman who declares, quite seriously, that his countrymen have chosen to drive on the wrong side of the road and ought to switch over to the American practice of driving on the right.

If the relativist is right about this, then we ought to be able to illustrate his point by finding an example of someone who criticizes and opposes on moral grounds some long-standing practice of his culture and who is to be judged, for that reason, to be either a kind of lunatic or seriously confused. And once more, it should not matter in the least what sort of example is chosen, what sort of practice is being opposed and criticized. The following example, therefore, should serve as well as any.

Robert Redfield, an anthropologist, presents us with the following account of Knife Chief and his son, Petalesharoo, of the Loup (or Skidi) band of the Pawnee:

> By ancient custom, this group of Pawnee each year sacrificed a captive to Venus, Morning Star, to ensure abundant crops. The victim, fattened and kept uninformed of the fate ahead, was on the proper day bound to a cross or scaffold, tomahawked, and shot with arrows. For several years Knife Chief "had regarded this sacrifice as an unnecessary and cruel exhibition of power, exercised upon unfortunate and defenseless individuals whom they were bound to protect; and he vainly endeavored to abolish it by philanthropic admonitions."
>   A young girl from another tribe was brought captive to the Pawnee village in the year before, or the second year before, the arrival of Long's party. She was bound to the cross when Knife Chief's son stepped forward "and in a hurried but firm manner, declared that it was his father's wish to abolish this sacrifice; that for himself, he had presented himself before them, for the purpose of laying down his life upon the spot, or of releasing his victim." He then cut the victim's cords, put her on a horse, mounted another, and carried her to safety. . . . in the year following Petalesharoo's act, another captive was made ready for sacrifice again, and again Knife Chief and his son tried to rescue the captive, in this case a Spanish boy. On this occasion a trader was present in the village, and Knife Chief, with manufactured goods obtained from this trader, bought the boy from the

Indian who had been his captor, and saved his life. Nor did this second attempt to end the custom succeed in doing so, for in John T. Irving's account of a visit to these same Pawnee made in 1822, we read that one Major Dougherty was summoned to the Loup Pawnee village to save a young Indian woman whom the Pawnee were about to sacrifice. Again it was the chief who showed himself favorable to saving the prisoner. (Was this chief again Petalesharoo's father? Irving's account refers to "Black Chief.") The other Indians were determined to perform the sacrifice. And so firm was the general opinion still, in spite of these three attempts by the chief to stop the custom, that when Major Dougherty and his white companions, with the aid of the chief, tried to carry off the captive, the Indians slew her with arrows.[4]

How Knife Chief and his son could have moral convictions so very different from those of their tribe will be considered in a later chapter. At issue here is what the relativist is obliged by his theory to say of such a case.

What picture do we get of Knife Chief? If he merely thought that human sacrifices were a waste of time because they failed to promote better crops, and if he was, for that reason, simply indifferent to these killings, this example would be of no interest. But that is not the case. Far from being indifferent (as he might have been had the ceremony involved, for instance, scratching designs in the soil), he went to great lengths to put a stop to these sacrifices, and he did so because he thought these killings wrong.[5]

Knife Chief, of course, knew that such killings were an accepted practice of his people, and therefore the relativist must say that Knife Chief's thinking is that of a moral absolutist. But moral absolutism, we are told, is an utter confusion. It is therefore the relativist's view that Knife Chief, in voicing moral objections to these sacrifices and acting on those objections, was a very misguided person. The mistake he has made is like that of an Englishman who insists that the English rule about driving on the left is the wrong rule and who undertakes to put an end to this practice. I am not certain that even among the English, who have their share of eccentric characters, there could be such a lunatic, but if so, he would be the relativist's model for understanding Knife Chief. This, then, is another lesson taught us by relativists. But again, is it a lesson they intended to teach? I think not, for when relativists are presented with examples like that of Knife Chief, they shy away from the real implications of their theory. Herskovits, for instance, when confronted with the fact that, during the years of racial segregation in the United States, some citizens tried to put an end to that practice (to be compared here to Knife Chief's attempt to end human sacrifice among his people), explains as follows how the relativist accommodates such matters:

It is something entirely different [from confused ethnocentrism] when we, as Americans, try to do something to correct "the racial caste system of the United States" of which we, as members of the society of whose culture this is a part, do not approve. In recognizing the validity of all ways of life for those who live in accordance with them, cultural relativism does not deny the dynamics of culture by insisting on an unchanging acceptance by a people of their preexisting ways of life, or by failing to take into account the influence of cultural transmission in making for cultural change. It accepts these, and in its acceptance achieves the most fruitful approach to the problem of the nature and significance of differential values in culture that has yet been devised.[6]

Herskovits is here attempting to accommodate someone like Knife Chief by saying: "Relativists do not deny that cultures may undergo changes brought about from within." But in making such a reply, Herskovits is failing to address the real issue. For the relevant question must be: How should moral relativists *describe* a person, such as Knife Chief, who not merely insists on *changing* the ways of his people ("Let's drive on the other side from now on") but insists that the old ways are *wrong* and *ought* to be abolished? Herskovits does not answer this question at all. Yet the answer he ought to have given is obvious. He ought to tell us that it makes no sense to say, "Our old ways are wrong and ought to be abolished." In other words, Herskovits's theory commits him to regarding Knife Chief as utterly confused.

Most of us, of course, will not regard Knife Chief in this way. We think we can well understand the moral objection he voices against human sacrifice: It is not only useless but cruel, and it deprives an innocent person of his or her life. But the relativist need not be disconcerted by the fact that we think this way, for his theory tells him how to regard this fact, too: We are just as much the dupes of moral absolutism as is Knife Chief. So the relativist need suffer no intellectual embarrassment over the fact that his theory teaches the foregoing lesson, even though it is not the lesson he meant to teach.

(4) When philosophers reflect on the nature of morality, they generally regard their resulting theories as being of little more than theoretical interest. Anthropologists who advocate relativism, on the other hand, while recognizing the philosophical character of their doctrine, also regard it as having great practical importance. They insist that relativism teaches people not to be judgmental about alien ways of life. If we take their doctrine to be true, we will think that we are debarred from having even the *thought* that we see wrongs that need righting in a culture other than our own—unless, of course, it can be shown that its own rules are being violated. And we will also think that we must in no case call for the reform of ongoing practices in other cultures.

This practical consequence became most apparent when, in 1947, the executive board of the American Anthropological Association submitted to the United Nations Commission on Human Rights a statement arguing that the UN should adopt moral relativism in formulating its "Declaration of the Rights of Man." Citing moral relativism as their grounds, these anthropologists insisted that the UN Declaration "be applicable to all human beings, and not be a statement of rights conceived only in terms of the values prevalent in the countries of Western Europe and America." The declaration, they said, should be "a statement of the rights of men to live in terms of their own traditions."[7]

This, of course, sounds most admirable when we think of the way in which major Western nations have, through Christian missionaries and foreign administrators, undermined the customs and disrupted the lives of peoples in preliterate societies, thereby often bringing about the demoralization and demise of these peoples. But moral relativism as a theory does not limit itself to opposing only such plainly deplorable interference in other cultures. On the contrary, it disregards *what* is being interfered with, and what the intervention may achieve, and simply declares that *any* interference in any other culture is unwarranted. So any example of interference that we care to choose should serve as well as any other for recognizing the great practical merit of relativism. Consider in this light the following case.

Recent reports from the Middle East tell of a small group of non-Arabs who have undertaken rescue missions to save the lives of young Arab women who would otherwise be killed by their families. The details are as follows. It has long been an accepted part of rural Arab folkways that if a woman becomes pregnant out of wedlock, she must be killed by her relatives in order to restore the family honor. (These are spoken of locally as "honor killings.") If she runs away, she is often lured back on the pretext that all has been forgiven and then, upon her return, is killed. The group attempting to rescue these young women is financed by a European foundation. Their modus operandi is to smuggle them into Israel by a secret "underground railway" and to then transport them to Europe, where a job is found for them. If they wish to correspond with their families, their letters are posted from another country, to keep their whereabouts secret.

This example, as I remarked above, should serve as well as any for demonstrating the practical significance of relativism. And what we learn is this: If relativism were taken seriously by everyone and put into practice, this small group would abandon its rescue missions, and consequently those endangered young women would be left to be killed. In other words, relativists, if they succeed in propagating their theory, must accept responsibility for costing others their lives. Is this what they intended? Probably not. They did not think of their theory as putting lives at risk. But this unintended consequence is unlikely to deter them. Herskovits, after all, declares that relativism is "a tough-minded" philosophy and "requires those who hold it to alter responses that arise out of the strongest enculturative conditioning to which they have been exposed, the ethnocentrism implicit in the particular value-systems of their society."[8] This is what I spoke of in chapter 3 as the relativist's moral recusal.

So let us hear no more from relativists about (in Herskovits's words) "the humility reflected in the tolerance of the cultural relativistic position."[9] The potential victim of an honor killing in Jordan is more likely to see mere hard-hearted indifference than "humility" in the moral recusal relativists call "tolerance." And when relativists next draft a statement on human rights, let them include not only "the rights of men to live in terms of their own traditions," but also the rights of women to die an unwelcome death as prescribed by those traditions.

(5) The relativist's doctrine amounts to this: Just as it makes no sense to say that the English drive on the wrong side of the road (as if driving on the left were wrong in and of itself, i.e., apart from some existing rule), so it makes no sense to say that a certain sort of conduct such as head-hunting or polygamy is, in and of itself, morally wrong. So we may expect to find relativists telling us that morality is arbitrary in the sense that it makes no difference which sort of conduct our culture morally condemns and which it condones.

Ruth Benedict has acknowledged that relativism, which she helped greatly to popularize, implies this sort of arbitrariness:

> [Cultural relativity] challenges customary opinions and causes those who have been bred to them acute discomfort. It rouses pessimism because it throws old [moral and social] formulae into confusion, not because it contains anything intrinsically difficult. As soon as the new [moral or social] opinion is embraced as customary belief, it will be another trusted bulwark of the good life. We shall arrive then at a more realistic faith, accepting as grounds of hope and as new bases for tolerance the coexisting and equally valid patterns of life which mankind has created for itself from the raw materials of existence.[10]

Benedict is not, of course, saying that when we cast off old values and adopt new ones, the new ones will be *better* than the old. (She would think that only an absolutist could say *that*.) Benedict is saying, rather, that when we adopt new values and abandon the old, we will be completely satisfied with the new values, *regardless* of what they may be. Why? Because all patterns of life are "equally valid." (Compare: If we switched over to driving on the other side of the road, we would eventually find no fault with the new arrangement, for there is nothing sacrosanct about either side of the road.)

This feature of relativism, which is of course absolutely essential to it, caused its proponents acute embarrassment once the horrors of Nazism became known. As Robert Redfield put it, "It was easy to look with equal benevolence upon all sorts of value systems so long as the values were those of unimportant little people remote from our own concerns. But the equal benevolence is harder to maintain when one is asked to anthropologize the Nazis."[11] Although relativists may find themselves embarrassed, they cannot now, without being guilty in their own eyes of ethnocentrism, become judgmental about Nazism. This need not, however, discourage the dedicated relativist. If he is prepared to follow his theory wherever it leads, he may yet continue to embrace relativism, thinking that it is the only sound moral philosophy available.

(6) There is another interesting consequence of the arbitrariness of morality implicit in the relativist's position. One critic of the doctrine, Frank Hartung, called attention to this consequence when he complained that "cul-

tural relativity deprives us of any possible rational basis for choosing a proper life. Tolerance and equal validity also seem to imply that no moral concepts, regardless of their derivation, can possibly be given any logical or empirical authority over the conventions of any individual."[12]

In saying that relativism does away with any moral "authority over the conventions of any individual," Hartung meant something like the following. If the relativist's doctrine is broadcast far and wide and people come to believe that morality is nothing but a set of arbitrary social conventions, people will cease to feel that they are genuinely *obligated* to do (or forgo) certain things. Or as Henry Veach has put it, "the lid would be off and all hell would break loose."[13] Veach instances "a teen-age youth with normal sex impulses" who has had a "strict upbringing" and is now persuaded by relativists that morality is "relative" and "without justification."

Perhaps another way to state this criticism is to say that the real upshot of moral relativism, although relativists haven't realized this, is that it turns morality into what Norman Mailer, in an essay on the Hipsters of the 1950s, called "absolute relativity":

> Character . . . enters then into an absolute relativity where there are no truths other than the isolated truths of what each observer feels at each instant of his existence. . . . What is consequent therefore is the divorce of man from his values, the liberation of the self from the Super-ego of society. The only Hip morality . . . is to do what one feels whenever and wherever it is possible, and—this is how the war of the Hip and the Square begins—to engage in one primal battle: to open the limits of the possible for oneself, for oneself alone because that is one's need.[14]

The Hipster, as Mailer says, is a "philosophical psychopath," and it has seemed to some that such philosophical psychopathy would be the inevitable result of adopting relativism. In his recent book, *The Moral Sense*, James Q. Wilson takes this view as his starting point. "The perils of accepting cultural relativism . . . can be very great," says Wilson, for if relativism is accepted as true, "then it will occur to some people . . . that they are free to do whatever they can get away with." Because of this, he adds, "the moral relativism of the modern age has probably contributed to the increase in crime rates. . . . It has done so . . . by supplying [potential criminals] a justification for doing what they might have done anyway. If you are tempted to take the criminal route to the easy life, you may go further along that route if everywhere you turn you hear educated people saying—indeed, 'proving'—that . . . moral standards [are] arbitrary."[15]

Is this a fair appraisal of the relativist's doctrine? At least some relativists have thought it is not. Herskovits replies that those who advance the foregoing objection have simply failed to realize "the power of the enculturative experience in shaping conduct and ideas. There is no cultural relativist, as far as I know, who asserts that his doctrine is based on, describes, or implies behavioral anarchy: there is no one who does not recognize that every society has rules of conduct, an ethical system, a moral code, that the individual members rarely question."[16]

This reply, however, seems to miss entirely the point of the objection it is meant to address. For the question being raised is not, as Herskovits seems to have thought, whether at present most people abide by the mores of their culture (to which, I suppose, the obvious answer is affirmative), but the very different question: How will people think and act if relativists succeed in winning general acceptance of their doctrine? Clearly, relativists hope to persuade people to stop criticizing alien ways, and now their critics are asking: What *other* practical consequence might result from people coming to believe that morality is arbitrary? To this question Herskovits offers no answer in the passage quoted above.

Hartung, Veach, and Wilson are confident that someone who really believed the relativists' doctrine would cease to feel bound by the mores of his culture, would cease, indeed, to feel constrained by any moral considerations. If we treat this as a prediction about how *in fact* someone might find in relativism a warrant for his conduct, that prediction finds confirmation in a passage from Benito Mussolini's *Diuturna:*

> In Germany relativism is an exceedingly daring and subversive theoretical construction (perhaps Germany's philosophical revenge which may herald the military revenge). In Italy, relativism is simply a fact. . . . Everything I have said and done in these last years is relativism by intuition. . . . If relativism signifies contempt for fixed categories and men who claim to be the bearers of an objective, immortal truth . . . then there is nothing more relativistic than Fascist attitudes and activity. . . . From the fact that all ideologies are of equal value, that all ideologies are mere fictions, the modern relativist infers that everybody has the right to create for himself his own ideology and to attempt to enforce it with all the energy of which he is capable.[17]

Moral absolutists might very well hold up Mussolini as proof of their contention that relativism leaves morality (as Hartung says) with no "authority over the conventions of any individual." And as an explanation, they might add: "A person will acknowledge that certain sorts of conduct are *morally wrong* only if he feels constrained in a way that he would *not* if he came to believe that such conduct merely violates of an arbitrary convention." Perhaps some philosophers will agree with this and then declare, with Mussolini, that morality is a "mere fiction."[18]

Herskovits, however, insists that relativism leaves moral authority undisturbed. This may not be evident from the passage quoted above, but in others he appears to reply more relevantly to those who see relativism as implicitly endorsing nihilism. In *Man and His Works,* Herskovits writes:

> We can dispose of the contention that cultural relativism negates the force of the codes that prevail at a given time in a given culture. . . . *Cultural relativism must be sharply distinguished from concepts of the relativity of individual behavior,* which would negate all social controls over conduct. . . . Conformity to the code of the group is a requirement for any regularity in life.[19]

Summing up this point, Herskovits remarks: "Cultural relativism . . . in no wise gives over the restraints that every system of ethics exercises over those who live in accordance with it. To recognize that right and justice . . . may have as many manifestations as there are cultures is to express tolerance, not nihilism."[20]

Perhaps we can grasp Herskovits's point by reintroducing Veach's concern with the "teen-age boy with normal sex impulses." Veach is evidently thinking that if this boy learns that teenagers among the Eskimos are permitted to engage freely in premarital sex, and if he is persuaded by the relativist that these Eskimo teenagers cannot rightly be thought to be doing something immoral, the relativist will have led the boy to think, "Well, then, even though my culture teaches that it's wrong for me to have sex, there is nothing *really* wrong in it." Herskovits appears to oppose this by saying: "Relativism, if properly understood, would *not* lead the boy to think this; rather, it would leave him thinking that it *would* be wrong for him to have premarital sex." What could Herskovits have meant by this? So far as I can see, he could only have meant the following: "Relativism demonstrates that the *only* meaning 'wrong' has is in connection with the mores of the culture; there is not some *other* sense of 'wrong' in which it would *not* be wrong for this boy to engage in sex, and therefore if he has understood relativism, he can only think it would be wrong for him to have sex." (I am putting this in the way Sumner did when, in a passage quoted earlier, he said that the word *immoral* never means anything but "contrary to the mores of the time and place.") Perhaps, then, Herskovits is saying that, because of this boy's enculturative conditioning, the only thought he could have is this: "In the only sense in which something *can* be wrong or immoral, it would be wrong and immoral for me to have sex."

If this is the proper interpretation of relativism, does it really leave that doctrine free of nasty consequences, as Herskovits seems to think? Consider once again that ancient Sicilian tradition by which a man could force a woman into marriage by raping her. What must a woman who has been raped in these circumstances think? If relativism has been explained to her as Herskovits explains it, she must think that if she defies the mores of her culture she is an immoral woman. But it is not at all likely that Franca Viola thought of herself in this way. She no doubt thought she was refusing to be cruelly manipulated. But Herskovits tells us that, unlike nihilism, relativism does not "negate the codes that prevail at a given time in a given culture," and this clearly implies that Franca Viola did do something wrong. On Herskovits's interpretation, then, moral relativism imposes a dreadful tyranny, for the Newspeak taught by the relativist would, if accepted, make it impossible for anyone to think that he or she was doing the right thing in violating the code of his or her culture, regardless of what that code might be.

This, then, is Herskovits's reply to those critics who claim that relativism, if adopted, would destroy all moral authority. He is completely at odds, then, with Hartung, Veach, and Wilson, who regard moral relativism as a nihilistic philosophy. How are we to choose between these two interpretations? Should we accede to Herskovits on the grounds that he is one of the architects of relativism? Or should we take the example of Mussolini as evidence of what actually happens to people's thinking when they embrace moral relativism? But does it really matter which interpretation a relativist settles on? For the consequences are equally bizarre: Either relativism promulgates a kind of tyranny over moral thinking or it justifies nihilism and frees its adherents from every sort of moral constraint. Perhaps those thinkers who have already embraced relativism have resigned themselves to one or the other of these alternatives, telling themselves that as defenders of the truth they would be intellectually dishonest were they to shun its bizarre implications. But they mustn't pretend that their doctrine is free of such implications.

(7) Relativists ask "What is morality?" and answer that morality is nothing but the accepted customs, practices, and sanctions regarding the conduct that, in any culture, is judged to be moral or immoral, right or wrong, good or bad. Where does this answer come from? Anthropologists pride themselves on giving accurate descriptions of the cultures they study, and they often insist that in order to achieve this accuracy it is necessary to understand the language of the people being studied. Since words such as *immoral, right, wrong*, and so on are our words, it would seem that we can expect relativists to have paid close attention to—and accurately reported—the way in which we actually use these words. To see whether they have done so, let us consider the following.

    (a) Sumner, as we saw, says that "immoral" never means anything but "contrary to the mores of the time and place." But this certainly does not reflect how we actually use the word *immoral*. For example, those who declared the Vietnam War to be not only wasteful but immoral did not think, nor did they mean, that that war was contrary to the current mores of the United States. Indeed, many critics of the war thought it was typical, all too typical, of this country's use of warfare as an instrument of national policy. Similarly, antiabortionists in this country declare that abortion is "immoral" while at the same time insisting that abortion has come to be *widely condoned and practiced* in this country. These examples show that people often declare something to be immoral although (contrary to what Sumner suggests) they do *not* mean to say that the conduct they condemn is "contrary to the mores of the time and place."

    (b) Relativism implies that if someone's actions are morally criticized, he can always defend himself by pointing out that he has acted as everyone in his society acts in such circumstances. That is, moral relativism implies that if someone responds to a moral criticism by saying, "But everyone else does it," he has given a moral justification for his action. But this implication of relativism is simply untrue. If someone is accused of, say, shady business practices and responds by saying, "But everyone else does it," he is offering the kind of lame excuse that

people give when they recognize that their position is morally indefensible.

Similarly, if an elected representative were shown to have accepted
bribes in return for his vote, and if he were then to say, "But everyone
else does it," we would not, even if we believed him, say, "Oh, in that
case you did nothing wrong." After all, he has misused his office, and
that is not altered by the fact that he happens to live in a country,
perhaps a South American country, where bribery is constantly practiced at all levels and has become an accepted "way of life." Indeed,
someone who is concerned about ethics in government may think that
the very fact that everyone *is* doing it gives him all the more reason
to oppose with vigor the acceptance of bribes by public officials.

Consider another example, reported by John Howard Griffin in his
book *Black Like Me*.[21] Griffin, a Caucasian, darkened his skin and
traveled through the southern United States posing as a black man in
order to record and publish his experience with racism. While hitch-
hiking through Alabama, he was given a ride by a man who appeared,
at first, to be (as Griffin puts it) "a decent white." The man asked him
about his children, and then proceeded in the following vein:

"You got a pretty wife?"

"Yes sir."

He waited a moment and then with lightness, paternal amuse-
ment, "She ever had it from a white man?"

I stared at my black hands, saw the gold wedding band and
mumbled something meaningless, hoping he would see my reti-
cence. He overrode my feelings and the conversation grew more
salacious. He told me how all of the white men in the region craved
colored girls. He said he hired a lot of them both for housework
and in his business. "And I guarantee you, I've had it in every one
of them before they ever got on the payroll." A pause. Silence above
the humming tires on the hot-top road. "What do you think of
that?"

"Surely some refuse," I suggested cautiously.

"Not if they want to eat—or feed their kids," he snorted. "If
they don't put out, they don't get the job."

I looked out the window to tall pine trees rising on either side
of the highway. . . .

"You think that's pretty terrible, don't you?" he asked.

"I guess I do."

"Why hell—everybody does it. Don't you know that?"

"No sir."

"Well, they sure as hell do."

Griffin adds: "Later I encountered many whites who freely admit-
ted the same practice my companion described." Moreover, none of
the white people he met in the South "denied that it was widespread."[22] But if the culture of that region condoned this practice, did
it, as relativism implies, constitute a genuine justification to say, "This
is what we [white men] do here"? Griffin did not think so, and surely
he is right about that.

Thus, what the relativist presents as the paradigm of moral justification is, in fact, no justification at all. One can, it is true, think of a few instances in which it would be wrong to go against a long-established custom, but this would be so not merely because the custom exists but because failure to continue the practice or observe the custom would cause some harm, such as offending someone whose sensibilities deserve consideration. (Grandmother would be deeply offended if the family's Thanksgiving dinner were not held at her house as usual.) But even in these cases the harm must be weighed against the nature of the practice or custom, which may be very bad indeed. Here again, then, moral relativism is not an accurate description of the way we actually think and talk about moral matters.

(c) Relativism equates morality with practices, customs, and the like, but this view disregards the fact that customs and practices are among the things that come in for moral scrutiny. We have already considered several instances of this, such as Knife Chief's opposition to the human sacrifices carried out by his people. And we can think of many more such instances. For example, among Russian gentlemen of the last century it was the custom to pay off their gambling debts to one another before honoring their debts to shopkeepers or paying wages to servants. Yet we can easily imagine some gentleman of the period suffering a troubled conscience over this and in the end deciding that he ought to pay first the servants and shopkeepers, for they were certainly more in need of payment, and in any case they had a better claim to payment because they had provided goods and services and would have no livelihood if not paid. It would seem, then, that relativism is wrong in identifying morality with what custom condones or requires.

(d) There is a serious error in the comparison of moral judgments to a rule that prescribes driving on the right or left side of the road. One difference can be brought out in the following way. If an American, while visiting England, were to start out driving his rented car on the right, someone might call out to him, "You're driving on the wrong side!" This person would, of course, mean that the American was driving on the side that is wrong in *that* place. But is this case analogous to the following? Suppose we are explaining to a child why her brother, who had gone on a rampage by driving against the traffic, was sent to prison. We tell her: "What your brother did was wrong because, by driving against the oncoming traffic, he was endangering other drivers. He almost killed someone." In this case we are rendering a moral judgment, but is it plausible to say that what we properly *mean* by this is only that in *this* place it is wrong to heedlessly endanger the lives of others? Surely not! So what we say in such a case is *not* like informing someone that he is driving on the wrong side of the road.

For the reasons I have just enumerated, moral relativism, if it purports to be a description of morality, is an utter and obvious failure. But is that what relativism purports it to be? One might think: It *must* have been intended by its proponents as a description of morality, for they present their doctrine as an answer to the question "What is morality?" and that question would seem to call for a *description*, for a recitation of such matters as those just mentioned in (a) to (d) above. Yet on the other hand, it would seem that relativists cannot have intended their doctrine to be a description of morality, for had that been their intent they would surely have noticed, for example, that customs and practices are among the things that come in for moral criticism and that it is no justification to say, "But everyone is doing it." Moreover, it seems clear that relativists intended to do something quite different from giving a description of morality. They believed they were drawing out the implications of certain discoveries made by anthropologists, two of which are the following: (i) It has been found in many instances that a mode of conduct that among one people is condemned as wrong is among other people viewed with indifference or enjoined as a duty, and (ii) We learn morality from the culture in which we are raised, that is, we acquire morality by the process of cultural conditioning.

These are the premises from which, according to relativists, their doctrine follows. Buried in these premises are several large assumptions we need to examine, but for now I want merely to point out that relativists believe that these—(i) and (ii) above—are the *facts* and that anyone who realizes this must accept moral relativism. That being so, what are we to think of the fact that relativism fails utterly as a description of morality? Does this failure prove that relativism is not true? Can we, that is, deduce that one or more of the relativist's premises is false from the fact that the relativist's conclusion does not square with the way we actually think and talk—as shown in (a) to (d)—about moral matters?

The dedicated relativist may happily accept the fact that his conclusion conflicts with the ways we normally think and talk about such matters. He may retort that the ways we think and talk simply reflect our propensity to as-sume that moral absolutism is true, whereas he has shown that it's false. And so he may argue that our ordinary ways of thinking and talking, far from be-ing a trustworthy guide to what morality is, are confused and in need of cor-rection (see note 5 of chapter 2). Yet, on the other hand, if the relativist does adopt this way of explaining the conflict between his doctrine and our ordi-nary ways of thinking and talking, he must ask himself what reason, if any, he can give for claiming that his doctrine is a doctrine about *morality?* For it would appear that the relativist is simply presenting a highly idiosyncratic and, as we have seen, highly paradoxical, way of using such words as *right, wrong,* and *immoral.* And if we try to imagine a form of life in which "Every-one else is doing it" really is always a sufficient rebuttal to a charge of wrong-doing and in which such considerations as the cruelty or unfairness of an act are wholly irrelevant, then it is difficult, at best, to see why we should think of that as *morality.* For this reason it seems merely quixotic for the relativist to insist that he has discovered what morality *really* is and that our familiar ways of thinking and talking are confused and in need of correction.

All the same, the relativist may remain unmoved. He may impatiently reply that our present ways of thinking and talking merely reflect our adherence to moral absolutism and that cultural studies have demonstrated that moral absolutism is a thoroughly confused doctrine. So if moral relativism is to be rejected, it cannot be rejected out of hand, despite the paradoxes it trails in its wake. What is called for, obviously, is a more thorough investigation of the whole subject. One of the questions that must be addressed is whether relativists are right in thinking that our familiar ways of thinking and talking presuppose the truth of moral absolutism. (In other words, are moral relativism and absolutism the only possibilities here? Couldn't they both be wrong?) We must also consider carefully the premises from which relativists derive their doctrine: What could it mean to say that we acquire morality by "enculturative conditioning," and what, if anything, can it mean to say that there are cultures that have different and conflicting moralities? But of far greater concern to the anthropologist is the question: Is relativism really essential to the proper conduct of anthropological research? Unless the answer to this question is negative, an anthropologist may refuse to take seriously a philosopher's criticisms of moral relativism. So before we start investigating possible philosophical criticisms of moral relativism, we had better figure out whether Herskovits was right to claim that "the relativistic point of view . . . is essential to the ethnographer who is to carry on field research successfully." In order to examine this claim, it is necessary to review various developments in anthropology at the end of the last century, for it is the contention of anthropologists that it was in those developments that it first became apparent that sound anthropology is impossible without moral relativism.

II

ANTHROPOLOGY AND MORAL RELATIVISM

The History of Relativism in Anthropology

The claims made by those who insist that relativism is essential to anthropology can be summarized in the following four propositions: (i) ethnocentrism is a hazard that anthropologists must scrupulously avoid, (ii) the means of being permanently on guard against this hazard is the adoption of relativism, (iii) Franz Boas demonstrated that relativism is essential to anthropology, and (iv) Boas did this by demonstrating that evolutionary theories of culture resulted from the ethnocentrism of their authors, notably E. B. Tylor and others.

Our principal concern is with propositions (i) and (ii), but (iii) and (iv) will be considered first, and in opposition to them I will argue that although Tylor and others were guilty of a serious error, and although Boas detected and clearly identified that error, that error was *not* the alleged sin of "ethnocentrism." If, then, the error anthropologists must guard against is that found in Tylor's work, there is no need for them to adopt moral relativism, with all its paradoxical consequences.

In order to support the foregoing claim, I will need to review the central theme of cultural evolutionism. It will be useful to begin this review by taking note of the circumstances in which evolutionary theories were devised. A very important circumstance was the fact that cultural anthropology as we know it today had hardly begun in the nineteenth century. The thorough and careful fieldwork that we take for granted today was not then the basis on which anthropologists grounded their theories. Tylor's *Primitive Culture* was published in 1871, and more than two decades later Boas could still complain of the quality and trustworthiness of reports of exotic cultures:

> The descriptions of the state of mind of primitive people, such as are given by most travellers, are too superficial to be used for psychological investigation. Very few travellers understand the language of the people they visit, and how is it possible to judge a tribe solely by the descriptions of interpreters, or by observations of disconnected actions the incentive of

which remains unknown? But even when the language is known to the visitor, he is generally an unappreciative listener of their tales. The missionary has his strong bias against the religious ideas and customs of primitive people, and the trader has no interest in their beliefs and in their barbarous arts. The observers who really entered into the inner life of a people, the Cushings, Callaways and Greys, are few in number and may be counted at one's fingers ends.[1]

Boas asks here: How is it possible to judge a tribe solely by observations of disconnected actions the incentive of which remains unknown? He asks this rhetorically, but in the middle of the last century and well into the present one anthropologists engaged in much theorizing on the basis of such inadequate observation. The accounts of travelers and missionaries were filled with tales of curious and exotic practices found among the preliterate peoples of the world: cannibalism, human sacrifice, witchcraft, self-torture, brothers marrying sisters, and so on. These sketchy and sensational reports gave the impression that a tour of other cultures was something like a stroll through a carnival freak show. It was not only the Chinese who were inscrutable; so, too, was everyone other than us. Boas, in a lecture given in 1888, described this state of affairs as follows:

Many books of travel give us descriptions drawn in the most abhorrent lines of the people inhabiting foreign countries, describing their mode of life as similar to that of wild beasts, denying that there is any indication of emotional or rational life deserving our sympathy. In early descriptions of Australians, Bushmen, Fuegians they are often described as the lowest forms of mankind, void of all feeling for social obligations, without law and order, without imagination, even without shelter and tools.[2]

It is understandable that with this view of other cultures as their starting point those who theorized about mankind were struck by the differences among cultures, so that their most urgent question was: What accounts for these differences? Prior to the development of evolutionary theories, various racial theories had been advanced as the answer to this question. Cultural differences, it was said, are traceable to hereditary differences. As one theorist put it, "Certain traits of the mind of the Mongol, the Negro, the Melanesian and of other races are different from our own and different among themselves."[3] These racial theories, then, claimed that, aside from man's common animal needs, there is little or no common humanity.

It was against this background that evolutionary theories were developed, and for our purposes it is useful to think of them as a reaction against the theory that cultural differences are traceable to the fact that culturally different people differ from one another because of their hereditary "traits of mind." The hypothesis that cultures evolve, that is, that some are more advanced than others, was put forth to explain why cultures differ so greatly. The "great differences" being explained, it should be noted, are those reported by ill-trained observers.

The explanation offered by these theories allows, unlike the earlier racial theories, that behind these alleged differences lies a common human nature, in other words, that there is an innate *human* mind, with its stock of basic desires, motives, emotions, reasoning powers, and so on. So, on this view, even the most exotic peoples are, beneath it all, just like us and should therefore be understandable to us provided we take the right approach to comprehending them. Such was Tylor's message when he wrote:

> It is, I think, a principle to be held fast in studying the early history of our race, that we ought always to look for practical and intelligible motives for the habits and opinions we find existing in the world. . . . The very assertion that [the savages'] actions are motiveless, and their opinions nonsense, is itself a theory, and, I hold, a profoundly false one.[4]

What Tylor says here may seem entirely admirable and quite in keeping with current approaches in cultural anthropology. What Tylor really meant, however, is a different matter. For although he claimed to find "practical and intelligible motives for the habits and opinions" in other peoples, he did not go about this by conducting thorough and careful fieldwork among these peoples to discover their actual motives. Instead, he fell back on something he merely *assumed,* namely, that among the peoples of the world there is a stock of common desires, aims, motives, emotions, reasoning powers, and so on.

So the methodological assumption of the evolutionists was that in order to understand the seemingly inscrutable people of other cultures, we must attribute to them aims and motives of the sort that we, too, have. This assumption about their aims and motives gives us the theme of the evolutionists' theories: Primitive peoples, according to Tylor, share our aims, and if they were to pursue those aims with the same unfettered use of their innate capacities as we do, their culture would be like ours, and therefore the *difference* between their cultures and ours can be explained in only one way: unlike us, they do *not* make unfettered use of their innate capacities. In other words, they have not *evolved* to the degree that we have.

To understand Tylor's reasoning on this point, let us consider several illustrations. He took the view, for instance, that the myths found among primitive peoples are attempts to explain various natural phenomena and are thus products of the same motivation as has led to our sciences. The difference is that myths are not founded on trained observation and experiment. Similarly, to take a second illustration, Tylor held that those cultures that make use of the long-bow have, in this regard, the same purpose as those that make use of the more effective cross-bow, and that the difference between the two cultures is to be thought of as a difference in technological development, so that to explain why the former culture continues to use the more primitive long-bow, we must discover what retarded its technological development. And the same holds for most other cultural differences, such as differences in family structure, in artistic styles, and in morality.

On the evolutionists' view, then, the key to understanding the motley array of cultural differences is to allow that primitive peoples stand at an early stage of development, that they have not evolved intellectually, technologically, artistically, and morally to the degree that European civilization has. A principal reason for our superiority is that in our culture the reasoning capacity of men has been given freer reign in shaping our lives. Primitive peoples, by contrast, are largely regulated by tradition and taboo. In consequence, they cling to methods and practices which are, and can be seen by us to be, ineffective or otherwise inappropriate. So if we are to understand primitive peoples, we must recognize the degree to which, although they share our general aims, they act both out of ignorance and without the full benefit of reason.[5]

On the evolutionist's theory, then, the history of a culture may be compared to the history of science. Initially people's ideas about natural processes were quite fantastic, yet people adhered to these ideas because, for one thing, suitable methods of investigation had not been devised and, for another, there is a natural inclination to adhere to what is familiar and widely accepted. Yet as reason prevailed over these handicaps, there was an inevitable development toward greater knowledge and understanding, and the outcome is science as we know it today. Similarly, cultures, that is, the beliefs, practices, and institutions of a people, follow a natural and inevitable progression as, little by little, reason is allowed to operate in the pursuit of human goals. Some cultures have come a great distance along the course of this natural evolution, while others, clinging to their traditional ways, have remained somewhere near the beginning.

Such was the evolutionists's picture of man and of cultural differences. Its principal innovation was that it rejected the idea that culturally different peoples are hereditarily different in their mental traits and insisted, instead, that in their basic mental makeup all people are innately alike. (Boas rejected both views and held that the relevant mental traits are not innate at all, and so are neither innately the same nor innately different in various culture groups.) The evolutionist's claim of the innate mental uniformity of man gave particular significance to the further claim that preliterate peoples are highly "conservative," that is, mired in tradition and taboo. For when these two claims are put together, it is extremely tempting to see all cultural change on the model of the historical development in the sciences or in technology.

It is this model and the resulting ranking of cultures as higher or lower, as more or less primitive, that cultural relativists attack with their relativistic doctrine. That is, they attack the idea that we can speak of "evolution" here at all, and they attack it on the grounds that it *makes* no sense to rank cultures as higher or lower, as more or less developed. Relativists, in other words, take a very short way with evolutionary theory. They do not stop to ponder the evidence adduced by evolutionists; they write off the theory as though it were founded on an initially incoherent assumption about "values," namely, that the anthropologist's own culture embodies the highest of all values (or standards).

Was this also Boas's way of assessing evolutionary theories? In chapter 6 we will see that this was not his view at all. He treated cultural evolutionism as a theory we could readily understand (it wasn't nonsense), but he found fault both with the methodology used to support it and with certain of its implications. Yet, despite his objections to the theory, he did not entirely dismiss it. He allowed, as we will see, that in some instances an evolutionist explanation may be correct.

Boas's Criticisms of Cultural Evolutionism

A premise essential to evolutionism is that preliterate peoples are extremely conservative, wedded to tradition, shackled by taboos. Is this premise open to criticism? Evidently not. Most anthropologists, whatever theories they may hold, agree that there is overwhelming evidence of such conservatism. On this score, then, the evolutionists' theory is not vulnerable to criticism. Boas nevertheless found reason to take issue with it. He criticized two aspects of the theory: the attempt to demonstrate that there is a common, innate human mind and the claim that in every instance of cultural change the change is always from a more primitive to a more advanced stage of culture. Let us consider this latter aspect first.

Because evolutionists wanted to demonstrate that humans have progressed (advanced, improved), they claim not only (i) that the cultural phenomenon out of which some later phenomenon develops will be the same in every culture but also (ii) that in each case the former will be more primitive than the latter. Now if (ii) is to be empirically testable, then the criterion for establishing which of the two phenomena occurred earlier in time must be different from the criterion for determining which of the two phenomena is the more primitive. If the criteria were not independent, then (ii), instead of being a *factual* claim, would be perfectly vacuous.

Bearing this in mind, consider the methodological proposal that Tylor makes the basis of this theory. He points out, first of all, that "development in culture is recognized by our most familiar knowledge," and to illustrate this he cites several examples of mechanical invention where crude devices were replaced by superior ones. (For example, in firearms, the clumsy wheel-lock model was replaced by the more serviceable flintlock, which in turn gave way to the superior percussion-lock, which was then altered from muzzleloading to breechloading. Similarly, the medieval astrolabe was replaced by the quadrant, which was then discarded by mariners in favor of the sextant.) Tylor says:

Such examples of progression are known to us as direct history [i.e., in instances where the chronology is known from historical records], but so thoroughly is this notion of development at home in our minds, that by means of it we reconstruct lost history without a scruple, trusting to general knowledge of the principles of human thought and action as a guide in putting the facts in their proper order. Whether chronicle speaks or is silent, no one comparing a long-bow and a cross-bow would doubt that the cross-bow was a development arising from the simpler instrument. So among the savage fire-drills for igniting by friction, it seems clear on the face of the matter that the drill worked by a cord or bow is a later improvement on the clumsier primitive instrument twirled between the hands.[1]

Tylor goes on to maintain that this manner of interpretation, which is so plausible in the case of mechanical invention, may be used for the whole range of cultural phenomena:

In the various branches of the problem . . . of determining the relation of the mental condition of savages to that of civilized men, it is an excellent guide and safeguard to keep before our minds the theory of development in the material arts. Throughout all the manifestations of the human intellect, facts will be found to fall into their places on the same general lines of evolution.[2]

In other words, Tylor is saying that it is sound methodology to take ethnic materials (myths, customs, artistic design, agricultural methods, family structure, and so on) of *unknown* date and arrange them according to some principle (e.g., from simple to complex) which *to us* seems a logical progression from more to less primitive and to then regard that ordering as being *also* their order of historical development. But this amounts to collapsing the two criteria, criteria which must be independent if the proof of parallel development is not to be question-begging.

This defect in Tylor's methodology was pointed out by Boas again and again. Typical of his criticism is the following:

If . . . we are to form an acceptable theory of the origin of decorative designs, it seems a safer method to form our judgment based on examples the history of which can be traced with a fair degree of certainty, rather than on speculations in regard to the origin of remote forms for the development of which no data [as to chronology] are available. . . . Looking at this matter from a purely theoretical point of view, it is quite obvious that in any series in which we have at one end a realistic figure and at the other end a conventional figure, the arrangement is due entirely to our judgment regarding similarities. If, without further proof [of chronological development], we interpret such a series as a genetic series, we simply substitute for the classificatory principle which has guided us in the arrangement of the series a new principle which has nothing to do with the principle of our classification. No proof whatever can be given [in this way] that the series selected according to similarities really represents an historical sequence. It is just as conceivable that the same series may begin [historically] at the conventional end and that realistic forms have been read into it [e.g., a native artisan interprets a diamond pattern as a lake and begins drawing more and more realistic lakes in place of the traditional geometric design], and we might interpret the series, therefore, as an historical series beginning at the opposite end.[3]

Boas's point is that, given Tylor's aim of showing that cultural change always follows the same pattern in different cultures, he is obliged to, and yet fails to, verify this by using materials whose chronological sequence has been established independently of the developmental sequence that seems logical to him. Because Tylor has failed to do this, his methodology is question-begging, that is, his conclusion derives from his methodology rather than from the ethnic materials themselves.

Boas makes a point of saying that he does not intend, by this criticism, to deny the evolutionists' conclusion but intends only to show that they have given us no reason to believe it: "While I do not mean to deny that this development may have occurred, it would be rash to generalize and to claim that in every case the classification which has been made according to a definite principle represents an historical development."[4]

This, then, is the first criticism Boas leveled at evolutionism, and it should be obvious that there is nothing in this criticism that resembles any sort of relativism. So far, then, no reason has been found to agree with the claim that Boas, in criticizing evolutionism, demonstrated that cultural relativism is essential to the proper conduct of anthropology. Let us consider, then, whether his other criticisms support relativism.

Evolutionists maintained that human beings all have the same innate mental apparatus, and they claimed to have good evidence of this. The evidence, they said, is that there are many known instances in which some ethnic phenomenon, such as taboo or totemism or nature myths, had arisen in cultures so isolated from one another that the phenomenon could not have spread by cultural contact, by "diffusion." The inference drawn from this was that the human mind is so constituted that at a given stage of cultural development the innate apparatus of the (common) human mind will generate the phenomenon in question, in other words, taboo, totemism, or whatever.

At different stages in his career Boas leveled different criticisms at this aspect of evolutionism. In an early (1896) article he put the matter as follows. The evolutionists' view, he said, is that

if an ethnological phenomenon has developed independently in a number of places, its development has been the same *everywhere;* or, expressed in a different form, that the same ethnological phenomena are always due to the same causes. This leads to the still wider generalization that the sameness of ethnological phenomena found in diverse regions is proof that the human mind obeys the same laws everywhere. It is obvious that if different historical developments could lead to the same results [i.e., to the same ethnic phenomenon], then this generalization would not be tenable.

And yet, says Boas, "even the most cursory review shows that the same phenomena may develop in a multitude of ways."[5]

In order for the evolutionists' claim to be true, the evidence would have to show that any given ethnic phenomenon, such as the manufacture and use of pottery or the use of geometrical figures in design, will always, in whatever culture it is found, have developed out of an earlier ethnic phenomenon that is the same in each instance. For example, if in several cases where the chronology is known we find that geometrical designs developed out of naturalistic, representational forms, the evolutionists' theory tells us that this is the order of development we will find in all other cases. But do we find this? No, says Boas, the facts run contrary to the theory. What we find is that, for example, geometrical design does not in *every* case develop out of the same preceding artistic form:

> Recent investigations have shown that geometrical designs in primitive art have originated sometimes from naturalistic forms which were gradually conventionalized, sometimes from technical motives, that in still other cases they were geometrical by origin or that they were derived from symbols. From all these sources the same forms have developed.[6]

Boas cites numerous instances in which actual findings go against the evolutionists' view that developments are always of the same sort in all cultures. He concludes, "We cannot say [as evolutionists do] that the same phenomenon is always due to the same causes, and that thus it is proved that the human mind obeys the same laws everywhere."[7] Notice that Boas is not denying that humans have a common mental apparatus; he merely says that its existence has not been proved. Notice, also, that in this criticism there is, once again, no hint of cultural relativism.

In later years Boas leveled a very different criticism at the claim that the same ethnic phenomenon always has the same cause. Instead of arguing that there is evidence contradicting this claim, he began to argue that the plausibility of this claim rests on a methodological blunder. What evolutionists claimed to have found is that in many instances some ethnic phenomenon, such as totemism, had sprung up independently, in other words, in cultures so isolated from one another that the phenomenon could not have spread by diffusion. In order for such a claim to be true, there would have to be no doubt that when various examples are treated as the *same* phenomenon and designated, for example, "totemism" or "nature myths," these examples are really alike in the relevant way. This is where Boas noticed an extremely important and interesting problem, a problem, as he put it, about the "comparability" of ethnic phenomena. This is a problem we will be much concerned with in what follows, for it was Boas's solution to it that came to be thought of as the justification for relativism.

The nature of the problem and its bearing on the evolutionists' theory was explained by Boas in the following passage:

> It must be borne in mind that ethnic phenomena which we compare are seldom really alike. The fact that we designate certain tales as myths, that

we group certain activities together as rituals, or that we consider certain forms of industrial products from an aesthetic point of view, does not prove that these phenomena, wherever they occur, have the same history or spring from the same mental activities. On the contrary, it is quite obvious that the selection of the material assembled for the purpose of comparison is wholly determined by the [anthropologist's] subjective point of view according to which we arrange diverse mental phenomena. In order to justify our inference that these phenomena are the same, their comparability has to be proved by other means. This has never been done. . . . On the contrary, whenever an analysis has been attempted we are led to the conclusion that we are dealing with heterogeneous material. Thus myths may be in part interpretations of nature that have originated [as Tylor had claimed] as results of naively considered impressions (*Naturanschauung*); they may be artistic productions in which the mythic element is rather a poetic form than a religious concept; they may be the result of philosophic interpretation, or they may have grown out of linguistic forms that have arisen into consciousness. To explain all these forms as members of one series [i.e., as if they were the *same* phenomenon] would be entirely unjustifiable.[8]

Boas is making the same point again when he writes:

A serious objection to the reasoning of those who try to establish lines of evolution of culture lies in the frequent lack of comparability of the data with which we are dealing. Attention is directed [by the anthropologist] essentially to the similarity of ethnic phenomena, while the individual variations are disregarded. As soon as we turn our attention to these [variations] we notice that the sameness of ethnic phenomena is more superficial than essential, more apparent than real. The unexpected similarities have attracted our attention to such an extent that we have disregarded differences.[9]

Evolutionists had inferred a common mental apparatus from the alleged fact that, again and again, *the same* ethnic phenomenon (myths or totemism or taboo or the idea of life after death, etc.) had arisen independently in many cultures. In the above-quoted passages Boas disputes this alleged fact by arguing that evolutionists are guilty of having treated diverse phenomena as the same.

In the first of the two passages quoted above he makes this point with regard to myths. Elsewhere he makes the same point about taboo, totemism, the idea of life after death, and many other things. Here, for example, is what he says about taboo:

Ethnic phenomena are, on the whole, exceedingly complex. And apparently similar ones may embrace quite distinct complexes of ideas and may be due to distinct causes. To take a definite example: Taboos may be arbitrarily forbidden actions; they may be actions that are not performed because they are not customary, or those that are not performed because associated with religious or other concepts. Thus a trail may be forbidden because the owner does not allow trespassing, or it may have a sacred character, or it may be feared. All ethnic units, separated from their cultural setting, are artificial units.[10]

Boas's point, once again, is that although anthropologists have found in cultures that are isolated from one another certain ethnic phenomena that they classify as "taboos," we must not allow this classification to obscure the fact that these so-called "taboos" are of different sorts and have not all come into existence by the same psychological process. The importance of recognizing these differences is that the failure to do so may lead us to think we have found proof that human minds always evolve in the same way. But this inference, says Boas, depends on the mistaken idea that the ethnic phenomena that have been classified as "taboos" are everywhere the same. And that being so, cultural evolutionism cannot be established in the aforesaid manner.

Such, then, is Boas's criticism of the evolutionists' reasoning. What is important for our purposes, and what we must examine in detail, are the methodological insights that enabled Boas to discern differences which others had failed to see. His achievement is of general significance for anthropology, and the fact that he developed it in criticizing cultural evolutionists is comparatively unimportant. We may therefore leave the evolutionists behind at this point and investigate the broader significance of Boas's insights regarding the comparability of ethnic phenomena.

Boas's Methodological Insights

In the preceding chapter we found Boas warning that faulty cultural comparisons may result from mistaking similar features of several cultures for the same feature. I have cited several of his examples, all of which involved an anthropologist comparing several cultures, none of which is his own. But Boas was also concerned with mistakes that are made in cases of another sort, those in which someone misunderstands another culture because it superficially resembles his own in some respect. These cases, as we will see, are of special relevance to our inquiry because what Boas says about them has been construed as an endorsement of cultural relativism. In this chapter we will examine his treatment of these cases and consider whether he deals with them in a relativistic fashion.

It is possible to distinguish two distinct insights in Boas's discussions of what he called "the comparability of ethnic phenomena": (i) his recognition that we have a tendency to jump to false conclusions about the people of other cultures, and (ii) his proposed method for avoiding this mistake. Both of these are mentioned in his review of Graebner's *Methode Der Ethnologie,* where Boas gives particular attention to Graebner's chapter on the interpretation of ethnic phenomena:

> He defines interpretation as the determination of the purpose, meaning and significance of ethnic phenomena . . . but he does not devote a single word to the question of how these are to be discovered. He accepts, without any attempt at a methodological investigation, myths as interpretations of celestial phenomena . . . as, for instance, the Jona theme as signifying the disappearance of a heavenly body; a conclusion which I for one am not by any means ready to accept. At this place [Graebner's] complete omission of all psychological considerations makes itself keenly felt. The significance of an ethnic phenomenon . . . must be studied by means of psychological investigations in which the different interpretations and attitudes of the people themselves toward the phenomenon present

the principal material. In the case of mythology, by means of which Mr. Graebner exemplifies his considerations, I should demand first of all an investigation of the question: why, and in how far are tales explanatory or [instead] related to ritualistic forms? The very existence of these questions and the possibility of approaching them has been entirely overlooked by the author. On the whole, he seems to assume that the psychological interpretation is self-evident in most cases.[1]

What I have called Boas's two insights regarding the comparability of ethnic phenomena are expressed in this passage as follows: first, there is his observation that in most cases Graebner appears to think that the psychological interpretation of ethnic phenomena is self-evident, and second, there is his insistence that an anthropologist's understanding of ethnic phenomena must be based primarily on the "interpretations and attitudes of the people themselves." Let us consider these in order.

(i) Boas, as I said, recognized that we have a tendency to jump to false conclusions about the people of other cultures, and in his remarks about Graebner, Boas seems to explain this by saying that an anthropologist may think that the psychological interpretation of other people's conduct is "self-evident." This is an important insight, but it needs elaboration. Why might we think, upon encountering people of another culture, that their motivations, beliefs, and so on are entirely obvious ("self-evident")? Part of his answer is that an anthropologist may misinterpret some aspect of an alien culture because he mistakes it for an apparently similar aspect of his own culture. Our question, then, comes to this: Why, according to Boas, do anthropologists tend to neglect or overlook certain subtle, but important, cultural differences.

Boas's explanation of this tendency consists of two closely related parts, one of which is the following:

> As long as we do not overstep the limits of one culture [i.e., our own] we are able to classify its features in a clear and definite terminology. We know what we mean by the terms family, state, government, etc. As soon as we overstep the limits of one culture we do not know in how far these may correspond to equivalent concepts. If we choose to apply our classification to alien cultures we may combine forms that do not belong together and separate what belongs together. The very rigidity of definition may lead to a misunderstanding of the essential problems [of interpretation] involved.[2]

To illustrate this sort of misunderstanding, Boas comments that there may be in another culture a term that we might translate as "soul" although they understand a "soul" to be a tangible object. Boas is evidently suggesting that a misunderstanding would arise in this instance if we translated their word as *soul* and took them to be saying what members of our culture say when they speak of their soul. As Boas remarks:

> One of the serious difficulties that has never been adequately dealt with is the lack of a precise understanding of the concepts with which alien

cultures are operating. These must be obtained from a study of the semantics of the language of the people whose culture we wish to study. . . .
Our knowledge of the semantics of primitive languages is wholly inadequate, and still, without [such knowledge], we can not understand the
world in which they live.[3]

Boas is no doubt right that we may jump to mistaken conclusions about
people of another culture if we have first used inappropriate English terms
for describing their beliefs and actions. But what accounts for our having
given—or having accepted—the misleading description in the first place?
After all, the mere fact that we are giving a description in English does not
force us to use words that are not altogether appropriate or force us to omit
whatever qualifying terms would prevent misunderstandings. So why would
someone go wrong in the manner Boas describes?

Here we come to the second part of his explanation of why the "psychological interpretation" of another people may seem "self-evident" to us. He
points out that when we come upon a culture quite different from our own,
we bring with us expectations and ideas derived from our own culture—
expectations about what people take the world to be like, ideas about what
motivates people to act as they do, and so on. As Boas puts it, our "psychological observations and conclusions are based essentially on experiences
[we have had] in our own culture," and mistakes can result from "transferring [to other cultures] the results of observations in our own culture."[4] Let
us consider how this part of Boas's explanation might go together with the
first part.

When an ethnographer initially encounters the people of an alien culture,
there is often nothing to tip him off at the outset that this or that English
word, unless explicitly qualified, will be misleading if used in describing the
beliefs or attitudes or actions, etc. of these people. To a considerable extent,
of course, there is no problem at all in using English straightforwardly to
describe what he observes of this other culture. People of all cultures sit and
stand, walk and run, eat and sleep, are born and die. For food they kill
animals or catch fish or raise crops or gather roots and berries and so on.
If they raise crops, they plant them, cultivate them, and harvest them. And
what they eat, they eat raw or cooked, and if cooked, it is roasted or boiled
or baked, etc. All of this and much more can be described in familiar English
words, and although we may add augmenting phrases, as in "baked in the
coals" or "baked in an adobe oven," this is not because the English word
("bake") is less than apt. When we encounter Eskimos or Bantus or Zunis,
we are not encountering an alien life form, so we can say much about them
in the same words and phrases we use in speaking of ourselves, and it is
obvious, even on our first encounter with them, that we can do so.

At what point, then, will it occur to us that we will be speaking mislead-
ingly if we continue, beyond the examples I have given, to describe them in
the same terms we use in speaking of ourselves? The problem is that when
someone first encounters a culture about which he knows absolutely noth-

ing, he will have no reason to suspect that they have beliefs he has never heard of and that they may have misconceptions about various natural processes, as some groups of Eskimos did when they thought that the role of sexual intercourse in procreation is, not to produce new life, but to feed the fetus in the mother's womb. It would be understandable, then, if such a novice were to proceed unhesitatingly to talk about these people without noticing that they are not always thinking and feeling and doing what he assumes they are thinking and feeling and doing. To see the kind of misinterpretation this can lead to, let us consider a particular instance.

Suppose that our novice encounters for the first time the Ojibwa Indians. One thing he would soon notice is that the Ojibwa frequently bring food to one another, and not merely to family members but to anyone whose hunting or fishing has been unsuccessful or who is too old or too feeble to catch their own fish or collect their own berries. Our novice could also easily discern that this activity is not dictated by tribal law, for there is no threat of public sanctions for those who do otherwise. It would therefore be natural for our novice to use the word *share* to describe these acts, and he might begin to speak of the Ojibwa's "food sharing." Perhaps he also uses such words as *giving, offering,* and *helping* in this connection. Understandably, then, he is likely to conclude that he has observed, in their "food sharing," many acts of generosity among the Ojibwa. Would he be right in this?

The truth of the matter is rather complex. First of all, living in a northern climate with extremely severe winters, any Ojibwa family may from time to time find itself without food. Fishing through the ice is often unsuccessful and trap lines are frequently empty. Parceling out their food, then, is a way of mitigating the hardships caused by an undependable food supply. In addition to this, the Ojibwa are great believers in the power of sorcery. (In 1945 Ernest Oberholtzer, who spent much of his life among the Ojibwa, related to me the following: A man at Red Gut claimed, with great satisfaction, to have brought about, by sorcery, the death of a man one hundred miles away at Lake of the Woods who had, he believed, sorcerized his two young sons, causing them to fall through the ice and drown.)

In view of the hardships resulting from an undependable food supply, it is understandable that an Ojibwa would suspect someone of malevolent motives who failed to share food with him during a lean period. Conversely, if he fails to share his food with a family in need, he can only imagine that they will suspect him of malevolent motives, and he must therefore live in fear of being sorcerized by them. In short, the ultimate motivation for food sharing among the Ojibwa is their fear of sorcery. Hallowell reports a confirming instance: "An Indian overlooked another man when he was passing around a bottle of whiskey. Later when this Indian became ill, he was certain that the man he overlooked got angry and sorcerized him. His illness was a revengeful act in retaliation for not sharing the whiskey."[5] What, then, are we to think of our novice's impression that the Ojibwa are acting from generosity when they share their food? We needn't conclude that the Ojibwa are lacking in generosity and share *only* when threatened, but once aware of the cultural circumstances, we can no longer regard their sharing food with others less fortunate as acts of generosity.

Yet it is entirely understandable that our novice should have mistaken the Ojibwa's food distribution for what it was not. Because our culture does not generally operate on the fear of sorcery, our novice, when he sees someone carrying a basket of berries to a hungry old woman or offering fish to a family that has none, will interpret this as an act of generosity. Why? Because of the resemblance of their actions to our own acts of generosity.

Here we can see how the various parts of Boas's explanation go together. First of all, we find here an instance of what Boas was speaking of when, in discussing faulty cultural comparisons, he warned that "there is [a] danger of overlooking, on account of general resemblance, significant dissimilarities."[6] But we can also see why the dissimilarities might be overlooked. In his encounter with the Ojibwa our novice is unaware that he is misled by expectations and ideas he has derived from his own culture. Moreover, the resemblances he notices lead him to describe the Ojibwa in terms drawn from his own language, not only "sharing" but also, perhaps, "giving," "offering," "helping"—terms that carry the suggestion of generosity. It is easy to see, then, how in cases such as this the failure to look beyond the superficial resemblances will lead to faulty cultural comparisons and how, in a case like that of the Ojibwa, one could misunderstand the moral character of an action, such as mistaking the Ojibwa's food distribution for acts of generosity.

Mistakes of this kind, which result from projecting some aspect of one's own culture onto another, were described by Boas in a passage quoted earlier, where he says that because our "psychological observations and conclusions" are based primarily on what we have learned in our own culture, mistakes can result from "transferring" them to other cultures. Henceforth I will refer to this kind of mistake as the Projection Error.

(ii) Let us turn now to Boas's own methodological proposals. In the passage quoted above from his review of Graebner, Boas insisted that the "principal material" for our interpretation of ethnic phenomena must be the "interpretations and attitudes of the people themselves." Elsewhere he says: "If it is our serious purpose to understand the thoughts of a people, the whole analysis . . . must be based on their concepts, not ours."[7] These proposals will hardly seem startling to those who are beneficiaries of the fieldwork done in this century, but Boas stood at the beginning of all that, and recalling the extent to which, in his day, anthropologists relied upon the reports of missionaries and world-travelers (see chapter 5), we can appreciate the revolutionary nature of his advice.

As early as his participation in the Jesup North Pacific expedition of 1898 Boas had been concerned to investigate the natives' own understanding of their actions, practices, and institutions. In presenting his Kwakiutl ethnography, which resulted from that expedition, he wrote:

It seemed to me well to make the leading point of view of my discussion, on the one hand an investigation of the historical relations of the tribes to their neighbors, on the other hand a presentation of the culture as it appears to the Indian. For this reason I have spared no trouble to collect descriptions of customs and beliefs in the language of the Indian, because in these Kwakiutl descriptions points that seem important to him are emphasized, and the almost unavoidable distortion contained in the descriptions given by the casual visitor and student is eliminated.[8]

We have already seen what it is that makes such distortions "almost unavoidable."

In other passages Boas combines his diagnosis of these distortions with his insistence on investigating the natives' own understanding of their actions, customs, and beliefs. One of these passages is the following:

The activities of the mind . . . exhibit an infinite variety of form among the peoples of the world. In order to understand these clearly, the student must endeavor to divest himself entirely of opinions and emotions based upon the peculiar social environment into which he is born. He must adapt his own mind, so far as feasible, to that of the people whom he is studying. The more successful he is in freeing himself from the bias based on the group of ideas that constitute the civilization in which he lives, the more successful he will be in interpreting the beliefs and actions of man.[9]

Boas repeats this point elsewhere as follows:

The data of ethnology prove that not only our knowledge but also our emotions are the result of the form of our social life and of the history of the people to whom we belong. If we desire to understand the development of human culture we [i.e., anthropologists] must try to free ourselves of these shackles. This is possible only to those who are willing to adapt themselves to the strange ways of thinking and feeling of primitive people. If we attempt to interpret the actions of our remote ancestors by our rational and emotional attitudes we cannot reach truthful results, for their thinking and feeling was different from ours. We must lay aside many points of view that seem to us self-evident. It is impossible to determine *a priori* those parts of our mental life that are common to mankind as a whole and those due to the culture in which we live. A knowledge of the data of ethnology enables us to attain this insight. Therefore it enables us also to view our own civilization objectively.[10]

In these two passages Boas combines his two insights: (i) his diagnosis of how it comes to pass that investigators give distorted accounts of other cultures, and (ii) his insistence on investigating the natives' own understanding of their actions, customs, and beliefs.

In these two passages, then, Boas provides us with an excellent account of his methodological proposals. The reader may be surprised, therefore, to learn that these passages are among those often cited as proof that Boas was a cultural relativist. Let us consider, then, what possible reason there might be for drawing such an inference from these passages.

I do not deny that these passages show that Boas was out of sympathy with cultural evolutionism. But was his lack of sympathy due to a relativistic strain in his thinking? We can answer this question by considering how he might have responded to what Tylor says in the following passage about the romantic idea of the Noble Savage:

> The ideal savage of the 18th century might be held up as a living reproof to vicious and frivolous London; but in sober fact, a Londoner who should attempt to lead the atrocious life which the real savage may lead with impunity and even respect, would be a criminal only allowed to follow his savage models during his short intervals out of gaol. Savage moral standards are real enough, but they are far looser and weaker than ours. . . . Altogether, it may be admitted that some rude tribes lead a life to be envied by some barbarous races, and even by the outcasts of higher nations. But that any known savage tribe would not be improved by judicious civilization, is a proposition which no moralist would dare to make; while the general tenor of the evidence goes far to justify the view that on the whole the civilized man is not only wiser and more capable than the savage, but also better and happier, and that the barbarian stands between [them].[11]

Boas would certainly have been critical of what Tylor says here. But does this make him a relativist? A relativist would reject Tylor's view because he thinks it makes no sense to say, as Tylor does, that the civilized man is "better" than both the savage and the barbarian. Would Boas have criticized Tylor in the same way?

No, Boas had quite a different reason for taking issue with Tylor. To understand this, there are three things to bear in mind about Tylor's remarks. First, he is clearly making a cultural comparison, a comparison of the actions of civilized men with those of "savages and barbarians," and for this reason Boas's warnings about the potential for errors in such comparisons becomes relevant to Tylor's remarks. Second, those warnings have particular relevance to Tylor's remark that "in sober fact, a Londoner who should attempt to lead the atrocious life which the real savage may lead with impunity and even respect, would be a criminal only allowed to follow his savage models during his short intervals out of gaol." Why would a Londoner be a criminal and confined to jail if he emulated the life which a savage may lead with respect? Because, so Tylor was thinking, certain of the savages actions are *the very same actions* which merit a criminal conviction under English law. In other words, Tylor was assuming that actions respected among savages and the criminal conduct of Londoners have the same motivation. Third, this comparison, which Tylor treats as a "sober fact," is a conclusion he derives from a lengthy recitation of examples of the (alleged) moral depravity of primitive peoples. Tylor cites the "wild-beast-like cunning" of the Papuans' attacks on European travelers, the "foul and brutal" character of the Eskimos, the "malignant ferocity" with which the Carib Indians "tortured their prisoners of war with knife and firebrand and red pepper, and then cooked and ate them in solemn debauch," and the "cruel and treacherous malignity" of the North American Indian, whose "religion expressed itself in absurd belief and useless ceremony."[12]

These descriptions of the Papuans, the Eskimos, and others are meant to show that they conduct themselves like the criminals in our midst, and this is where Boas would have found reason to take issue with Tylor. He would have raised the question whether these descriptions present us with "sober facts" or are merely the result of Tylor's being guilty of what I have called "the Projection Error." Boas might have raised this question by pointing out, for instance, that cannibalism is culturally sanctioned where it is believed that a warrior, by eating certain parts of his enemy's body, can acquire his enemy's courage or skill. He might have pointed out also that when the torture of enemies is culturally sanctioned, the motivation for this is not (or not always)—as in *our* culture it might be—a malignant desire to watch someone suffer. As Redfield says about this practice among the Huron indians: "I learned that torture of captives was performed, not just to cause pain but to test and exhibit demonstrations of fortitude—a virtue and value shared by the torturer and the tortured. The custom remains terrible, but it has, with this understanding, become more human."[13] Thus, Boas might say that Tylor, in attributing to "savages" the vicious motives behind the criminal conduct of Londoners, has failed to understand their thinking and has then projected onto them the motives that superficially similar actions might have in our culture.

We find Boas taking such a position when, in discussing the comparability of ethnic phenomena, he speaks of "crimes like murder" and writes:

> From an ethnological point of view murder cannot be considered as a single phenomenon. Unity [of ethnic phenomena] is established by introducing our juridical concept of murder. As an act murder must be considered as the result of a situation in which the usual respect for human life is superseded by stronger motives [such as jealousy, greed, rage, etc.]. . . .
> [A] father who kills his child as a sacrifice for the welfare of his people, acts from such entirely different motives [i.e., motives so different from jealousy, greed, and rage], that psychologically a comparison of their actions does not seem permissible. It would seem much more proper to compare . . . the sacrifice of a child on behalf of the tribe with any other action performed on account of strong altruistic motives, than to base our comparison on the common concept of murder (Westermarck).[14]

Here we find Boas insisting that the motive for performing a human sacrifice can be very different from the motivation for conduct we declare to be murder. His allusion here to Edward Westermarck is significant because Westermarck makes much the same point when he writes:

> We find . . . among many people the custom of killing or abandoning parents worn out with age or disease. . . . This custom is particularly common among nomadic hunting tribes, owing to the hardships of life and the inability of decrepit persons to keep up in the march. In times when the food-supply is insufficient to support all members of a community it also

seems more reasonable that the old and useless should have to perish than the young and vigorous. . . . What appears to most of us as an atrocious practice may really be an act of kindness, and is commonly approved of, or even insisted upon, by the old people themselves.[15]

It is obvious why Boas would cite Westermarck with approval: Not only in this case, but in others as well, Westermarck calls attention to situations in which we may be guilty of the Projection Error, guilty of projecting on to the people of another culture vicious motives that they do not have. And Boas might have pointed out that Tylor, in his recitation of savage "atrocities," shows no awareness of this.

The fact that we do misjudge people in this way was Boas's reason for declaring that "the general theory of valuation of human activities, as developed by anthropological research, teaches us a higher tolerance than the one we now profess."[16] What Boas claims to have found through anthropological research is that an appearance of vicious conduct can arise simply from the fact that, because we do not understand the beliefs and motives of another people, we are prone to project onto them assumptions derived from our own culture. The tolerance we learn from this discovery, far from being a wholesale and indiscriminate exoneration of culturally condoned practices, is tolerance of only those actions and practices which we, in our failure to understand them, may *mistakenly* believe to be analogous to actions in our own culture that are unfair or cruel or in some other way vicious. As Westermarck says of his example from Eskimo life: What *appears to us* to be atrocious may be, in reality, an act of kindness.

Here there arises a question that, although a digression from our present concerns, must be addressed: Is Boas implying that Knife Chief was mistaken in his moral criticism of the human sacrifices carried out by his own people? Was he implying that Knife Chief should have been more tolerant of that practice? The answer to this question cannot be a simple one, but it is hinted at in what Redfield says about the Hurons, namely, that once we understand their treatment of captives, we will conclude: "The custom [of torture] remains terrible, but it has, with this understanding, become more human." The phrase "becomes more human" is unhelpfully vague, but it means, I take it, that we won't think that the Hurons were acting like a vicious dictator who tortures political prisoners to extract information or to his intimidate political opponents. Even so, says Redfield, the custom remains terrible, that is, we shouldn't want to see it continued.

Boas might say something like this about human sacrifices: They are not like murders committed from greed or jealousy, but even so we shouldn't want to see this practice continued—and not just because it does not have the efficacy its practitioners suppose but for the moral reasons given by Knife Chief. In this case, then, the "tolerance" of which Boas speaks would come to this: While we might, if the opportunity arose, interfere, as Knife Chief did, with the performance of a human sacrifice, we would not think that those who perform such sacrifices by custom and from sincere belief deserve to be tried and punished for murder. Even so, this case is quite different from that mentioned by Westermarck: One could not say of a human sacrifice what Westermarck says of the Eskimo practice. One could not say that the sacrifice, although it appears to us to be atrocious, may really be an act of kindness. Although Boas, in his remark about tolerance, makes no distinction between such cases, there is no reason why he should not have, and I will assume henceforth that his position allows such a distinction.

It should now be clear that it would be a mistake to think that Boas, in his criticism of cultural evolutionism, was advancing a relativistic argument. The tolerance he urges upon us is tolerance of conduct whose moral character we may wrongly estimate because we do not understand it, which does not amount to anything like relativism. Such misunderstandings arise, Boas points out, when, as the result of being seduced by superficial similarities, we project onto the people of another culture ideas derived from our own about what people believe and why they act as they do. Accordingly, his proposed method for avoiding such unwitting projections is that we should guard against being seduced by superficial resemblances and proceed, instead, to fathom the actual beliefs and motives from which people act. Clearly, there is nothing in this proposed method that moral absolutists could not accept, for there is nothing in their doctrine that precludes them from trying to understand other cultures as fully as possible.

The fact that Boas's proposed method is not incompatible with moral absolutism should, together with other reasons I shall mention below, lead us to expect that there would be widespread recognition that Boas was no relativist. Yet this goes very much against the conventional wisdom of modern anthropology. The claim that Boas endorsed cultural relativism is commonplace in the literature and has, so far as I can discover, gone unchallenged among anthropologists. Herskovits, in his forward to the 1963 edition of Boas's *The Mind of Primitive Man*, states that Boas in this book "adumbrates what we have come to call *cultural relativism*."[17] David Bidney, another anthropologist, is more explicit: "In contrast to the monistic theory of cultural evolution involving mankind as a whole, Boas and his followers in America preferred a pluralistic theory of the history of cultures. The notion, accepted by Tylor, that our Western European civilization represents the highest point of cultural development seemed to [Boas] obviously ethnocentric, and he therefore preferred the alternative of cultural pluralism and cultural relativity."[18] Elvin Hatch has recently written that "Boas . . . was largely responsible for developing cultural relativism in American anthropology."[19]

As remarked above, one reason for disputing this reading of Boas is the fact that absolutists could, without modifying their view, endorse the use of Boas's method of cultural comparisons. This is not, however, the only reason for dismissing the claim that Boas was a relativist.

A second reason for doing so is the following. Relativists maintain that a practice, regardless of what it may be, can never be morally criticized if it is culturally sanctioned. This has two implications: (a) We will never come upon a culture that deserves moral rebuke on account of some practice it condones. (b) Someone who morally criticizes a practice condoned by his own culture will be talking nonsense because this would be comparable to an Englishman declaring that his countrymen regularly drive on the wrong side of the road. Nothing that Boas says implies either of these things. Consider (a): Boas's method enables us to recognize that certain alien practices are not, as they initially seem, cruel or unfair or in some other way vicious, but it does not guarantee that *every* alien practice will be found harmless or less than vicious once it is fully understood. Boas could perfectly well allow, for example, that once we know everything of relevance about the Carib Indians we may find, as Tylor claimed, that their treatment of captives was sheer cruelty. As for (b), we have the example of Knife Chief, who was morally critical of the human sacrifices regularly practiced by his own people. Unlike relativists, Boas offers no reason for thinking that Knife Chief's criticism is nonsensical.

A third important difference between Boas's method and the relativist's doctrine lies in the different ways in which these are used in criticizing cultural evolutionism. Relativism deploys a thoroughly general argument against the evolutionist's conclusion that cultures stand in an order of higher and lower in development, including moral development. This conclusion must be rejected, according to relativism, because such ranking, which allows Tylor to say that civilized men are "better" than savages and barbarians, would be legitimate only in case moral absolutism were true, which it is not. Boas proposed no such general argument; he did not argue that evolutionism *cannot* be true. Moreover, he did not direct his criticism at the evolutionist's conclusion but argued instead (see chapter 6) that the methods Tylor used to prove that conclusion were so defective that we have, as yet, no reason to believe that cultural evolutionism is true.

Had Boas been truly a relativist, he would have dismissed out of hand all theories of cultural evolution. This, in fact, is what David Bidney (see above) and many other commentators take his attitude to have been. But this is a mistake, for Boas did not categorically dismiss evolutionism. On the contrary, he was constantly at pains to insist that his disagreement with the evolutionists, as well as with other anthropological theorists of his day, was a disagreement over methods, not conclusions. What he was opposed to, he said, is "forcing phenomena into the straight-jacket of a theory."[20] In place of such dubious a priori theorizing, Boas proposed "another method, which in many respects is much safer," namely, "a detailed study of customs in their relation to the total culture of the tribe practicing them."[21] Anthropologists must undertake this intensive study of existing cultures, said Boas, and "relegate the solution of the [evolutionists'] ultimate question of the relative importance of parallelism of cultural development in distant areas, as against worldwide diffusion, . . . to a future time when the actual conditions of cultural change are better known."[22]

Thus, unlike relativists, Boas leaves it an open question whether and in what respect or to what degree one culture is superior to another. There is nothing in what Boas says to rule out sensibly thinking that the elimination of slavery from our modern means of production is a definite improvement, or that modern military planning, which envisions the use of nuclear weapons, is, as Bertrand Russell has said, the most evil in history.[23]

The fourth difference is this: Relativism, as noted earlier, has a number of paradoxical implications, such as that Franca Viola was guilty of wrongdoing when she refused to be manipulated by the rejected suitor who raped her. Boas's method has *no* such implications. The reason for this difference, of course, is that relativism presents a certain philosophical theory of morality, whereas Boas presents no such theory at all.

The fifth and final difference for purposes of this discussion is that Boas's methodological proposals, unlike relativism, provide anthropologists with some practical guidance, guidance that is genuinely useful for avoiding mistakes of a kind that anyone comparing cultures is prone to make. That mistake can be illustrated by a line from the last passage quoted above from Tylor. Tylor says that despite the romantic idealization of the savage, "in sober fact, a Londoner who should attempt to lead the atrocious life which the real savage may lead with impunity and even respect, would be a criminal only allowed to follow his savage models during his short intervals out of gaol."

Relativism teaches that such remarks are nonsensical, and anthropologists who receive their training from relativists will undoubtedly refrain from making comparisons like Tylor's. But how will such restraint make them competent anthropologists? Consider once again the example of someone for the first time coming upon an Ojibwa campsite and observing that they frequently share food with one another. How are relativistically trained anthropologists rendered competent to understand what is going on in this case? Perhaps they will *refrain* from saying that the Ojibwa, as evidenced by their foodsharing, are generous people. But merely refraining from such remarks is not, in itself, a contribution to anthropology.

Compare this with the fruits of Boas's method. The point of his method, as he tells us, is to get behind cultural similarities that are merely superficial in order to discover the motivations, conceptions, and other impulses that are at work in other cultures. How might anthropologists be trained in this method? One would, I suppose, present them with numerous examples and require them to do two things: first, to take note of similarities of conduct that might mislead one if one assumes that they are more than superficial (e.g., an Eskimo may leave a parent to freeze to death and someone in Chicago may do that, too) and, second, to look further in other cultures for evidence of how the conduct in question is explained and understood by the people themselves. Doing this will not always be easy. Who would guess, for example, that what the Ojibwa do with their food needs to be understood in connection with their fear of being sorcerized?

In other cases the task will be less difficult. Boas himself discusses such a case in an early (1894) article in which he criticizes certain racial theories. One of his criticism is that travelers who claim to have found that different races exhibit different mental qualities are guilty of making faulty comparisons. As an illustration of this Boas writes: "The traveller, desirous to reach his goal as soon as possible, engages men to start on a journey at a certain time" and is then disgusted to find them dallying and not ready to travel. From this, says Boas, the traveler mistakenly concludes that these people are "fickle," lacking in perseverance. The traveler makes this mistake, Boas explains, because he "measures the fickleness of the people by the importance which he [the traveler] attributes to the actions or purposes in which they do not persevere," whereas "the proper way to compare the fickleness of the savage and that of the white is to compare their behavior in undertakings which are equally important to each." If we observe him engaged in matters important to his own life, such as the manufacture of his utensils and weapons or awaiting the appearance of his guardian spirit as he fasts on a mountain top, we find that "primitive man perseveres," said Boas, but does so "in certain pursuits which differ from those in which civilized man perseveres."[24]

This is a nice illustration of Boas explaining his method. And my point is that what Boas teaches—not only in this instance but in many of his discussions of the comparability of ethnic phenomena—has a practical bearing on the conduct of anthropology, whereas relativism never could. In order to avoid the Projection Error, it is no use joining relativists in their general resolve not to be judgmental about the people of other cultures, for this general resolve is no guarantee that when it comes to actual cases one will discern the real motives of Ojibwa or Dyaks and thereby avoid being taken in by superficial similarities. That is to say, when I walk into an Ojibwa encampment for the first time and observe them passing along food to those in need, there is nothing in the relativists' resolve that enables me to understand this conduct. I could be a relativist and still think the explanation is, as Graebner put it, self-evident.

The importance of this last observation will become apparent in chapters 10 and 11, where we will find that relativists themselves commit the Projection Error and that they do so because, unlike Boas, they have not realized that the key to the problem of fathoming the actual motives of alien peoples is to avoid being seduced by superficial similarities.

There are, then, these five important differences between Boas's method and relativism. It should not be surprising, therefore, that Boas, in his only published comment on moral relativism, explicitly rejected that doctrine. Anthropologists, he said, are "easily led to a relativistic attitude" because the diversity of cultural "forms" is so great that "there might seem to be no common ground on which to base absolute standards." But this is a mistake, he continued, for "the ethical standards in the group are the same everywhere." "Thus, the study of human cultures," Boas concluded, "should not lead to a relativistic attitude toward ethical standards. The standards within the group are the same everywhere, however much they may differ in form."[25]

These remarks show clearly that Boas was opposed to moral relativism. They also reveal two other things. First, they show that he had the mistaken idea that moral relativism is false because, although cultures differ in superficial ways, they are, beneath these differences, alike as regards their moral standards. In other words, he had the mistaken idea—so common among nonphilosophers—that moral relativism can't be true if there are "cultural universals."

In addition, Boas's remarks leave no doubt that he believed that his own views do not support moral relativism. This presents us with the puzzling fact that his two most famous students, Herskovits and Benedict, were leading proponents of moral relativism and believed themselves to be expounding Boas's ideas. Clearly, they had gravely misunderstood him. How was this possible? How, that is, could Herskovits and Benedict—along with many other anthropologists—have mistaken Boas's ideas for relativism? How could they have failed to appreciate those great differences that I have pointed out in this chapter? This is the question to which we now turn.

8

Relativism and Ethnocentrism

Those who claim that relativism is essential to the proper conduct of anthropology argue as follows: (i) Ethnocentrism is a hazard that anthropologists must scrupulously avoid. (ii) The way to be permanently on guard against this hazard is to embrace relativism. (iii) Boas demonstrated anthropology's need of relativism. (iv) He did this by demonstrating that evolutionist theories of culture resulted from the ethnocentrism of those who devised these theories. In the preceding chapter, propositions (iii) and (iv) were shown to be false. This leaves us, however, with two questions: Are propositions (i) and (ii) nevertheless true? and Why have anthropologists thought that they are? This latter question is of more than merely historical interest, and it is this question that I want to take up next.

The question can be put this way: If, as we have seen, Boas was *not* demonstrating anthropology's need of relativism, why then have anthropologists thought that they did need that philosophical doctrine? One possibility is that, having seen that Boas's method is unquestionably essential to anthropology, anthropologists have then made the mistake of equating Boas's method with relativism and so have mistakenly reasoned that anthropologists, because they cannot dispense with Boas's method, must be relativists. This is not the only possibility, but we will do well to consider it, for by doing so we may come to understand the perplexity some anthropologists have felt about this whole matter.

Is there good reason, then, for thinking that anthropologists have mistakenly equated Boas's method with relativism? I believe there is and that evidence of this mistake can be found in their writings. One sort of evidence is the group of passages (see chapter 7) in which Herskovits, Bidney, and Hatch declare Boas to have been a relativist. Such passages do not, however, help us to understand how anthropologists could have made this mistake. More revealing is the following passage by Robert Redfield, an anthropologist who struggled throughout his career with the difficulties surrounding relativism, for it reveals how Boas's method might become confused with relativism.

> For a time in the course of anthropological development the prevailing conclusion of theoretical . . . importance was that anything might be found right and good. The foundation of morality appeared to lie only in the judgments of each particular local community. This was the anthropological rejoinder to both a theologically justified morality and that philosophical morality that assumed or declared the presence of moral faculties or inherent moral insights. Westermarck's well-known book was such a rejoinder. Later anthropologists dropped his method of taking a custom here and a custom there and turned instead to the study of custom and morality as these appeared in the life-ways of particular societies, usually primitive, and studied intensively by direct observation. As anthropologists came to work themselves more intimately into exotic human societies, they came to understand that, if the unfamiliar human being does something even shockingly different from what educated Western people generally do, the "rightness" often lay in how the thing done entered into and was further explicable by something in the total way of life of that people. It was no longer possible to stop with the assertion, "Those people think it right to kill their fathers, or practice cannibalism, or marry one's sister." Seen in its full context, there was much more to be said as to why these things were done and thought right and good. The Eskimo who walled up an aged parent in a snow house and left him to die, did so because in their hard, migratory life the old person could no longer travel, endangered his close kinsmen by his presence, and perhaps himself endured an almost unbearable existence. Furthermore, good reporters of actual cases of these assisted suicides—for that they were, rather than homicides—show the tenderness, even the filial respect, with which the thing was done. Cannibalism, found to be not one custom but many different kinds of customs, showed in one of its forms, a ritual partaking of the flesh of a slain enemy into which entered, among other elements of feeling and belief, a respect for the valor, one might say the spiritual strength, of that enemy. . . . I am, of course, not trying to represent primitive life as high-minded and supremely ethical; there is much that is cruel and terrible in what people do. I am merely trying to make the point that to the anthropologist the shock of the different began to disappear as it came to be understood that each traditional way of life was a somewhat coherent statement, in thought and action, of a good life. Seen in context, most customs then showed a reasonableness, a fitness with much of the life, that allowed the outsider more easily to understand and more reluctantly to condemn. At this point in the development of the understanding of differences in group-ways the phrase "cultural relativism" came into use. The basic tenet of cultural relativism is the proposition that the rightness of what is done by another people follows from *their* view of things, not from ours.[1]

Redfield's remark that anthropologists abandoned Westermarck's way of thinking when they recognized the necessity of understanding actions in their "full context," presumably tells us how anthropologists abandoned relativism (which is the position Westermarck espoused) and replaced it with Boas's method. That this is what Redfield meant to say is confirmed by his handling of the examples he gives, for he treats them, not relativistically, but as Boas might have. Yet, surprisingly, toward the end of the passage, Redfield declares this newer approach to be cultural relativism. But of course it is not. (There is nothing in his treatment of those examples that an absolutist could not accept.) So there is a curious vacillation in the passage, a confusion that Redfield was unaware of.

This confusion shows through also in Redfield's ambiguously saying that the "basic tenet" of relativism is "that the rightness of what is done by another people follows from *their* view of things, not ours." Does this describe relativism or Boas's method? Is Redfield saying that an individual who acts from the beliefs and motivations current in his own culture is necessarily beyond moral reproach (relativism), or is he saying that we must discover what beliefs and motivations people are acting from in order to decide whether they are acting generously, selfishly, cruelly, or unfairly (Boas's method)? I would guess that Redfield did not have either of these alternatives clearly and exclusively in mind and that his ambiguous wording reveals that in his own thinking he had confused these.

In both these respects, then, Redfield's remarks tend to confirm my suggestion that Redfield has failed to distinguish Boas's method from relativism, has mistakenly equated the latter with the former, and so came to think that adopting Boas's method is the same as embracing relativism. (Incidentally, Redfield's remarks elsewhere leave no doubt that he understood cultural relativism to be that philosophical doctrine identified in earlier chapters of this book, i.e., the doctrine having a variety of paradoxical implications, such as that it is a mistake for outsiders to be morally critical of Nazism.)[2]

The reason that Redfield, as well as many other anthropologists, have made this mistake is that the following equation has become entrenched in their thinking: Whoever is not a relativist is an absolutist, and absolutism necessarily involves ethnocentricity. In later chapters we will examine the assumption that one must choose between relativism and absolutism, that is, that there is no other alternative. But for now, *given* that assumption, it would seem inevitable to anthropologists that if they are *not* to regard Boas as a relativist, they must regard him as an absolutist, which is unthinkable because absolutism is inherently ethnocentric. Notice how A. L. Kroeber, an anthropologist, puts the matter:

> An absolute standard involves two qualities. First, it must be extranatural, or supernatural, to be an a priori absolute. And second, ethnocentricity is implied in the elevation of any one actual standard as absolute. By contrary, standards or value-systems conceived as parts of nature [i.e., as *social* in origin] are necessarily . . . relative and comparative. That the first condition to the scientific study of culture is the barring of ethnocentrism has been a basic canon of anthropology for three-quarters of a century.[3]

Kroeber presents the issue in terms of the following dichotomy: One must either be a moral absolutist, in which case one is bound to have ethnocentric attitudes, or be a moral relativist and thus be free of ethnocentrism. If most anthropologists accept this dichotomy (and I suspect they do), how will they classify Boas? Inasmuch as he was, in many ways, the father of modern anthropology, anthropologists would find it unthinkable to suppose that Boas was anything but a relativist. And this, I submit, explains why Redfield and others have failed to notice the enormously important differences between Boas's method and relativism. They have not taken the trouble to understand properly Boas's method because they have assumed that they understood it perfectly well: It was just the well-known doctrine of cultural relativism.

Can it now be said that there are overwhelmingly good reasons for anthropologists to abandon relativism and acknowledge that it is of no use at all to their discipline? To answer this question we need only recall that Boas, as we saw in chapter 7, was prepared to leave open the question whether, or in what respect, one culture may be superior to another. In short, he was not in principle opposed to making cross-cultural moral comparisons. So an anthropologist who is prepared to follow Boas and dismiss relativism will have to allow that it may be perfectly appropriate, in *some* cases, to make (unbiased) moral criticisms of other cultures. But for many anthropologists this presents a problem because, as we saw in the preceding chapter, it is widely assumed both (a) that only moral absolutists can think it legitimate to make moral criticisms of other cultures and (b) that absolutists are predisposed to rank their own culture superior to all others. Given this assumption, the *only* way to avoid a prejudicial ranking of cultures would be to embrace relativism. For this reason some anthropologists—we might call them *philosophical* relativists because of their eagerness to do battle with absolutists—would reject any proposal to abandon relativism and replace it with Boas's method.[4]

These philosophical relativists will want to press the following objection against Boasians:

> You have not demonstrated that relativism is inessential to anthropology, for its use lies in combating ethnocentrism, and you haven't shown that it's no longer needed for that purpose. What you have shown is that *in certain cases* Boas's method enables us to see that an alien practice that we might at first think was atrocious can, when properly understood, be reconciled with our moral attitudes. But you have given no reason for thinking that *all* problematic cases can be disposed of in this way, and surely it's implausible to think that they can. Yet it's precisely where we cannot, by means of Boas's method, reconcile an alien practice with our own moral attitudes, that is, cases in which our moral objections remain, that ethnocentrism will rear its ugly head. For in these cases people will adopt the absolutists' view that they are superior to those who engage in the alien practice. This is especially true of cases in which religiously based

moralities conflict, for in such cases each sect believes it is following divinely ordained principles and that infidels violate divine law. So Boas's method, although valuable in itself, is no substitute for cultural relativism; we need the latter doctrine as well. It's our only safeguard against ethnocentrism.

This rejoinder makes two claims: first, that there are cases in which Boas's method does not suffice for removing moral condemnations of alien practices, especially when religiously based moralities are in conflict, and second, that it can be seen that whoever makes those condemnations is guilty of ethnocentrism. Are both of these claims true?

The first is unquestionably true. Consider, first, the case of religiously based moralities. Catholicism, for instance, maintains that the use of contraceptives to prevent pregnancy is contrary to God's law. So let us ask: When an orthodox Catholic anthropologist comes upon a culture whose members employ contraceptives to prevent pregnancy, could he or she, by employing Boas's method, come to see that these people are doing nothing wrong? Of course not! He would think that these people are in need of moral instruction.

When we turn to secular examples, we find something similar. For even if we invoke no religious teachings, how will we think of, for instance, the case of Franca Viola? When we have learned all there is to know about the motivations and cultural circumstances of those Sicilian men who rape women in order to force them into unwanted marriages, we are not going to think, "The man who raped Franca was within his rights to do so" or "That man did nothing wrong." No, our moral objections to that Sicilian practice are not going to be removed by a Boasian inquiry into the motivation of Sicilian men.

So it is easy to see that the relativist would be right in making the first of the above claims. But is the second claim true as well, that is, are we guilty of ethnocentrism when we refuse, in cases like that of Franca Viola, to withhold moral condemnation of an alien practice? Consider once more those Europeans who have undertaken to rescue Arab women from "honor killings"—can we rightly say that they are guilty of ethnocentrism?

To answer this question, we must recall the meaning of the technical term "ethnocentrism." A moral judgment is said to be the product of ethnocentrism if those making the judgment have failed to realize that a moral principle cannot be stated in an entirely general way (e.g., "Rape is wrong") but must be formulated in such a way as to include a reference to the culture(s) that espouse the principle. Those who have embraced this relativized account of morality argue: "Since there was no moral prohibition *in Sicily* against a man's raping a woman to force her into marriage, Franca Viola's rapist cannot be morally condemned for what he did, and if *we* say that he did wrong, we are guilty of ethnocentrism."

Obviously, the term "ethnocentrism" presupposes that the relativistic account of morality is correct. For that reason, only someone who has already embraced relativism could think that if we condemn the rape of Franca Viola we *are* guilty of ethnocentrism. This brings us back to the question: How does anyone ever get so far as to think that relativism is true?

As we saw in chapter 1, it is a mistake to think, as some relativists have, that their doctrine is shown to be true by the fact that some cultures condemn what others condone, for this is not something an absolutist denies. What the absolutist holds is that when two cultures differ morally, only one of them embraces *true* moral principles. This is what the relativist is obliged to attack, and he does so, as we have seen, by arguing that *all* moralities are acquired in the same way, namely, by a process of "enculturative conditioning" and that therefore none of them is known to be true. This is what relativists claim to have discovered by means of ethnographic research. In order to assess this claim properly, we will have to resume our search for the evidence anthropologists adduce in support of it. At this point, then, we are not in a position to decide whether an anthropologist who proposed to reject moral relativism and employ Boas's method could defend himself against the relativist's accusation that he will be prone to make prejudicial cultural comparisons.

9

Is There Evidence Supporting
Moral Relativism?

We turn now to the claim that the truth of moral relativism has been established by data anthropologists have gathered by studying various cultures. This means, of course, that until someone had done the relevant research, it was not known that morality is relative. Our investigation, therefore, must proceed with the following idea: There was a time at which an anthropologist was not yet a relativist, then he came upon some ethnographic data that led him to conclude that morality is relative. So we need to ask: What sort of data might that have been? What sort of discovery could persuade someone who is not yet a relativist that moral relativism is true?

One thing we already know is that the data we are looking for supposedly show that there are *different moralities* among the world's various cultures. We also know that cultures are said to have different moralities when "a mode of conduct which among one people is condemned as wrong is among other people viewed with indifference or enjoined as a duty." And, as I have already noted, if there *are* cases that fit this definition, even nonrelativists must be able to recognize that they fit it. Let us see whether we can find examples that meet these requirements.

At first sight it may seem that evidence of the right sort can be easily discovered by considering instances in which the adherents of a religious faith condemn as immoral certain conduct that is unobjectionable to people who don't share their beliefs. A case of this sort was mentioned at the beginning of chapter 4: the case of a Christian missionary who declared that the Tahitians, on account of their sexual conduct, were "sunk . . . in brutal licentiousness and moral degradation." Here we have a case in which the conduct that is condoned in one culture, the Tahitians', is condemned in another, the missionary's. But does this demonstrate the existence of different moralities? Let us assume that the Tahitians engaged in extramarital sexual relations and that the missionary believed that there is a divine prohibition against such conduct. The Tahitians, of course, did not share this belief. So in this case there is plainly a difference of *belief*. But who is going to describe this as a clash of two *moralities*? We know that relativists will so describe it, but our question is whether anyone else will.

Here we should notice that the phrase "different moralities" does not already have a common use *before* relativism comes on the scene. In this respect "different moralities" is not like "different religions." The latter phrase has a very common use, as when someone says, "Sixty different religions are practiced in the United States" or "Various members of my family practice three different religions." By contrast, if someone who had never heard of moral relativism were asked, "How many different moralities are there in the world?" or "How many different moralities are there among your classmates?" it isn't likely this person would understand the question right off. It would sound peculiar. Or, to put the same point in another way, when we encounter someone who disagrees with us about some moral issue, such as whether to use animals in medical research, we don't commonly say that that person has "a different morality." We say that we "don't agree" with them or that they "disagree with" us about the matter. It is important, then, to bear in mind that the phrase "different moralities" gets introduced by relativists, and it gets introduced with a particular meaning. For saying that two people from different cultures exhibit by their actions that they have *different moralities* must mean that each of those people is, in his own way, acting morally.

That being so, does the case of the Tahitians and the missionary provide us with evidence of the sort that relativists can use to prove to us that their doctrine is true? If so, then anyone, even the missionary himself, must be able to see that he and the Tahitians have different moralities, that is, that the Tahitians were acting *morally* but according to their own principles. But is this, in fact, what the missionary thought? No, he concluded that the Tahitians were depraved and in need of moral instruction. He certainly would not have allowed that the Tahitians' conduct shows that there are different ways of being moral, his own way being merely one among several.

This result suggests that cases such as this—cases involving religious convictions—may not provide evidence for the relativists' view of morality, that is, evidence that will convince people who are not already relativists that there are different and conflicting moralities. Some moral relativists have conceded this, and in chapter 13 we will investigate this matter in greater detail. For the present, then, let us confine ourselves to cases in which, although no religious beliefs are involved, one culture condemns as immoral the very same conduct that another either views with indifference or enjoins as a duty. I will henceforth refer to these as type A cases. As we will see, there is no difficulty in finding type A cases. But will nonrelativists think that they are examples of "different moralities"?

Type A cases are of two kinds. This is because the conduct that is morally condemned in one culture is, in the other culture, either (i) regarded as a duty or (ii) regarded with indifference. Let us consider these separately, beginning with the first. An example would be the "honor killings" mentioned in chapter 4. In the rural areas of some Arab countries, if a young woman becomes pregnant out of wedlock, her male relatives regard it as their duty to restore the family honor by killing her. People who are not members of this community regard the matter very differently: We regard these killings as morally wrong, and efforts have been undertaken by Europeans to rescue potential victims. Here, then, we have a case in which the same conduct is regarded as a duty in one culture and morally condemned in another. But is this an example of different moralities? How is that to be decided?

Are we to assume that this can be decided simply by observing how members of the several cultures conduct themselves and what they say? This assumption would be in keeping with the relativists' idea that moral rules are like rules specifying which side of the road to drive on. For in order to discover that two countries have different driving rules, one need only observe what their drivers do and say. So if relativists are right about the nature of morality, it should be easy to study a culture to learn what its morality is and how it may differ from others: We need only observe what the people typically declare to be right or wrong and whether they act accordingly. (We need not, that is, investigate how they came to say what they say and need not use our critical faculties to evaluate the moral cogency of what they say, e.g., whether the moral justifications they give are self-serving or dishonest rationalizations for their conduct.) So if we proceed on the aforementioned assumption, we will have to allow that the Arabs in question have an obligation to kill certain of their female relatives, for they *say* they are obliged to and act accordingly. And having allowed this, we will be forced to conclude that they have a morality that is different from ours, for *we* do not think that "restoring the family's honor" justifies killing someone.

This much, then, is clear: *If* we assume that the relativists' view of morality is correct, then when we come upon type A cases of this sort, we will think we have found evidence proving that cultures have different moralities. But such reasoning would beg the question, for we are supposed to be able to find evidence for relativism *without* first assuming that it's true. So let us remind ourselves of how matters stand when we do not begin by taking for granted the relativists' view of morality.

Suppose we had an Arab friend who came to us in anguish over the fact that his parents had ordered him to carry out an honor killing of his younger sister. Would we say to him, "She's unmarried and pregnant, so it's *your duty* to kill her"? If moral relativists are right, this is what we would say, for we would *know* that our friend has the duty to kill his sister. We would know this because we know what his community says and does in such situations. But of course we would *not* say that! We would no more say that than we would say that Franca Viola's rapist did nothing wrong because what he did was standard practice in his Sicilian culture. Instead, we would try to convince our troubled friend that he does *not* have a duty to kill his sister.

It must be, then, that our ordinary understanding of morality is not the same as the relativists'. The latter think that to discover what a person's moral obligations are we need only observe what members of his or her culture typically say their obligations are and whether they act accordingly. One can, obviously, learn much in this way, but there is also much that this procedure may fail to detect. As I remarked above, one will not learn in this way how people came to say what they say, nor will one have evaluated the moral cogency of what they say, for instance, whether the moral justifications they give are self-serving rationalizations. If we are not already relativists, we are likely to think that these are important matters. For we understand that people can be morally obtuse, self-deceiving, lacking in imagination, and overly conventional, that their thinking can be riddled with cliches, burdened with misconceptions, and ruled by fear or hatred. What people, even whole cultures, think and say about moral issues may be no more than what has been drummed into them by propaganda, as in the case of Nazi Germany. Are we going to say that the Nazis had a morality, albeit one that differs from ours? Surely not! Rather, they had a fascist mentality and a trumped up hatred of Jews and other minorities, whom they used as scapegoats for the economic woes that beset Germany after World War I. Hitler was a megalomaniac, and his followers were sycophants, opportunists, cowards, and self-deceivers. Their program of genocide was not the outcome of their earnestly and honestly inquiring how people ought to be treated.

As I said, we would try to convince our Arab friend that he is not obligated to kill his sister, but this, I am now pointing out, doesn't mean that we would merely say the opposite. Rather, we can lead our troubled friend through several lines of inquiry, one or another of which may enable him to see the practice of "honor killings" in a new light. Perhaps he will come to regard the notion of "family honor" as a bizarre anachronism and so come to think it grotesque to place the "honor" of one's family above the life of one's sister. This will not involve—as a relativist would think—his merely switching allegiance from one set of rules (or principles) to another. It will be more like a man's coming to see in a new light the macho attitude that he and his fellow countrymen grew up with—coming to see machismo as a ludicrous sort of preening and strutting.

My point is that if we are not already relativists, we are likely to understand that morality involves much more than the relativists' account of it suggests. I will explore this in greater detail in later chapters, but I think I have said enough to show how we would regard type A cases of the sort we have been considering: We will not be inclined to think that they constitute evidence that cultures can have different moralities.[1] I think we may conclude, then, that type A cases of this sort do not constitute the empirical evidence that relativists claim to have found.

Let us consider now some type A cases of the other kind: those in which the conduct that is morally condemned in one culture is condoned or regarded with indifference in another. It is easy enough to find cases we could describe in this way. For instance, we know of cultures that have condoned slavery, and slavery is something we most definitely "condemn as wrong."

We know, too, of cultures that have condoned cockfighting, bullfighting, and other bloody amusements that are regarded in our culture as plainly cruel. Also, cultures have condoned the painful and debilitating practices of footbinding and clitoral circumcision, which most other cultures would regard as wholly unjustifiable mutilation. And we know that many cultures have condoned wife-beating—indeed, some African cultures still do, whereas in our culture a wife-beater is regarded as a cruel bully.

These are all obvious examples of one culture condoning or viewing with indifference the very same conduct or activities or practices that another culture morally condemns. But do such cases constitute evidence that obliges us to embrace moral relativism? If they do, then anyone who contemplates the examples just cited should think: "So there *are* different moralities!" And yet this is not, in fact, what we would think—at least not if we haven't already embraced moral relativism. The reason, of course, is that we think of people who beat their wives, for example, as callous or cruel. We are not about to dignify wife-beaters as having "a morality of their own." Nor do we think of Sicilians as having "a different morality" because they condone raping women to force them into unwanted marriages. We do not, that is, think of those Sicilian rapists as being concerned to do the right thing; we think of them as selfishly manipulating women, and we are ready to applaud any woman who refuses to be thus manipulated.

What about slavery? It is sometimes maintained that slavery in ancient Greece, unlike slavery in modern times, cannot appropriately be condemned by us because of the way the Greeks thought of it—as being natural and inevitable or as being simply the fate or bad luck that befalls some human beings. In opposition to this view it has been argued that the ancient Greeks can't rightly be shielded in this way from moral criticism because, not only were they capable of understanding that slaves suffered, but we can rightly say that the Greeks' way of thinking of slavery was self-serving or that they were guilty of willful ignorance.[2] I am inclined to accept the latter view of this matter and to say, therefore, that someone who is not already a relativist will not be moved to embrace that doctrine upon learning of the practice of slavery in ancient Greece. But even if we are inclined to adopt the other alternative and exempt the ancient Greeks from moral censure, this would not amount to our conceding that the Greeks had a "morality of their own." This is so because that alternative does not declare that those Greek slave-holders decided, after earnestly considering whether their practice was morally justified, that owning slaves is a good or decent or honorable thing to do. Rather, that alternative declares that the ancient Greeks lacked the conceptual wherewithal to ask moral questions about slavery or, if not that, then they viewed slavery through concepts of a nonmoral sort, such as fate. So no matter which alternative we deem most reasonable, that is, whether or not the ancient Greeks, on account of their use of slaves, are morally blameworthy, this example does not force us to think: "So there *are* different moralities!"

My general point about type A cases can be made as follows. Suppose that a friend arouses herself from a reverie and says to us: "Some cultures condone the very conduct that others condemn as immoral." Suppose also that, upon hearing this, our thoughts turn immediately to some well-documented type A cases, such as the practice in Thailand of parents selling their daughters—girls as young as twelve or thirteen—into prostitution. Thinking that such cases illustrate our friend's musings, we respond in agreement, "You are surely right about *that*!" But would we amplify this by saying: "There are *several* different moralities, perhaps more than we know of"? Of course not! Since we are thinking exclusively of the conduct involved in type A cases, we will be inclined, not to any conclusion about there being "different moralities," but to a conclusion about man's inhumanity to man—and woman! Thinking of the countless victims in type A cases—slaves, rape victims, women who have been mutilated or severely beaten, twelve-year-old girls forced into prostitution, and on and on, we might say, echoing Joseph Conrad's Kurtz, "Oh, the horror! The horror!"

It seems, then, that type A cases are not of the right sort to start someone thinking relativistically. Or it might be more accurate to say: Noticing type A cases will not start us thinking relativistically *unless we play fast and loose with words*. In chapter 1 I quoted Kroeber and Kluckhohn as saying that "sincere comparison of cultures leads quickly to recognition of their relativity." I went on to point out that something more must be involved, for moral absolutists are not going to embrace relativism upon learning about certain cultural differences. And yet there is a way that someone might become a relativist as quickly as Kroeber and Kluckhohn think we should. It is very common to find the issues involved in this topic being presented by use of the word *values*. It is said, for example, that cultures differ in their values. So we must ask: "Consider some particular type A case, such as wife beating. Does the fact that culture X condones and that culture Y condemns such conduct demonstrate that these cultures differ in their values?" I have already pointed out that we should not want to say that they have different *moralities*. But what about their *values*? The trouble here is that "values" is a word that is commonly used very sloppily. What are we to include in an account of a person's or a culture's values? Does a person's depravity or his callousness, for example, reveal his values? If "values" were used with some precision, we could answer. But we can't. For this reason when people use the word *values* in discussions of moral relativism, they are prone to define the word as they please. Moreover, it is quite easy to see how someone might define it in such a way that—given the fact that type A cases exist—the truth of moral relativism is decided by his or her definition. Suppose someone reasoned as follows:

> The question whether relativism is true is the question whether cultures differ in their values, where the term *values* is defined as follows: A culture's values are constituted by what its members are and are not permitted or required to do, and that, in turn, is revealed in the conduct of its

members, that is, in whether or not certain conduct (or its omission) is commonly punished or stigmatized or condoned. This being so, cultures that condone or give their blessings to, for example, wife-beating or the coercive use of rape (and there *are* such cultures) are cultures whose values *differ* from ours, since we condemn, rather than condone, such conduct. So there are cultures having different values.

If we found someone reasoning in this fashion, should we think that they have proved that there are different moralities? Of course not! They have certainly proved that cultures have different *values*, but this is of no interest at all. No one wants to dispute this reasoner's claim that cultures have different "values," because the word *values* has been defined so sweepingly that *any* conduct—even the most depraved and vicious—must be allowed to reveal someone's values. Therefore, not even moral absolutists have an interest in denying that values, as *thus* defined, are relative! And yet I suspect that there are those who, having defined "values" in that way, believe that they have shown that *moral relativism* is true. This is perhaps why Kroeber and Kluckhohn thought that anyone who compares various cultures will *quickly* conclude that relativism is true.

Returning now to my point about type A cases, it seems they are not of the right sort to start someone thinking relativistically. For this reason I am disposed to think that those who have become moral relativists did not do so by surveying a number of type A cases. Prior to becoming relativists they would have regarded such cases just as others do. As proof of this I offer the following observation. When the atrocities of Nazi Germany became apparent in the 1940s, many relativists beat a hasty retreat from the doctrine. What can we infer from this fact? Plainly, if type A cases (of which Nazism would be a paradigm) had been the data that originally led them to embrace relativism, the revelation of Nazi atrocities would have been received by them as *additional* proof that relativism is true. The fact, then, that they did *not* so receive it shows that they did not have type A cases in mind when they initially thought they had found evidence for moral relativism.[3]

We are told by relativists that the study of many different cultures provides the data from which relativism follows. Yet our search for the relativists' data has met with failure at every turn. Must we, then, abandon the search for such evidence? I think this would be premature. Relativists have said so often and so emphatically that their doctrine is supported by evidence that I suspect that there are cases of some sort that have at least *seemed* to relativists to provide the evidential grounds for their view of morality. The problem is to figure out what sort of cases these might be.

In trying to figure this out, we can take guidance from two considerations. First, we are looking for cases which make us think that there are *different* moralities, but in order for that to be so, there must be something—one and the same thing—that these moralities differ *about,* and that means that the mode of conduct that is condoned or enjoined in one culture must be—or at least *appear* to be—the same mode of conduct that is morally condemned in another. Now type A cases meet this requirement, for when we condemn wife-beating as vicious, we are condemning the *same* conduct for which excuses are given in cultures which permit wife-beating. But type A cases, although they meet this requirement, cannot, as we have seen, be the cases we are looking for. That being so, we can formulate a second requirement as follows: The conduct that is condoned in the one culture must not be conduct, such as wife-beating or rape, which a nonrelativist would regard as obviously cruel or brutal or unfair, etc.

It is difficult to see how anything could satisfy both of these requirements, for they seem to cancel each other out. And they would do just that were it not for the fact that the first of the above requirements contains the phrase "or at least appear to be." Evidently, then, we must take seriously the following possibility: The cases that have led relativists to think that there are different moralities—which I will call "type B cases"—are cases in which the conduct that is condoned in some cultures, although it may *appear* to be the same conduct that is condemned in others, is *not* the same conduct.

What sort of cases might these be? We already have a clue to this in Boas's insights about the comparability of ethnic phenomena, such as his remark, quoted in chapter 5, that the ethnic phenomena found in several cultures are often treated by anthropologists as the same, when in truth "the sameness of the ethnic phenomena is more superficial than essential, more apparent than real." What I am suggesting here is the following. When anthropologists believe that they have found evidence which supports their doctrine, they are making the mistake that I have called the Projection Error, that is, they have *mistakenly* thought that the conduct which is condemned in our culture is the *same* conduct that is condoned in some other.

If they do make this mistake, that would not by itself explain why they come to embrace a relativistic account of morality. Someone guilty of the Projection Error in a given instance might simply conclude that the people in question, because they condone vile conduct, are morally lax or depraved. If so, he would be mistaken, but he would not be a relativist. Something more, then, is involved, something that makes relativism seem plausible.

To illustrate this, I will present a fictitious example of my own devising. In this example the Projection Error will be clearly in evidence. Moreover, an additional error—one that leads straight to relativism—will be present in such a transparent way that there will be no difficulty in recognizing it. My fictitious example is the following.

Suppose that in a tribe, known as the Mobimtu, it is expected that when a boy reaches the age of passage his father will begin to talk a great deal about the boy's greatness and goodness. He is to speak often, and even with some exaggeration, about his son's prowess, exploits, and possessions. To fail in this parental duty is regarded as a failure to provide the son with the self-confidence that is necessary for meeting the rigors of tribal life. Now if we should happen upon this tribe and notice a man going on in this fashion about his son's prowess, exploits, and possessions, we might be reminded of some neighbor of ours back home who constantly brags about his chil-

dren. We might then think: What an obnoxious fellow, always puffing himself up with exaggerated tales about his son! And as we notice more and
more of this going on in the tribe, and notice also that no one castigates
these men for their constant and (as it seems to us) insufferable bragging,
we might conclude that the Mobimtu have no scruples about bragging.

It is at this point that the turn toward relativism may occur. Anthropologists studying the Mobimtu would soon recognize that this "bragging"
occurs under prescribed circumstances and that it has the social function of
preparing boys for adult life. And having recognized this, they might think:
"It is a mistake for outsiders to scorn the Mobimtu for their bragging, for
although it sounds vainglorious to our ears, they see nothing wrong in it,
and it serves a valuable purpose in their lives. The Mobimtu simply have a
different morality from ours: We think that bragging is wrong, but they do
not."

Let us suppose that the Mobimtu were an *actual* tribe and that someone
who has observed or read about the Mobimtu were to reason in this manner.
If he were also given to philosophizing, what conclusions might he reach?
At the very least, he would conclude that he had found empirical proof that
cultures can have different and conflicting moralities. He might also reach
the further conclusion that the evidence he has found shows that the morality that is alien to him, the Mobimtu's morality, does not, at least as far
as their bragging is concerned, deserve his censure. This is an incipient form
of moral relativism, but it is not full-blown relativism because it applies only
to this one instance and because this instance is quite a tame one. By this
last remark I mean the following. If we are to arrive at a form of relativism
that will do the job assigned to it by most anthropologists, it will have to
be capable of going up against the views of evolutionists, who support their
claim that our civilization is superior to others by citing (what they take to
be) the most egregious examples of savage and barbarous conduct. (See the
remarks by Tylor quoted in chapter 7.) What is needed, in other words, is
a form of relativism that extends even to type A cases. But how does our
philosophizing anthropologist arrive at this more robust form of relativism?

We already know the answer: Having gotten himself onto the slippery
slope to relativism by way of the Projection Error, and having no inclination
to second-guess himself, our theorist plunges ahead to bring type A cases
under the tent of relativism. And he does so by means of what, in chapter
1, I called the relativist's Fully Developed Argument, which cites the (alleged)
fact that there are different moralities as evidence showing that morality is
acquired, not by a truth-finding procedure, but by a process of enculturative
conditioning. Armed with this conclusion, the relativist is ready to oppose
the claim that certain cultures, because they condone the conduct involved
in type A cases, are morally deficient.

We can now see how one might, by starting with actual cases that resem-
ble my Mobimtu example, eventually arrive at full-blown moral relativism.
We can also see the several ways in which this reasoning would be flawed.
The first mistake involved is the Projection Error, which in this case leads

one to think that the Mobimtu fathers are great braggarts. They are not, of course, for although they talk in ways that sound to our ears like bragging, the Mobimtu are not extolling their sons in order to reflect credit or glory upon themselves.[4] Also they differ from braggarts in that they are doing only what is expected of them. (There may be braggarts among them, but if so, this would have to show itself in other ways than by their carrying out this parental duty to their sons.) The first mistake, then, is what Boas noted when he warned against thinking that "the psychological interpretation is self-evident" and that we can describe other cultures using words (e.g., "bragging") already in our vocabulary.

The second mistake incorporates and compounds the first. It consists in retaining the idea that these men are bragging and then, having noticed that this is prescribed behavior, concluding that *bragging* is morally approved of by the Mobimtu. One could also describe this compounding of the first mistake, the Projection Error, in the following way. One's first impression of the Mobimtu was that they are insufferable braggarts, and now one tries to correct this mistake, tries to dispel one's disgust, but *without* retracting the word *bragging*. How does one do this? By adopting a relativistic account of morality, by telling oneself: "Each culture has its own morality and there are no grounds for thinking that ours, which condemns bragging, is superior." It will be useful to have an additional name for this compounded error, so I will call it "the Relativizing Ploy."

Here, incidentally, is also where the term "ethnocentrism" gets invented. It comes from having made the compound error that I have been describing. Only as the result of this error could one come to think that "ethnocentrism" (as contrasted with ordinary bigotry or xenophobia)[5] actually occurs and needs to be combated. In other words, one will think that the term "ethnocentrism" means something only if one fails to recognize the Projection Error for what it is and consequently undertakes to combat its consequences in the wrong way, with the Relativizing Ploy.

The right way, the Boasian way, to combat that error in the foregoing example would be to bring out the fact that Mobimtu fathers are doing something very different from bragging. A relativist would say: "Your disgust with the bragging of the Mobimtu fathers is a sign of your ethnocentrism. But you must overcome your disgust because the Mobimtu have, after all, a different morality, and there is no way of proving that ours is superior." Boasians, by contrast, would have no need for the term "ethnocentrism" because they would dispel the disgust by pointing out, quite simply, that the Mobimtu fathers are *not* bragging.

It is when the Relativizing Ploy is generalized as a philosophical theory of morality—a theory that compares morality to rules of the road which (arbitrarily) prescribe which side to drive on—that moral relativists encounter embarrassment over cases such as Nazism and the rape of Sicilian women.

It should now be obvious that one way to become a relativist is by failing to make the right use of Boas's insight that we sometimes introduce distortions when we describe in our own terms the people of another culture. It is therefore surprising that two of the greatest champions of relativism were Boas's protégés, Benedict and Herskovits. They, of course, thought that in espousing relativism they were following Boas's lead. Although they were mistaken about this, their confusion is understandable. They and other relativists thought they were following Boas's lead because he does show that, in cases like the one I have invented, our criticism of or contempt for the people of another culture is unwarranted. But this similarity of result is no reason for thinking that relativism is a proper development of Boas's insight. On the contrary, relativism perpetuates the very mistake—the Projection Error—that Boas detected and warned against.

I have now explained as clearly as I can the *kind* of confusion I am attributing to anthropologists who claim to have found, in actual cases, evidence that has led them to embrace moral relativism. It remains to be seen, however, whether my diagnosis is correct, whether we can discover relativists actually making this mistake when they present their evidence. This is not an easy thing to discover. (If it were, no one would ever make the mistake.) So in the writings of anthropologists, the dual mistake illustrated by my Mobimtu example will not be as transparent as in that fictitious case. In particular, we should not expect always to find the two parts of the dual mistake occurring separately. That is, if the Mobimtu were an actual tribe being studied by an anthropologist, who happens also to be a relativist, we should not expect that in his published research he would first write, "The Mobimtu fathers are insufferable braggarts!" and then later on write: "Their bragging, I have come to realize, deserves our tolerance because these men are carrying out a parental duty." Rather, we should expect the published version to suppress the initial reaction ("Insufferable braggarts!") and to say simply: "The bragging of the Mobimtu fathers is a parental duty, and this shows that their morality differs from ours where bragging is concerned." Here the two parts of the dual mistake are telescoped; the only sign that the first mistake—the Projection Error—has been made is the retention of the word *bragging*. It is this telescoping of the two mistakes that we should expect to find in the writings of anthropologists if they have come to embrace relativism in the manner I am suggesting.

This last fact may lead some to wonder whether that first mistake is ever made at all, especially by trained anthropologists. To allay this suspicion, I will cite in the next chapter the admissions by several people, including anthropologists, that they have made the first mistake, the Projection Error. In these instances those who made the mistake came to recognize and correct their error and so did not proceed, as relativists do, to compound the Projection Error with the Relativizing Ploy. Once we have examined these self-confessed instances of the first mistake, we will proceed to consider examples of the compound error.

10

Some Obvious Instances
of the Projection Error

Let us recall what the Projection Error consists of. It occurs when, having witnessed (or perhaps read about) certain actions of an alien people, one misconstrues their actions because of the following circumstances: (a) one is ignorant of the actual motivation of those people, and (b) their actions appear similar in some way to actions of a sort that might occur in—or that one is familiar with from—one's own culture. These are the circumstances in which it is possible to commit the Projection Error. The error itself consists of thinking, on account of their similarity, that the actions of an alien people are actions of the *same* sort as actions that might occur in—or that one is familiar with from—one's own culture.

This error can take somewhat different forms, depending on which sort of familiar actions one takes the foreign actions to be. Our Ojibwa example is one in which the error was to mistake Ojibwa foodsharing for familiar acts of generosity. Someone who made this error might, in consequence, form a highly favorable opinion of the Ojibwa. There are, however, cases in which the Projection Error would readily lead someone to form an unfavorable opinion of another culture. My Mobimtu example is designed to illustrate this. In this case the error consisted of mistaking the conduct of the Mobimtu fathers for familiar acts of bragging, and had this been an actual case, someone who made this error might form the opinion that the Mobimtu are insufferable braggarts. (And in a more extreme version of this, the foreign action might be mistaken for some sort of criminal conduct that one is familiar with from one's own culture, in which case one would form the erroneous opinion that the foreign culture condones conduct that is vicious or dishonest or in some other way morally unacceptable.) Finally, the Projection Error can also occur in cases in which no evaluations will result because the actions in questions are neither laudable nor despicable. In the general conduct of anthropology, mistakes of all three sorts are of equal significance, that is, it is equally important to correct the mistake involved in them. But they are not of equal significance in our investigation of moral relativism, for the only relevant cases are those in which there may be a temptation to introduce relativism as the means of thwarting unfavorable evaluations of another culture. The cases we are looking for, then, are those in which the Projection Error results, as it does in my Mobimtu example, in an unfavorable evaluation.

To show that people actually make this mistake, I will present several cases in which those who made the mistake came to recognize and acknowledge their error. As a result, they did not go on, as relativists do, to compound their error by means of the Relativizing Ploy, that is, by trying to exonerate the misunderstood action on relativistic grounds.

The first example is provided by Peter Freuchen, a Dane, who spent half a century among the Eskimos, beginning in 1906, when he went to Greenland on the Denmark expedition of that year, eventually marrying an Eskimo and living among her people as a trader. In his *Book of the Eskimos* he tells us of a young orphan boy named Ungarpaluk on whom he took pity because of what he regarded as the callous indifference shown him by other members of the Eskimo community. Freuchen's account runs as follows:

> The boy was reduced to foraging for himself. . . . He was so full of lice that nobody liked to have him sleeping in their house, and he usually slept in the tunnel of an abandoned house. He was happy, though. He played with the other children and looked well fed. But he was always hungry, so when the hunters were feeding their dogs he came running to get his share of the walrus hide or meat. He jumped in among the voracious, battling dogs, who often bit him in the face and on the hands, and he saved himself a bite or two. . . . When I first saw him at Cape York, I pitied him, and I announced that I thought it was shoddy of the great hunters there that they couldn't bring home enough food to give a poor orphan suitable clothes and nourishment. I referred to their own children, whom they watched over and stuffed with all the delicacies the house had to offer.

Such was Freuchen's initial reaction; he thought that the Eskimos were callously indifferent to the plight of orphans and treated them badly. He soon recognized, however, that this was a mistaken impression. He goes on to say that the hunters, whom he had been chiding,

> listened to me a little—patiently, as they always did. But then one of them said: "Pita, you speak both wisely and at the same time like the newborn man that you are in this country! An orphan who has a hard time should never be pitied, for he is merely being hardened for a better life. Look and you will see that the greatest chief hunters living here have all been orphans. Myself, I can remember how Quisunguaq was left behind by starving foster parents and still made out by seeking out the winter depots of the foxes and at the same time training himself more in hunger than people thought possible. Today it is impossible for Quisunguaq to feel cold. Look at Angutidluarssuak, who always manages to cross the tracks of the game animals, and who endures all hardships and can live without sleep more

than anybody else. His childhood was spent in constant starvation, and for several winters his only food was stolen from the hunters' meat graves. Look at little Iggianguaq here. Here see a man who may be slight to look at, but who outdoes everybody in bear hunting because he never gets tired of long-time sled driving.

Thus I understood that the Eskimos had their own method of caring for orphans, and perhaps not such an inhuman one.[1]

In Freuchen's initial reaction we have a clear example of the first mistake: He thought that the Eskimos treated Ungarpaluk with callous disregard for his welfare.

He did not go on to invoke the Relativizing Ploy by saying that Eskimos think it right to treat orphans cruelly, and he was saved from this by being shown that his first, uninformed impression was mistaken: The Eskimos were not as "inhuman" as he had imagined for they were preparing Ungarpaluk for "a better life," to become a great hunter. Perhaps, for all we know, they regularly watched Ungarpaluk with great interest and remarked among themselves on his courage as he dove in amongst the dogs for his food. It is easy to imagine that they were even quite fond of him. To think that their treatment of him showed they had no regard for his welfare is like thinking that an American mother is being heedless of her child's welfare when she permits a doctor to stick needles in its arm.

Let us now consider examples in which respected anthropologists admit to having made the Projection Error.

Raymond Firth tells us that early in his study of the Tikopia he "came to the conclusion that there was no such thing as friendship or kindness for its own sake among these people." It seemed to him that, far from offering him assistance when he plainly needed it, they were constantly demanding that he give them things. Understandably, he took them to be a greedy and calculating people. Eventually, however, he came to realize that he had been wrong about this. It was not that these people were greedy and lacking in kindness; it was rather that among these people "the most obvious foundation of friendship was material reciprocity."[2] Their constantly asking to be given things was not greediness, as he had thought, but overtures and a testing of the waters of friendship. Like Freuchen, Firth made the first mistake, the Projection Error, but did not go on to invoke the Relativizing Ploy: He did not compound his error by saying that these people think it right to be greedy.

In some cases the Boasian insight may serve merely to partially, rather than fully, exonerate a person or a practice. My final example is of this sort. It is taken from Malinowski's reflection on his initial impression of life among the Trobrian Islanders:

> At first it might appear, not only in the preconceived ideas of the layman, but also to the casual reader of ethnographic accounts, that early forms of monarchy or sovereignty are characterized by despotism, abuses of power on the part of the chief—in short, political as well as economic tyranny. . . . In my own field, I was at first impressed by the enormous

tribute claimed by the chief, by the rigorous and cumbersome etiquette imposed upon his subjects, an etiquette almost Polynesian in its elaboration and in the strict rules of physical lowliness followed by those of lower rank; and by the advantages, sexual, personal and economic, which polygamy bestows on the ruler. My views were shared by the early administrators of the district, in whose opinion the best way of advancing the interests of the commoner and community alike was to break down the power of the chief. Fuller knowledge, however, convinced me that I had been in error. The enormous tribute which the chief collects in food he does not, in fact he could not, consume himself. He employs it in ceremonial re-distributions, in financing war, enterprise and tribal festivity. In doing this he of course enhances his own prestige, and displays his chiefly power and dignity. At the same time, without this organizing power given to the chief and without the means offered him by the tribal constitution of accumulating and then dispersing a large part of the tribal income, the commoners would be deprived of most of the things which make life worth living for them. The partial decay of tribal custom has in the Trobrians reduced the interest in life, an expression which actually covers a multitude of concrete facts which I was able to observe and record.[3]

The Boasian insight here is clearly expressed. Malinowski tells us that his initial impression was one of tyranny, but he goes on to say, "Fuller knowledge, however, convinced me that I had been in error." He did not, like a relativist, say, "These people approve of unmitigated tyranny; that is their morality, and so in this case we must be tolerant of tyranny." On the contrary, he came to see that the chief was not exacting tribute out of sheer greed; he was providing the commoners with what makes "life worth living for them." Malinowski is not, of course, saying that this is a system we would want to adopt. Nor is he saying that the Trobrian Islanders, even if they became aware of other possibilities, would continue to prefer their system. Rather, he is saying that their system is not the *unmitigated* despotism that he had at first imagined.

These three examples demonstrate that people do, in fact, make the mistake I have called "the Projection Error." Yet in each of these examples the author eventually recognized his mistake and did so in the way Boas recommended: by getting a better understanding of the thinking or motivation of the alien culture.

As we will see in the next chapter, not all anthropologists are as astute in recognizing and correcting the Projection Error. Some persist in thinking of the alien culture in the terms suggested to them by their initial impression, and they then invoke the idea of "different moralities" (or "different standards") as a way of nullifying the implications of those terms. In this way, then, they arrive at the idea that morality is relative and so become defenders of moral relativism.

Some readers may find this to be an implausible explanation of how people come to be moral relativists because two staunch proponents of moral relativism were Boas's students, Melville Herskovits and Ruth Benedict. So if my explanation is correct, his most famous students failed to understand what he was getting at in his many discussions of the comparability of ethnic phenomena. Could that really be? In chapter 8 I showed how Boas's method could be confused with relativism, but did his students actually make this mistake?

To show that this is exactly what happened, I will turn to a discussion of a famous article by Ruth Benedict, "Anthropology and the Abnormal."[4] Her claim in this article is that ethnography proves that standards of sanity and insanity (or normality and abnormality) are "relative" to a culture. She purports to have found cases in which people who are regarded as perfectly sane (or normal) in one culture act no differently, in the relevant respect, from people who are declared to be insane (crazy, abnormal) in some other culture. From this she concludes that what is regarded, in any culture, as a mental aberration or form of insanity is largely arbitrary. Those whom we declare to be insane or neurotic are not, as we think, in some way deficient or ailing; rather, our society has simply not condoned or honored the sort of character and conduct these people exhibit. We tend to think of them as deviating from some absolute standard of normality, but this idea of psychological normality, Benedict argues, is largely illusory.[5]

In order to examine her argument, we must consider carefully the cases Benedict cites in support of this conclusion. In one of her most prominent examples she compares our culture with that of the Kwakiutl Indians of the Pacific Northwest. She claims to have discovered that members of our culture whom we (correctly) diagnose as megalomaniacs and paranoids are indistinguishable from Kwakiutl Indians who are accepted, in their own culture, as being entirely normal, perfectly sane. As proof that the Kwakiutl are, by our standards, megalomaniacs she cites their potlaches and remarks that on these occasions "there was an uncensored self-glorification and ridicule of the opponent that it is hard to equal in other cultures outside of the monologues of the abnormal."

But what sort of proof is this? No doubt we can grant Benedict that the hyperbole of the potlach, along with the amassing of blankets and their destruction, bear some resemblance to the ravings and antics of a megalomaniac. But is this resemblance more than superficial? Benedict is claiming that the Kwakiutl, in the course of their potlaches, are doing the *same thing* as a bookbinder in Peoria who has gone berserk, whose self-aggrandizement and ostentation have exceeded the bounds of sanity. But surely this ignores a great deal about both the Kwakiutl and (genuine) megalomaniacs. The latter are acting out some pathological fantasy of their own, perhaps overcompensating for what they take to be their own insignificance. This is not at all what the Kwakiutl are doing, for their conduct at potlaches does not spring from a condition that has developed in them individually. They have been taught since childhood to participate in potlaches, and what they say on those occasions is largely a matter of ritual form.

While there may be megalomaniacs among the Kwakiutl, the affliction would have to reveal itself in other ways than by their participation in potlaches. A Kwakiutl's megalomania might reveal itself in, for example, the way he talks to his children and other relations and in how he comports himself at tribal meetings. It is in these situations, and not in their potlaches, that indications of megalomania might be found.

Benedict has overlooked all this. She has also neglected the fact that a Kwakiutl is born into a culture in which even minimal self-esteem requires successful participation in potlaches. If a Kwakiutl Indian were to give up in resignation and decline to participate in any further potlach competition, he would not be at all like a megalomaniac who, perhaps with psychiatric help, ceases his self-aggrandizing diatribes. The latter is a person who is no longer compulsively overcompensating for feelings of unworthiness; his pathological fantasies cease as his self-esteem returns. By contrast, a Kwakiutl who declined to compete any longer in potlaches must be someone whose self-esteem has, *by any standard,* suffered an unhealthy decline, like that of a middle-class American who is a failure at earning a living and supporting his family.

If we bear all this in mind, we will have no inclination to think that the Kwakiutl are, in relevant respects, like those whom we diagnose as megalomaniacs. Benedict has made the mistake of equating actions in one culture with those in another because of their superficial resemblance. In short, she is guilty of the Projection Error, for she has asked us, in effect, to imagine a bookbinder from Peoria doing, in his own community, what the Kwakiutl do during a potlach, as if such a comparison made sense. (And let there be no mistake about what Benedict thinks of herself as comparing: She insists that "it is with the motivations that were recognized in this contest [the potlach] that we are concerned in this discussion. The drives were those which in our own culture we should call megalomaniac."[6]) Then, having overlooked the salient differences between the Kwakiutl and genuine megalomaniacs, she is led to think that a Kwakiutl is someone whom we, because of his potlatch conduct, would regard as insane and that therefore we and they have different standards in regard to such matters.

Benedict makes these same mistakes throughout her discussion of this subject. I will mention briefly two other instances.

As proof that normal people among the Kwakiutl are like our paranoids, she cites the fact that they see "all of existence . . . in terms of insult" and permit themselves to retaliate for all sorts of accidental mishaps, as when one is cut by an axe that slips. On such occasions, she reports, "the first thought one was allowed was how to get even, how to wipe out the insult."[7] But does this demonstrate, as Benedict claims, a genuinely paranoid pattern of thought and conduct?

First of all, even perfectly normal people among us do not, and are not expected to, suffer insults gladly, and a most common response is some form of retaliation. Thus, if one of us found himself, like the Kwakiutl, thrust into a situation in which he was bombarded with insults, his quite healthy response would be to give as good as he gets, trading insult for insult. In this respect, then, the (normal) Kwakiutl is no different from the (normal) New York cab driver.

But what are we to make of the fact that the Kwakiutl see insults everywhere, even in purely accidental events? Benedict thinks that, by "our" standards, this would call for a diagnosis of paranoia. Here, however, she is forgetting that it makes a great difference that the Kwakiutl are taught to see things in this way, that unlike a genuine paranoid, a Kwakiutl does not, as the result of some idiosyncracy in his own psyche, come to see himself as bombarded with insults. His seeing mere accidents as insults is not the outcome of some irrational fear or suppressed hostility that betokens a deficiency in him. He is merely following a pattern he has learned from his elders. This being so, we must reject Benedict's contention that the Kwakiutl are no different from people whom we diagnose as paranoid.

Her account suggests that the Kwakiutl would find the paranoids in our society to be quite sane. But if the Kwakiutl could grasp the facts relevant to our diagnosing someone as paranoid, they would surely concur that the persons we so diagnose are not in sound mental health. Here again Benedict has been led astray by superficial similarities between Kwakiutl thought and conduct and the thought and conduct of genuine paranoids.

As our final example, consider a case that Benedict draws from Fortune's study of the Dobu. The Dobu believe in black magic and malignant spirits, and since everyone else is a potential threat to oneself, especially by poisoning, people are constantly vigilant and no one will work with, or share food with, another person. Among the Dobu, however, Fortune found a man of sunny, kindly disposition, who kept no vigil against poisoning and offered to help others with their work. The Dobu regarded him as simple and definitely crazy.[8]

Benedict claims that this clearly proves that the Dobu do not share our notions of what is and is not crazy. In fact, however, the case proves nothing of the sort. Benedict has neglected a crucial detail. Did this man share the others' belief that they were all in constant peril? If, as the Dobu must have assumed, he did believe this, then they were right to think him crazy. For who but someone insane would fail to take well-known and readily available precautions against what he understands to be imminent peril?

More than likely, however, this man did not share the others' belief, in which case it is no mere cultural bias that we would find his helpfulness to be perfectly sane behavior. After all, even the Dobu would not think that a person was crazy who took no precautions where he saw no peril. (I would surmise that the man was a victim of brain damage and simply did not understand all the fuss about poisoning. The mentally retarded generally have sunny dispositions, as did this man.) Contrary to Benedict, then, there is nothing in this example to show that assessments of psychological abnormality are "relative" to a culture.

Benedict claims to have shown, by means of evidence drawn from ethnography, that neuroses and psychoses are nothing but deviations from the typical pattern of thought and conduct of one culture or another. Having reviewed her proffered examples, we can see that what she presents us with is not in fact *evidence* but rather a confused mishandling of the facts.

The following consideration will help us to see what kind of mistake Benedict has made. She is claiming that the concepts "psychotic" and "neurotic" are like the concept "unfashionable" in the following respect. A person can be fashionable one year and unfashionable the next, even though her manner of dress *remains the same* over that period of time, that is, she becomes unfashionable because of a change in her surroundings. (If you observe a person ever so closely—including her manner of dress, those observations alone will not enable you to say whether she is unfashionable.) In the same way, according to Benedict, a person could be normal at the age of twenty-five and neurotic at thirty, even though there has been no change *in her,* that is, in her emotions, thoughts, and behavior. The only reason for describing her, at the age of thirty, as being neurotic is that certain changes have gone on *around* her: *she* has remained constant but her culture has changed. Benedict is saying that no matter how intensely you study a person (including her thoughts, emotions, and conduct), you will not, on the basis of what you observe *about her,* be able to say whether she is neurotic. This is what her relativism amounts to here.

Benedict, however, is entirely wrong about this. Karen Horney, a well-known psychiatrist, states the relevant objection succinctly: "If we regard a neurosis only from the sociological point of view as a mere deviation from the behavior pattern common to a certain society, we neglect grossly all we know about the psychological characteristics of a neurosis, and no psychiatrist of any school or country would recognize the result as what he is accustomed to designate a neurosis."[9]

Horney goes on to point out that, contrary to Benedict, "persons may deviate from the general pattern [of their culture] without having a neurosis," and "on the other hand, many persons may have a severe neurosis who according to surface observations are adapted to existing patterns of life."[10] What, then, constitutes a neurosis? Horney mentions two reliable diagnostic symptoms: "a certain rigidity in reaction and a discrepancy between potentialities and accomplishments."[11] (She adds that a psychiatrist when diagnosing an individual must distinguish between truly neurotic rigidity and conduct that is inflexible merely because the culture prescribes it, such as the invariable thriftiness of the American middle-class—at the time of her writing.) A more reliable, but less easily detected, symptom is that "the neurotic person . . . suffers invariably more than the average person. . . . In fact, the neurotic is invariably a suffering person."[12] When this suffering is related to the other two symptoms (rigidity and inability to function) we have a genuine neurosis.

It would therefore be a fundamental mistake to think that correctly diagnosing someone as being neurotic amounts to the same thing as observing in that person's conduct a "deviation from the behavior pattern common to [his or her] society." Yet Benedict's relativism involves precisely this mistake. This is most obvious when she remarks, in reference to the Kwakiutl and Dobu, that "an adult shaped to the drives and standards of either of these cultures, if he were transported into our civilization, would fall into our categories of abnormality."[13]

No doubt, if a Dobu were somehow transported into our midst while retaining his beliefs and reactions, we, in our ignorance of his background, might mistake him for a paranoid, but if psychiatrists were asked to examine this man, they would try to understand his conduct, and if they succeeded in this, they would not think that he was paranoid. Benedict can think otherwise only because she made no attempt to understand, and properly describe, the conduct in the cultures she is comparing. Instead, she has treated superficially similar conduct from two cultures as being the same. It is this mistake that serves as the premise of her relativism, of her claim to have shown that standards of sanity and insanity (or normality and abnormality) are "relative" to a culture.

This should overcome the incredulity with which, as I said above, anthropologists may greet my claim that Boas's most famous students became proponents of moral relativism because they failed to realize that they were making the very mistake Boas attempted to explain in his discussions of the comparability of ethnic phenomena. In the next chapter we will see how easy it is to arrive in this way at a relativistic view of morality.

The Projection Error as a Source
of Moral Relativism

To see how easily one can slip into a relativistic view of morality, let us consider a case everyone is familiar with from popular discussions of relativism: the case of Eskimos leaving their old people to freeze to death. The argument, as we've all heard it, goes as follows: "People in our culture think this Eskimo practice cruel, and if one of us were to treat an aged parent like this, he would be prosecuted for murder. But the Eskimos see nothing wrong in leaving their old people to freeze to death. Even the old people themselves accept this practice. Obviously, then, they have a different morality from ours."

The implication is that the Eskimos do what someone in our culture does when committing a murder. (This is an essential part of the argument, for what the relativist is obliged to show is that the *same* action that one culture condemns is condoned by another culture.) But this comparison is a mistake—a further example of what I have called "the Projection Error." Suppose that the Eskimos learned that more and more Americans each year had been chucking Granny out the back door and leaving her to die in a snow bank. If the Eskimos were familiar with the circumstances in which the American people live, would they think that each year we were becoming more like them? Of course not! No typical Eskimo would say to an American who had left his grandmother to freeze in a snow bank in Peoria: "I did that to my grandmother, too." The typical Eskimo does not act with murderous motives, and in order to give a correct account of his actions, our account must include mention of the cultural circumstances and environmental exigencies within which he acts. And this, of course, makes it a mistake to think the typical Eskimo is doing what a murderer in our culture does. But only by making this mistake can the relativist support his argument.

In a way, the relativist knows that these Eskimos are not rightly to be thought of as murderers, but although the relativist in some sense knows this, he does not correct his idea that these Eskimos do what murderers do. Instead, he tries to make allowances for them by saying that Eskimos have a "different morality." But "making allowances" in this way is the second mistake, which incorporates and compounds the first, for it can only mean that the Eskimos condone what we condemn, namely, murder.

An example of this dual mistake is Westermarck's claim that "the custom of killing or abandoning parents worn out with age or disease" is an instance of "the variability of moral valuation."[1] He says this despite the fact that he also acknowledges that what the Eskimos do on these occasions can be "an act of kindness, . . . commonly approved of, or even insisted upon, by the old people themselves."[2] Where, then, is the difference in "valuation"? Westermarck apparently thinks he exhibits this difference when he remarks that this practice of the Eskimos "appears to most of us as an atrocious practice." He does not, of course, mean that we think it atrocious although we know it to be an act of kindness. No, he means that we think it is atrocious because we fail to realize that it *is* an act of kindness, because we are thinking of the Eskimos as murdering their old people. But if that is what he means, how can he also say that there is here a difference in "valuations"? The Eskimos do not condone the *murder* of family or friends; nor do we, on the other hand, condemn acts of kindness. What we have here is not a difference in "valuations" (whatever that might mean), but rather a case in which "we" have misunderstood what the Eskimos are doing.

Another example would seem to be that mentioned by Fürer-Haimendorf in a passage which the reader may recall from chapter 1, the passage in which he remarks that a European who beheaded "a woman from a neighboring village whom he happened to encounter on her way home from the fields, would be locked up as a criminal lunatic; whereas in a Naga village a youth returning with a human head captured under similar circumstances earns the insignia of a successful headhunter." He goes on to remark: "Examples of such extreme differences in the moral assessment of conduct could easily be multiplied." Plainly, in order to think that his example shows that there are "differences in moral assessment," Fürer-Haimendorf must have thought that a Naga tribesman who beheads someone is doing the *same* thing as the European he describes. I do not know what, exactly, those Naga headhunters were doing, but I feel fairly sure that there is no precedent for their actions in the murderers in our midst. If I am right about this, then Fürer-Haimendorf first commits the Projection Error and then compounds his error by treating his example as proof that different moral assessments are made in the two cultures.

The same confusion is found in some remarks by L. T. Hobhouse about the Dyaks of Borneo, with whom, he tells us,

> it is a delight to dwell, so courteous are they, so hospitable, so full of brotherly kindliness. We begin to think there is truth in the idyllic picture of savage life so popular in the days of our great-grandfathers, until we stumble upon the fact that these same Dyaks are inveterate headhunters, and make a practice of murdering not men only, but women and children

in satisfaction of the duty of blood-vengeance, and to obtain the magical virtue inherent in an enemy's skull. At once the deamon picture takes the place of the angel, and the savage world is seen as a Gehenna rather than a Paradise. We . . . can hardly believe that men capable of acts so fiendish can have any trace of genuine humanity about them. The fairer view about them is that the Dyaks have a morality of their own, for many purposes as good as ours, but limited by the conditions of their life and coloured by their ideas of the supernatural.[3]

Why does Hobhouse think that this latter view is "the fairer view about them"? Well, you might ask, isn't it fairer than the other view, which paints them as "capable of acts so fiendish" that we must think of them as devils? But do they *not* perform such acts? After all, Hobhouse himself tells us that they regularly "murder" men, women, and children. If that is not fiendish, what is? Moreover, Hobhouse does not retract this description of them, that is, that they *murder* men, women, and children. In fact, he depends on that description to give substance to his claim that they have a "different morality."

But what does this claim mean? Would Hobhouse say that all murderers have a "different morality"? No, I am sure he would not. Anyone who kills with a murderous motive would not be accorded the "fairer view" Hobhouse extends to the Dyaks. But why, then, do the Dyaks get special treatment? Hobhouse's explanation is that they do not kill with a murderous motive, but rather act out of their superstitious belief in the magical virtues inherent in an enemy's skull. (If they gave up their superstitious belief, they would not go on killing in this way.) Even so, we may think that Hobhouse is too quick to exonerate the Dyaks, for we may think that their conduct is like that of someone in our culture who needs a liver transplant in order to stay alive and who kills someone in order to obtain his liver. That would be murder plain and simple. I assume, however, that Hobhouse would dismiss this comparison, perhaps by saying that the Dyaks, when they kill "to obtain the magical virtue inherent in an enemy's skull," are acting analogously to a soldier who kills an enemy in order to take his weapon so that he can defend himself and his troops. Given this view of the Dyaks, then, their killing an enemy for the magical virtues of his skull amounts to a kind of self-defense, for they must have the idea that foregoing those magical virtues would leave them fatally vulnerable. But in that case, surely, it is highly misleading to say flatly, as Hobhouse does, that the Dyaks *murder* men, women, and children, for what they are doing is not at all what we would be doing if we committed murder.

As Boas points out in a passage quoted earlier, it can only lead to confusion to use our term "murder" to speak of the actions of people in whose culture their actions are understood very differently from the way we understand actions which, in our culture, lead to criminal charges of murder. But if we withdraw the term "murder" once we realize that the Dyaks are acting on their superstitious belief, where do we find them to have a "different morality"? After all, we have no reason to think that they would see nothing wrong in an American murdering his wife in order to inherit her fortune. In any case in which we and they agree on all the facts there will be nothing that we condemn and they condone. The only difference consists in the fact that they have superstitious beliefs and act on them in a certain way.[4]

Hobhouse, then, is guilty of the first mistake—the Projection Error—in that he depicts them as murderers, and he is guilty of invoking the Relativizing Ploy when he tries to block the implications of this, in other words, tries to take a "fairer view," by saying that they have a "morality of their own." Here again, then, the relativist's idea of "different moralities" results from the dual mistake illustrated by my Mobimtu example.

12

Pulling the Strands Together

It is time to retrace our steps in order to survey the path we have followed through the preceding chapters. Relativists tell us that their view of morality is supported by observations anthropologists have made in their study of many different cultures. If this were true, it should be easy to discover how they became moral relativists. There was a time at which they were not yet relativists, then they came upon, or read about, some ethnographic data which persuaded them that there are different moralities in different cultures, that is, that there are cases in which people of one culture morally condemn the *same* actions that people of some other culture view with indifference or regard as a duty. This first step, as we saw in chapter 1, does not by itself constitute their relativistic view of morality, but having taken this step, they go on to propound their Fully Developed Argument, which takes them the rest of the way to relativism. For the moment I want to review only what we have discovered about the first step, the one that seemed so easy: finding cases of different moralities.

I examined a number of cases that seemed to meet the relativists' requirements, some of which involved religious differences and some of which did not. For a variety of reason I found it necessary to reject all of these candidates. None of them provided grounds for saying that there are different moralities.

I had to consider, therefore, whether there might be cases of some other sort which look to relativists like ethnographic data that necessitate a relativistic account of morality. To show how such cases are possible, I proposed my Mobimtu example. In constructing this example I was guided by two considerations: The example must not fail in the way type A cases fail, and the example must seem (at least) to give sense to the idea that there are different moralities. These considerations dictate that the example have an oddly dual character: The conduct involved must be such that it tempts someone who is not yet a relativist to indulge in a moral criticism across some cultural divide, but at the same time it must be such that he can also see that the criticism he is *tempted* to make would be *unwarranted*. Cases of this sort I have called "type B cases," and the question is: How could there be a case that has this oddly dual character? It would have to be one of those cases that concerned Boas, that is, those in which someone who voices criticism of another culture is misinterpreting the actions of the people in that culture. These are cases, in other words, in which we are prone to commit the Projection Error: Although we see that the actions are quite innocent, we misinterpret them to be the very actions that our own culture condemns.

By inventing my fictitious Mobimtu example I did not, of course, establish that any anthropologist has ever been guilty of the Projection Error, nor did I show that this is the route by which anyone has become a moral relativist. My example merely illustrates how this *might* come about. So it remained to be shown, as I did, that misinterpretations of the sort Boas warned against in type B cases do occur (the cases of Freuchen, Firth, Malinowski, and Benedict). And finally, with my remaining examples (Westermarck, Fürer-Haimendorf, and Hobhouse), I established that relativists do make the dual mistake illustrated by my Mobimtu example, that is, they lack Boas's insight about the proper description of other cultures and consequently try to deflect unwarranted criticism of other cultures by declaring that type B cases involve "different moralities."

What makes that a mistake is that in type B cases what the people of one culture condemn is *not* (despite appearances) the *same* thing as what people in the other culture condone. (For example, the Mobimtu fathers are not bragging; they are carrying out a parental duty.) Therefore, if this is how anthropologists have arrived at moral relativism, they have not really found support for this doctrine in genuine ethnographic data. Instead, they have, by way of the Projection Error, misrepresented a particular sort of cultural difference and have then treated their own misrepresentations *as though* they were data.

What, if anything, have I established by this argument? Have I shown that moral relativism is not true? No, I have been concerned only to display the mistakes involved in the train of thought that leads from type B cases to relativism. I have also shown that, as regards type B cases, the very phrase "different moralities" incorporates these mistakes, as does the term "ethnocentrism."

Because I can claim to have accomplished no more than this, it is possible that a relativist might concede everything I have argued for thus far and yet think that there must be some way to resuscitate moral relativism. And the way to go about this, he might think, is to breathe new life into the idea that we acquire morality, not by any rational means, but by the causal process of "enculturative conditioning." In the relativists' Fully Developed Argument, this idea was supported by the claim that there are many different moralities. Since we have now found this claim to rest on an error, we can dismiss that reasoning, but someone might point out that I have so far said nothing to discredit the idea that morality is acquired by enculturative conditioning. So long, then, as relativists continue to think that we acquire morality in this way, they may feel that their cause is not yet lost. To complete our inquiry, therefore, we need to pursue a number of additional questions about morality—about what it is and how it is acquired. This we will do in the next section of the book.

III

PHILOSOPHY AND MORAL RELATIVISM

13

Westermarck's Concession and the
Philosophical Argument for Relativism

We have reached a transition point at which the anthropologist's version of the problem must give way to the philosopher's. We have seen that relativists take the view that the "analysis of moral concepts" is properly a job for anthropologists, rather than philosophers, for only the former have a sufficient knowledge of the ethnographic research that shows morality to be relative. Yet, in examining the claim that data gathered by ethnographers demonstrates the relativity of morals, we discovered that what has been treated as data is not, in fact, data at all. But we still need to consider the claim that, to find examples of different moralities, we need only consider the various religions that give rise to conflicting moral judgments.

Westermarck, alluding to cases that involve differences of belief, acknowledges the following:

> In innumerable cases the variations of moral estimates are due to differences of beliefs. Almost every chapter of this work has borne witness to the enormous influence which the belief in supernatural forces or beings or in a future state has exercised upon the moral ideas of mankind. . . . It has introduced a great variety of new duties and virtues, quite different from those which are recognized by the moral consciousness when left to itself.[1]

But having acknowledged this, Westermarck, unlike some relativists, refused to concede that the differences between the moral views of various religions is proof of the relativity of morals. Commenting on such cases in *Ethical Relativity*, he wrote:

> In so far as differences of moral opinion depend on knowledge or ignorance of facts, on specific religious or superstitious beliefs, on different degrees of reflection, or on different conditions of life or other external circumstances, they do not clash with that universality [i.e., universal

agreement] which is implied in the notion of the objective validity of moral judgments.[2]

In his earlier book, *The Origin and Development of the Moral Ideas,* he put the matter as follows: "A diversity of opinion regarding the moral value of certain modes of conduct [may result] from circumstances of a purely intellectual character—from the knowledge or ignorance of positive facts—and involves no discord in [moral] principle."[3]

Westermarck's reason for holding that the cases in question may involve no discord of moral principles was as follows. It is at least possible, he pointed out, that if the differing parties could come to an agreement about the facts, so that no difference of *beliefs* remained, the differing parties might very well agree also in their moral convictions.[4]

Does this mean that Westermarck abandoned the idea that there are "different moralities"? Not at all, for he goes on immediately to say: "But although in this way [i.e., by reaching agreement about the relevant facts] many differences may be accorded, there are points in which unanimity [on moral matters] cannot be reached even by the most accurate presentation of facts or the subtlest process of reasoning." He elaborates this point as follows:

> No intellectual enlightenment, no scrutiny of facts, can decide how far the interests of the lower animals should be regarded when conflicting with those of men, or how far a person is bound, or allowed, to promote the welfare of his nation, or his own welfare, at the cost of that of other nations or other individuals. Professor Sidgwick's well-known moral axiom, "I ought not to prefer my own lesser good to the greater good of another," would, if explained to a Fuegian or Hottentot, be regarded by him, not as self-evident, but as simply absurd; nor can it claim general acceptance even among ourselves. Who is that "Another" to whose greater good I ought not to prefer my own lesser good? A fellow countryman, a savage, a criminal, a bird, a fish—all without distinction?[5]

We can see from this that Westermarck believed that he could produce examples of genuine *moral* differences. But he insisted that in our search for such examples we must consider only those cases in which the differing parties agree on all the relevant facts.

It is now evident that Westermarck's original explanation of what constitutes a difference of morality must be qualified in some way. As we saw in chapter 1, his explanation is that there is a difference of morality when "a mode of conduct which among one people is condemned as wrong is among other people viewed with indifference or enjoined as a duty." To this we must now add: "even though the people in question are agreed on all the relevant facts."

This qualification is addressed to cases such as the following. Some Christians insist that abortion is murder and do so because they believe that the fetus has been "ensouled" by God and is therefore a person from the moment of conception. People who hold different religious beliefs—or none at all—may not share this belief about the fetus and so do not regard abortion (in the first trimester, at least) as murder. But this is not a genuine *moral* difference, if Westermarck's qualification is taken into account, because the differing parties are not agreed on a fact that is plainly relevant, namely, whether the day-old fetus (or zygote) has been ensouled by god. So in our search for examples that demonstrate the relativity of morals, Westermarck would tell us to ignore those in which religious or superstitious beliefs play a role.

Westermarck, by conceding the irrelevance of such cases, has substantially reduced the stock of cases from which to pick out examples that support the cause of relativism. Yet he insists that we can find examples of purely moral differences if we confine ourselves to those in which the differing parties agree on all the relevant facts. This, however, raises a new problem: Which facts *are* the relevant facts? Or, to put it differently, how is the *relevance* of a fact to be determined?

Westermarck gives us no help with this. He does not even produce any actual examples for our inspection, although in the passage last quoted he alludes to several sticky problems and expects us to agree that on these matters, such as the treatment of the lower animals, people can know all the relevant facts and still differ about what is right and wrong. In *Ethical Relativity* he is equally vague, saying simply that "we all know that there often is a conflict between moral convictions of thoughtful and well-educated people, 'nay, even between the moral 'intuitions' of philosophers, which prove to be irreconcilable."[6] It is tempting to agree, but before doing so, let us be sure that we understand what we would be agreeing to.

One thing we can readily agree to is this: In a situation in which two people know all the relevant facts, one may insist that the other is doing something terribly wrong and yet not succeed in getting the other to cease doing it. Consider the torture of political prisoners. Idi Amin, the Ugandan dictator, engaged in this on a massive scale, and for that reason, among others, most of us regard him as a vile and corrupt man. He, of course, does not share this view. Yet there is nothing that we know and he does not, or vice versa. We know well enough what advantages for staying in power a dictator may gain by the use of torture to intimidate and extract information from political opponents, and he knows well enough what agonies are caused by torture. But if one of us had had the opportunity to protest to Idi Amin that he was doing a dreadful thing, our protest would have fallen on deaf ears. So this case might seem to fit Westermarck's prescription for a genuine moral difference.

Examples need not be multiplied. This is one of the type A cases that were dismissed in the previous chapter on the grounds that they provide no support for moral relativism. More exactly, I dismissed them because it seemed obvious that anyone who is not yet a relativist will remain unpersuaded that someone like Idi Amin simply has a "different morality." On the contrary, we will think of him as callously and ruthlessly pursuing his own selfish ends. And we would stick by this verdict even if we found, not an individual, but an entire culture that went in for torture in a big way. I am thinking here of what Tylor said about the Carib Indians, namely, that they delighted in watching their victims suffer. If we found this to be true, we would not think that such conduct revealed to us a unique moral principle of the Carib Indians.

So if Westermarck meant to say that cases of this sort demonstrate that there can be "different moralities," his position would seem to be plainly absurd. It seems, however, that he was not thinking of cases of this sort, for he speaks of disagreements between "thoughtful and well-educated people," and this would leave out anyone like Idi Amin. The question, then, is this: How are we to describe moral disagreements between thoughtful and well-educated people who know all the relevant facts?

Westermarck's view is that such cases come down to a clash of principles, principles that are so fundamental that nothing can be said about them to persuade others of their truth. And because of this he can reason as follows: If moral absolutism were true, thoughtful and well-educated people would all share the same moral principles, but we know that such people can fail to reach agreement on some moral issue despite their knowing all the relevant facts, which implies that their disagreement results from a discord of principles, and this, in turn, implies that absolutism is false.

Westermarck is aware that others might dispute his view of such moral disagreements, and at one point he anticipates that an opponent of relativism might propose the following alternative: The disagreement persists in such cases, *not* because (as you imagine) the differing parties hold different moral principles, but because at least one of the parties lacks a sufficiently developed moral consciousness.

Westermarck could not allow this objection to go unanswered, for were he to do so, he would have dealt away the last of the examples that seem to provide evidence against moral absolutism. Accordingly, he replied to this objection as follows:

> It will perhaps be argued that on this, and on all other points of morals, there would be general agreement, if only the moral consciousness of men were sufficiently developed. But then, when speaking of a "sufficiently developed" moral consciousness (beyond insistence upon a full insight into the governing facts of each case), we practically mean nothing else than agreement with our own moral convictions. The expression is faulty and deceptive, because if intended to mean anything more [i.e., if we mean "a moral conscious whose principles are *true*"], it presupposes an objectivity of moral judgments which they do not possess, and at the same time seems to be proving what it presupposes [namely, that there *are* universal moral truths].[7]

Westermarck's argument here is that there are only two possible meanings his opponent might give to the phrase "a sufficiently developed" moral consciousness and that *neither* meaning enables one to show that there cannot be different moralities. The first possible meaning, according to Westermarck, is this: When his opponent speaks of people whose moral consciousness is "sufficiently developed," he might mean "people whose moral principles are the same as *mine*." But if *this* is what his opponent means, he is only in a position to say: "There would be no moral disagreements if everyone, in addition to having a full insight into the relevant facts, shared *my* moral principles." This, of course, would be perfectly irrelevant, for it in no way conflicts with moral relativism. So if *this* is what his opponent means, his purported criticism is no criticism at all. The second possible meaning, according to Westermarck, is the following: When his opponent speaks of a person having a "sufficiently developed" moral consciousness, he might mean that this person's moral principles are *true*. If *this* is what his opponent means, then he may say: "When there remains a moral disagreement between parties who have a full insight into the governing facts of a case, the reason that the disagreement remains is that at least one of the differing parties does not hold *true* moral principles." The trouble here, says Westermarck, is that this opponent means to be *refuting* relativism, but he cannot do so by simply *asserting* that one of the parties to the dispute holds true moral principles and the other does not, for if all that he can do is assert (rather than prove) this, he has merely begged the question. So whichever meaning is adopted, says Westermarck, his opponent fails to prove that there cannot be different moralities. What are we to think of this argument?

The opponent Westermarck meant to address with this argument is the moral absolutist, and it is pretty clear that his argument is decisive when addressed to that opponent. By this I mean, not that he has proven that moral relativism is true, but only that he has shown that a moral absolutist will fail if he tries to refute relativism in this way. Suppose, however, that, rather than wanting to defend either moral relativism or absolutism, we want only to inquire into the nature of morality: Should we agree that Westermarck has found the *only* meanings we might assign to the phrase "a sufficiently developed moral consciousness"? Might we not think that it has a meaning quite different from either of those he proposes? We will consider this in the next chapter.

14

A Preliminary Assessment of the
Philosophical Argument

Westermarck's view of moral disagreements implies that we are all equals in our capacity to think about moral matters: Two people can hold conflicting moral principles, but since there is no legitimate sense in which one of them can be said to have "a superior moral consciousness," neither of them can be said to be on the right side of the issue. We might, therefore, call this his "argument for universal moral equality." This would be absurd, of course, if it meant that Idi Amin is as capable as anyone else of thinking about moral issues, that his use of torture proves nothing to the contrary. But let us give Westermarck the benefit of the doubt and assume that he would not defend his position by insisting that a psychopath differs from us in having different moral principles. Even so, we may still wonder whether, with such people excluded, it is plausible to maintain that everyone is equally capable of thinking about moral matters. Can we, for example, credit children—or even teenagers—with the moral sagacity of a mature adult? And even if we confine ourselves to adults, can we not say that some reflect on moral matters more carefully and honestly than others?

At the end of the preceding chapter I suggested that someone who opposed Westermarck's view might have in mind a meaning quite different from either of those he proposed for the phrase "a sufficiently developed moral consciousness." I will now explain this alternative.

Moral issues are not like chess problems ("White to mate in eight moves"), where it is known in advance what it is relevant to consider, so that no matter how complex the problem may be, any chess player could with patience, or a computer, work out the winning moves. In moral matters the great difficulty is often to discern or acknowledge what is relevant, what has a legitimate bearing on the matter. We are often blind to aspects of a situation that we would need to be mindful of in order to think usefully about it. Let us, therefore, suppose that Westermarck's opponent had explained himself in the following way.

Once you have set aside cases involving psychopaths and cases involving a difference of religious (or superstitious) belief, the *remaining* cases of moral disagreement are *not* cases in which (as Westermarck puts it) the differing parties hold different "moral principles"; rather, at least one of the differing parties lacks (what might be called) "a sufficiently developed moral consciousness." By this I mean that he fails to reflect on moral matters in an honest and careful way. He may be, for example, a very conventional person who has a comfortable life and never asks himself searching questions about the long-standing practices of his community. It's not that he is *unaware* of those practices, but if he thinks about them at all, he thinks: "That's just the way things are." In consequence, he fails to see that some of those practices are grossly unfair. So although he is not a thoroughly *evil* person, he could not be said to be a morally thoughtful or insightful person. Now, what is the difference between him and other, more thoughtful, people? The difference has nothing to do with *principles*. It is a difference, rather, in the ways people *think* about matters, in how earnestly, honestly, and diligently they think.

This explanation of the phrase "a sufficiently developed moral consciousness" is quite different from either of those Westermarck considers. Let us explore this further.

Consider again the conventional fellow leading a comfortable life who never asks searching questions about the practices of his own culture or community, practices that a more insightful person might recognize as being unfair or even cruel. By developing our account of this person more fully, we can portray his culpability, and the extent of it, in various ways. It may be, for example, that he is such a conventional fellow, so lacking in imagination and so little given to critical reflection, that it never occurs to him that there are searching questions that *ought* to be asked about his culture. In that case we might say that he is morally obtuse or naive. It might be, however, that he simply does not let himself dwell on such disquieting facts as that many of his countrymen are forced to live in squalor and work in wretched conditions, and he makes no attempt to learn more about the lives of these people. In that case we could say that, in his failure to ask searching questions, he is being willfully ignorant. Or he may, when he thinks about— or is asked about—the lives of these people, minimize what he knows ("It's not so bad, really"), in which case we might say that he is deceiving himself. Another possibility is that, to avoid being distressed by what he has seen and heard, he forms a sentimentalized—and hence falsified—picture of the lives of the less fortunate around him. Or it may be that he has accepted uncritically the demagoguery of those who attack all social reformers as purveyors of treacherous lies and dangerous schemes, in which case we could accuse him of being inexcusably gullible. These are a few ways in which a person can be blind to—or can blind himself to—morally relevant facts.

Consider another case, that of Franca Viola's rejected suitor. Let us, for the sake of argument, assume that he was not a vicious person, not thoroughly evil. He was, let us assume, smitten with the lovely Franca and eager to make her his wife. But while he may not have been thoroughly evil, he was not without moral deficiencies. When he raped Franca, he was not a conscientious young man trying to do the right thing; he was attempting to manipulate her in a degrading way and thought he could get away with it because his culture had for centuries condoned the practice. What more can we say about his moral deficiencies?

Let us suppose that when Franca realized she was about to be raped, she screamed at the man, "You are trying to dictate the rest of my life to me! Don't you see how *wrong* that is?" We could readily imagine that this had no effect, and yet it was not that the man failed to realize that he was, indeed, aiming to dictate the rest of her life. If Franca's protest fell on deaf ears, it must be that the man, if he was not simply callous, was blind to or willfully ignorant of such relevant considerations as the needs, potentialities, and aspirations of women. Perhaps, having known of other rapes that resulted in the victim marrying the rapist, he fortified himself with the self-deceiving lie that women, despite appearances, like to be pursued in this way. By describing him in these ways we are not, of course, exonerating him, for being blind to, or willfully ignorant of, or deceiving oneself about considerations that are morally relevant to one's conduct is itself a moral shortcoming.

What I want to suggest, then, is that people may differ from one another in the degree to which they have moral shortcomings of this sort. And this sort of difference is what we might mean if we were to speak of people as having a more developed (or less developed) "moral consciousness." So if we were to dispute Westermarck's view in the manner described above, we would not accept either of the meanings he assigns to the phrase "a sufficiently developed moral consciousness." Rather, we would say that people differ from one another by being, for example, more or less morally obtuse or prejudiced or willfully ignorant or disposed to sentimentalize or given to self-deception, and so on.

Is everyone in our culture aware of these morally relevant differences among people? Perhaps not, but most of us are aware of them in one degree or another, and we have an extensive vocabulary for speaking of them. In thinking about people, we distinguish between those who are fair-minded and others who are prejudiced, between those who take heed and those who are willfully ignorant, between the insightful and the obtuse, the self-critical and the self-deceivers, the responsible and the perverse, the callous and the sensitive, the thoughtful and the thoughtless. These distinctions are concerned with the degree of earnestness, honesty, and patience with which a person thinks about, investigates, and discusses certain matters, and Westermarck seems to have taken no account of this.

Had Westermarck taken sufficient notice of such differences among people he might have seen that there is a way of thinking about moral disagreements that is very different from his, namely, that moral disagreements have their source, not in the fact that people hold different "moral principles," but in the fact that people often fail to think honestly and carefully about moral matters. So we need to consider why he overlooked such differences among people. I suspect that there are several reasons for this, and in the remainder of this chapter I will suggest two.

One reason, I suspect, is that, although he speaks of a person having "full insight into the governing facts of each case," he was inclined to think of "facts" in the following way:

> If we have a full compliment of normally functioning sense organs, then all we need do, in order to ascertain the facts, is to direct those senses to the left and right, and up and down, and the facts will all be apparent to us. And although someone may try to keep us in ignorance by deliberately concealing something from us, that only means that we must leave no stone unturned when we direct our sense to the left and right and up and down.

This view of what a "fact" is—or of what is involved in ascertaining the facts—may seem plausible if we think only of cases like that of looking to see whether the sky is cloudy or listening for thunder, but in most cases it has no plausibility at all. It is especially misleading when we try to philosophize about moral matters, where we need to allow that a person may go about with his eyes wide open and his head full of distortions. Yet this is something commonly overlooked by people trying to think about moral philosophy. One result of this is that they, like Westermarck, take the view that, since people can easily discover—and come to agreement about—all the relevant facts, when they find themselves in disagreement over some moral matter, this is because they hold conflicting moral principles, that is, principles so fundamental that when they conflict no further discussion could lead to agreement.

In this picture there is no room for regarding one or more of the parties to the dispute as being callous, perverse, prejudiced, willfully ignorant, self-deceiving, or the like, for within Westermarck's picture whatever anyone does or says in regard to moral matters simply reflects his "ultimate principles." This is why Westermarck thought he could insist that people have "different moralities." Given his idea that people are equals in their capacity to think about moral matters, he can say: A culture can have moral principles that differ from yours, and you cannot dispute theirs by claiming that you alone have a "fully developed moral consciousness."[1]

Let us consider now a second reason Westermarck may have had for thinking of morality in the way he did. I proposed above that an opponent might attack Westermarck's position by insisting that moral disagreements have their source, not in the fact that people hold different "moral principles," but in the fact that people often fail to think honestly and carefully about moral matters. In reply to this someone may wish to say: "We will grant you that *some* moral disagreements have this character, but you are surely wrong if you think that none of them results from (as Westermarck says) 'a discord of principles.' Why, just consider what people say about sexual conduct: Here there are moral differences that have exactly the character Westermarck alleges."

It does seem that the way people think about sexual conduct lends itself in an especially promising way to Westermarck's picture of morality. The terms "moral" and "immoral" are, of course, very commonly used (in our culture, at least) in connection with sexual matters, and one may readily suppose that people can, even if they hold no religious beliefs, differ over the morality of certain sexual conduct in a way that fits Westermarck's view. To test this idea, we need to consider several examples.

Let us begin with a case in which, regarding sexual conduct, there is a very striking difference between cultures. It is sometimes said that a culture that practices monogamy has a different morality from one that practices polygamy. The matter cannot, however, be quite this simple. For I think we may suppose that if the Eskimos, a monogamous people, were told of the polygamous arrangements of other cultures, it would not occur to them that the members of those other cultures were doing something wrong or bad. They might find polygamy surprising and something to be wondered at but not immoral. So the mere fact of cultural difference does not imply a moral disagreement.

It is, of course, commonly the case that people believe that their form of marriage is sanctioned by a deity and that other forms violate divine law, and where that is so they may regard alien forms of marriage as being immoral. But cases of this sort will not support Westermarck's view of morality, for he himself excludes cases in which religious beliefs play a role. He wants us to deal only with cases in which, as he puts it, moral consciousness has been "left to itself." What would it be like, then, for there to be a purely moral disagreement between two cultures because the one is monogamous and the other polygamous?

Consider the following example involving two cultures, both thoroughly secular, which I shall designate by the letters "A" and "B." Suppose that the people of culture A, who now practice monogamy, had at one time been a polygamous people. The change came about because the women began to chafe under the old system and eventually led the men to realize that polygamy is unfair to women, that it is an important element in a pervasive pattern of male chauvinism. From that time onward only monogamous marriages have been permitted. So we can rightly say that the people of culture A have a moral objection to polygamy. If, now, we suppose that they voice this objection to the people of culture B, who practice polygamy, they may find that the objection falls on deaf ears when addressed to the men of culture B. This is not, however, because the people of culture B believe that polygamy is divinely ordained, for we are supposing that B is a secular culture. Why, then, would they dismiss the moral objection raised by the people of A? Here is one possibility: The men of B, whose prerogatives are being challenged, simply refuse to see that polygamy *is* unfair to women. (This is not, of course, surprising, for it often happens that when moral objections are raised against something we greatly prize, we become defensive and refuse to give serious attention to the objection raised.) We may also suppose that the women of B are so accustomed to deferring to their fathers, brothers, and husbands that it has not yet occurred to them that they might raise serious objections to their form of marriage. (Recently, when the government of an African country prohibited wife beating, some women in positions of authority to enforce the ban did not do so, saying that a woman should expect to be beaten if she displeases her husband.) So the men of B remain intransigent, and culture B remains polygamous.

Here we have a clear moral difference between these two peoples, but is it the *sort* of difference that would support Westermarck's view of morality? Surely not. For we do not find that the men of B are invoking some "principle" about which nothing can be said. Rather, they simply refuse to give serious thought to the criticism of polygamy that is voiced by the people of A. They refuse to acknowledge that polygamy is unfair to women, but also they have not viewed the matter with complete candor.

What must we do, then, to make our example conform to Westermarck's view of morality? Apparently, we have to describe two thoroughly secular cultures, one monogamous and the other polygamous, in which each says of the other's form of marriage, "That's immoral." Also, of course, to ensure that this disagreement be unresolvable, we must specify that they are each voicing an ultimate—or fundamental—principle, which means that neither can say anything by way of explaining what is wrong with the other's form of marriage; they can't say *what* its immorality consists in. But if we sketch such an example, have we sketched an imaginable state of affairs? Can we imagine people saying, "That's immoral," and then drawing a complete blank when asked why? What is the word *immoral* doing here? Does it have anything to do with morality? Since they cannot explain themselves, I see no reason to think that it does. Indeed, is "immoral" even a word in this sketch that I have given? It is not clear to me that it is. Additional surroundings seem to be needed. So far, then, I have not produced an example that supports Westermarck's view of morality.

Perhaps I could come closer to what is needed by describing something we find in our own culture. When the words *moral* and *immoral* are used in our culture in regard to sexual matters, it is generally in connection with such things as premarital sex, homosexual intercourse, masturbation, nude sunbathing at public beaches, topless dancing, and the like. Until recently, most people in our culture frowned on such activities, and many, even if they held no religious views about them, were inclined to call these activities—or some of them—"immoral." Moreover, if they were pressed to say what they found immoral about such activities, they could make no very cogent response. They might say, "It just *is* immoral, that's all!" Here, then, we may seem to have the sort of case that supports Westermarck's view of morality: We have found their "ultimate moral principles." Moreover, it seems obvious that cultures can differ about these. In regard to premarital sex, for example, consider Freuchen's account of the Greenland Eskimos:

Parents never worry when their teen-agers fail to return home at the usual hour. They take it for granted that the young people have found a vacant igloo nearby and are spending some time there, either as a couple or as members of a larger party. In fact, at a larger settlement there will always be a house called the Young People's House where young people can sleep together just for the fun of it, with no obligation outside of that certain night. Nobody takes offense at this practice, for no marriage can be a success, Eskimos believe, without sexual affinity.[2]

How different this is from what we find in our own culture!

Could it be, then, that in this difference we have finally found a living illustration of Westermarck's "ultimate moral principles"? To answer this question, let us look more closely at the two cultures to see what is going on.

Freuchen helps us to understand the Eskimos by telling us more about their sexual ethics:

> People are used to going naked inside their houses while their clothes are being cleaned. This is not only to get away for a time from the warm skin clothing and to get fresh air for their bodies; it also allows them to pick out the lice from the garments that are bundled together and hung by a string from the ceiling. . . . From their childhood, therefore, Eskimos are used to seeing men and women in the nude, and absolutely no shame is connected with the human body and its needs. This is not to say that wherever Eskimos get together there is promiscuity. On the contrary, if several families should happen to occupy the same house, there is a strict order in sleeping arrangements. . . .
>
> More important in understanding the Eskimos' sexual ethic is their point of view that sexual desire is entirely natural and normal, something like desire for food and sleep. . . .
>
> Man and woman are indispensable to each other; they form a basic economic unit. Consequently, marriage between Eskimos is usually a matter of mutual interest and sheer necessity rather than of love in the sense in which we use the term. On the other hand, married people are generally very devoted to each other and as a rule remain faithful to each other throughout life. But Eskimo love for—or rather devotion to—each other has very little to do with sex. It is considered rather ludicrous if a man can find pleasure in only one woman; as for the woman, it is considered a great honor if she is desired by many men and can give them pleasure. For this reason, Eskimos have never understood why white people put so much significance on their so-called wife-trading.[3]

This account presents Eskimo life as being very different from the lives of most Americans and Europeans. One difference comes out in Freuchen's remark that the Eskimos "have never understood why white people put so much significance on their so-called wife-swapping." Does this difference between the cultures support Westermarck's view of morality?

It is important to bear in mind that in our culture attitudes regarding sexual matters have a long history that includes strong prohibitions against many forms of sexual conduct—against not only premarital sex but against adultery, homosexuality, masturbation, and other things. (A Surgeon General of the United State was recently cashiered for having responded affirmatively to the suggestion, put to her at a press conference, that the pregnancy rate among teenagers might decline if they were taught that it's all right to masturbate.) Moreover, these prohibitions—and denunciations—still ring from the pulpits of many of today's churches. (In recent years, for example, the leaders of several Protestant denominations have declared that the AIDS virus is the punishment God has visited upon homosexuals.) It is hardly to be wondered at, then, that even those in our culture who no longer hold *explicitly* religious views about sexual matters are still influenced to some degree by the religious currents—past and present—in our culture. They grew up, after all, in a cultural context very different from that of the uninhibited Eskimos. Freuchen tells us: "From their childhood . . . Eskimos are used to seeing men and women in the nude, and absolutely no shame is connected with the human body and its needs." Very few people in our culture have experienced anything like this. On the contrary, most of us have grown up in a prudish atmosphere and accordingly have developed strong inhibitions about sex. Although this state of affairs is gradually changing, the change has not come about as the result of people discussing the matter in candid and thoughtful ways. Many people in our culture still have strong inhibitions about discussing sexual matters.

As a result there are still many who, although they would not say that God forbids homosexual conduct, insist that homosexuality is *wrong*. And if asked to defend this, they have nothing enlightening to say about the matter. Public opinion polling has revealed something important about this: Those who have a friend or relative whom they know to be homosexual are far less inclined than others to declare that homosexuality is immoral. This shows that many people, in their ignorance, tend to build up a false picture of what homosexuals are like, a false picture of their character. (They may, for example, regard homosexuals as being, by their "nature," sexual predators.) Such false pictures, then, are among the elements governing attitudes about sex in our culture.

This being so, is it really useful, or even accurate, to say that we and the Eskimos have "different moral principles" in regard to sex? One reason for saying so is that, as it happens, the words *moral* and *immoral* are probably most frequently used in our culture in connection with sexual matters. It may therefore seem very strained to deny that our sexual mores and attitudes amount to a *morality*. Yet when we think about what lies behind those particular mores and attitudes, it seems misleading at best to say flatly that, in regard to sex, our *morality* differs from that of the Eskimos. It is even imaginable that someone might want to insist that, because most of us do not *think* about sex in any honest and useful way, most people in our culture have no *morality* about sexual matters, that we have only a conglomeration of neurotic defenses and permissions onto which we have grafted the language of morality. Perhaps someone will say that many of us have *taboos* regarding sexual conduct but have nothing worthy of being called "ethics" or "morality."[4]

I had hoped to find in the differences between our culture and that of the Eskimos in regard to sexual matters an unproblematic example of Westermarck's "ultimate moral principles," but it seems that I have failed. The most we can say is that Westermarck's account, if it fits the ways we think and act in regard to sexual matters, does so only problematically because a moral attitude is *not* the same thing as a taboo.

But I can imagine other people, those who are cynical about morality, wanting to say that Westermarck's account fits us perfectly, that our taboos about sexual conduct are perfect illustrations of "ultimate moral principles." Such people will say that moral principles are nothing but mindless taboos. In chapter 18 I will discuss this attitude toward morality and try to show what it springs from.

I began this chapter by considering whether Westermarck's argument for universal moral equality is a cogent argument. I have offered several reasons for thinking it is not. Even so, his argument raises some deep questions about the nature of morality, and in subsequent chapters we will look into these.

15

What Is Morality?

Relativists think of their doctrine as a radical departure from the traditional theories of moral absolutists. In fact, however, moral relativism and absolutism are no more than variations on a common theme: Both derive from the idea that morality consists of moral rules or principles, that these constitute the bedrock of moral thought and reasoning. If there is a fundamental flaw in the relativists' doctrine, it is that they fail to be radical enough, that they share with absolutists this underlying picture of morality and differ from absolutists only after they have, hand in hand, taken the fatal plunge. In this chapter we will consider more carefully their common conception of morality.

We may take as our guide in this matter the anthropologist Raymond Firth, who has sketched the main elements of this picture as well as anyone. There are three such elements, and Firth describes the first of them as follows:

> By the moral attributes of an action is meant its qualities from the standpoint of right and wrong. Morality is a set of principles on which such judgements are based. Looked at empirically from the sociological point of view, morality is socially specific in the first instance. Every society has its own moral rules about what kinds of conduct are right and what are wrong, and members of society conform to them or evade them, and pass judgement accordingly. For each society, such rules, the relevant conduct, and the associated judgements, may be said to form a moral system.[1]

The first part of the story, then, is that "morality is a set of principles," that moral judgments about particular actions are "based on" those principles (or "rules"), and that in such judgments we weigh actions and say that they are right or wrong.

Firth goes on to expound on the nature of moral principles, this time calling them "standards":

> From the empirical point of view, . . . what are the essential elements in
> the exercise of moral judgements? There is the recognition that conduct is
> measurable by certain standards, commonly known as those of good and
> bad, right and wrong. These standards are regarded as not emanating
> from the person giving the judgement, but from outside him; they are
> external, non-personal in their origin. Linked with this, as Durkheim has
> pointed out, they are invested with a special authority; they are credited
> with an intrinsic virtue which demands that they be obeyed. The felt ne-
> cessity of obedience to this authority is termed *duty*. Yet this moral obli-
> gation is not of the order of mere yielding to superior weight. These moral
> standards have the character of being thought desirable in themselves—
> the character of goodness. Given this, moral standards tend to be regarded
> as absolutes.[2]

So, according to Firth, it is an essential feature of moral standards (rules,
principles) that they be regarded as "not emanating from the person giving
the judgment." This seems to mean that the role of the individual in morality
is limited to following rules (or applying principles) that he has had no hand
in fashioning.

The account given thus far is meant, not as a theory, but as a neutral
description of familiar facts of daily life, a description on which all thinkers
will agree. Absolutist and relativist theories enter the picture only at the next
stage, which presents us with their different accounts of the "external origin"
(or "source") of moral principles. Firth, once again, can serve as our guide:

> What can be said about the source of these moral standards? The com-
> monest answer, probably, in the history of Western society is that the
> source of all morality is God, that he provides both the absolute desira-
> bility of the standards and the unquestionable authority for following
> them. On such a view, the distinction between right and wrong is absolute,
> universal. . . . On this and similar views the moral rules to be found in
> different types of society are various forms of approximation (according
> to the perception or ignorance of the members of the society) to the ab-
> solute criteria springing from the central divine source. At the opposite
> extreme from this are the various views that morality is a thing of circum-
> stance . . . [and is] lacking any absolute character of external necessity, any
> validation of universal principle. In Westermarck's conception of ethical
> relativity, for instance, conduct can be judged to be right or wrong only
> within its own social setting. . . . On the [absolutist's] view, morality is
> human by endowment and social by practice, but its origin is sought be-
> yond [both] man and society altogether. On the [relativist's] view, morality
> is essentially a social product.[3]

Relativism and absolutism, then, are both answers—competing answers—
to the question: What is the source of moral principles?

It is understandable that discussions of these doctrines have focused on
their differences, but as such discussions have failed to produce unanimity,
we may suspect that there is more to be gained from attending to what
relativism and absolutism have in common, namely, their shared picture of
morality, and especially the idea that it is something "external, non-

personal" in origin. As Frank Ramsey once remarked, when the conflict between two theories appears incapable of resolution, "it is a heuristic maxim that the truth lies not in one of the two disputed views but in some third possibility which has not yet been thought of, which we can only discover by rejecting something assumed as obvious by both the disputants."[4] The application of this maxim to the dispute between relativists and absolutists would lead us to expect that, by rejecting their shared view of morality, we might discover a new possibility. In recent years a few philosophers have undertaken precisely this line of inquiry.

One of the deficiencies they have pointed out in the common picture of morality is the following. Because that picture represents morality as consisting of principles, and because these are conceived of as saying what one ought or ought not to do, morality gets represented as pertaining essentially to human actions, to what someone can be ordered or forbidden to do. But as we saw in the preceding chapter, this picture fails as an account of morality, for it neglects the fact that we make moral assessments also of the way in which people *think*, that is, it neglects our familiar understanding of the differences between, for example, callousness and sensitivity, insightfulness and obtuseness, reasonableness and perversity, fair-mindedness and prejudice, self-deception and self-criticism, wisdom and fanaticism. Insofar as traditional moral theories deal with these at all (and typically they do not) they try to account for them in terms of the two intellectual capacities they are prepared to recognize: knowing and reasoning, where knowing is thought of as simply opening one's eyes and ears and letting the data pour in, while reasoning is thought of as a kind of calculating with premises. What this picture completely neglects is the kind of inner struggle that is very often involved in overcoming one's prejudices, self-deception, smugness, and so on, and also the kind of temptations there are to be perverse, callous, and willfully ignorant. And yet once we come to a full appreciation of such matters, it seems fairly obvious that these temptations and the struggle to resist or overcome them must lie at the very heart of morality. For what is the use of having a command of those *other* moral terms ("good," "fair," "cheat," "steal," "lie," etc.) if one is callous or prejudiced or is constantly deceiving oneself? Could a person who feeds his prejudices by dwelling on imagined grievances be aiming to do the right thing? Does racism or homophobia limit a person's capacity for right action? The answer is plain. In our philosophical reflections about morality, we must assign priority to moral assessments of how we think about matters and of how we perceive and represent them to ourselves; moral assessments of actions must take second place. Hence the importance of literature that explores the ways people think and perceive the world.

The point I am getting at here has been made very forcefully by Iris Murdoch, the Oxford philosopher and novelist. She remarks that "morality is essentially concerned with change and progress [in a person's capacity for insight and understanding],"[5] and she illustrates the sort of "change and progress" she is speaking of by means of the following example:

A mother, whom I shall call M, feels hostility to her daughter-in-law, whom I shall call D. M finds D quite a good-hearted girl, but while not exactly common yet certainly unpolished and lacking in dignity and refinements. D is inclined to be pert and familiar, insufficiently ceremonious, brusque, sometimes positively rude, always tiresomely juvenile. M does not like D's accent or the way D dresses. M feels that her son has married beneath him. . . .

This much for M's first thoughts about D. Time passes, and it could be that M settles down with a hardened sense of grievance and a fixed picture of D, imprisoned . . . by the cliché: my poor son has married a silly vulgar girl. However, the M of the example is an intelligent and well-intentioned person, capable of self-criticism, capable of giving careful and just attention to [D]. M tells herself "I am old-fashioned and conventional. I may be prejudiced and narrow-minded. I may be snobbish. I am certainly jealous. Let me look again." Here I assume that M observes D or at least reflects deliberately about D, until gradually her vision of D alters. . . . D is discovered to be not vulgar but refreshingly simple, not undignified but spontaneous, not noisy but gay, not tiresomely juvenile but delightfully youthful, and so on.[6]

Because morality is essentially concerned with the sort of "change and progress" this story illustrates, and because people vary greatly in this respect, "we cannot," says Murdoch, "be as democratic about [morality] as some philosophers would like to think."[7] Plainly, she is rejecting Westermarck's claim that we can make no legitimate distinction between a more developed and a less developed "moral consciousness."

This will seem shocking, no doubt, to dedicated relativists, whose cause has been "the equal validity of all moralities." And they may suspect that Murdoch's position is a covert form of moral absolutism. This would be a misguided interpretation, however, for an important part of Murdoch's position is that she attacks the common underpinning of both absolutism and relativism, namely, the idea that "right," "wrong," "good," "bad," and "ought" are the fundamental moral terms. Far from being fundamental, such terms could, she says, be dispensed with altogether.[8] Clearly, if Murdoch is right about this, the picture of morality as consisting of moral principles is seriously misguided. I will return to this matter in due course. But let us first explore further Murdoch's suggestion that because people cannot all be credited with the same degree of insight and understanding, we cannot be as democratic about morality as some philosophers would like to think.

What Murdoch is saying here is something that should not take us by surprise, for she is calling attention to something that most of us are, to one degree or another, already familiar with. Her story of M's perception of D, clouded as it is by jealousy, is but one of many familiar and varied examples of someone's thought and perception being morally flawed.[9]

What ought to surprise us, then, is Westermarck's claim that people cannot be regarded as being more or less capable of thinking about moral matters. I have challenged that view in much the same way as Murdoch, but for good measure I want to present here one more example.

For this purpose I will turn to some passages from Lillian Smith's *Killers of the Dream,* where we get an account, not by an outsider looking into an alien culture, but by an insider looking at the racism she grew up with in the southern United States. The following passages capture the essentials of her account:

> Hypocrisy, greed, self-righteousness, defensiveness twisted in men's minds. The South grew more sensitive to criticism, more defensive and dishonest in its thinking. For deep down in their hearts, southerners knew they were wrong. They knew it in slavery just as they later knew that sharecropping was wrong, and as they know today that segregation is wrong. . . . [Yet] they could not say, "We shall keep our slaves because they are profitable, regardless of right and wrong." A few tough old realists . . . probably did say it. But to most, such words would have seemed . . . fantastic. . . . Our grandfathers' conscience compelled them to justify slavery and they did: by making the black man "different," setting him outside God's law, reducing him to less than human. . . . And once doing it, they continued doing it, and their sons continued doing it, and their grandsons, telling themselves and their children more and more and more lies about white superiority until they no longer knew the truth and were lost in a maze of fantasy and falsehood that had little resemblance to the actual world they lived in. . . .
>
> Most of our families could not take these traumatic experiences [i.e., the changes that came with the abolition of slavery] in a sane, creative way. There was too much. And their past life, their values, their beliefs, their mental habits had not prepared them for this kind of trouble. Insight was not a quality their culture valued; nor intellectual honesty; nor self-criticism; nor concern for human rights; nor could they laugh at themselves . . .
>
> Yet there were individuals, all over the South, who kept themselves without hate, admitting the South's mistakes, and refusing to believe in the tenets of white supremacy. . . . But most [people] gave up, did things the easy way regardless of human consequences, thought the easy way, and identifying with the group, dissolved their scruples by substituting for a personal conscience and a clear brain this thing our politicians call "loyalty to southern tradition." . . .
>
> Our people were meeting trouble by closing up their lives, minds, hearts, consciences, trying not to see, not to feel things as they really were.[10]

These remarks serve nicely to illustrate the point Murdoch is making when she says that we cannot be democratic about morality. Her point is that morality is essentially concerned with the sorts of things mentioned by Lillian Smith: the self-serving ways in which we see ourselves and others, the dishonest ways we may talk about such matters, and the struggle one must undertake in order to break through to an honest perception of things.[11]

It is a fatal deficiency of traditional moral theories, whether absolutist or relativist, that they fail to accommodate Murdoch's insight about morality. In the next chapter we will consider some of their other defects.

Problems in the Philosophical
Description of Morality

The conception of morality shared by relativists and absolutists contains a number of ideas that deserve scrutiny: (i) It represents morality as being concerned only (or at least primarily) with actions. (ii) It describes morality as consisting of moral principles. (iii) It treats the words *right, wrong, good, bad,* and *ought* as the primary moral terms. (iv) It represents our (alleged) moral principles—on which our familiar moral comments (judgments) about people's actions are "based"—as being "external, non-personal in their origin," which implies that one's role in morality is limited to that of following rules (or applying principles) which one had no hand in fashioning.

I will consider these four ideas in order. I should say first, however, that I do not believe that an adequate treatment can be given of these ideas taken separately. They hang together, each supported by the others. Therefore, although I shall make some brief remarks in this chapter about each of these ideas, I do not think of this procedure as yielding anything very conclusive. Subsequent chapters will deal with these matters in a more substantive way.

"Morality Is Concerned With Actions"

This idea is very much the result of the further ideas that morality is largely a matter of passing judgment and that the operative words in such judgments are "right," "wrong," "good," "bad," and "ought." For these further ideas would seem to be most plausible, if they are plausible at all, in connection with actions, with things people do or contemplate doing. We say, "It was good of you to do that," "You ought not to do that," "I want to do the right thing," "Would it be wrong of me to do that?" and so on. This is a prominent feature of our lives, and for that reason it is not, perhaps, surprising that when people philosophize about morality they should think that it is concerned only with actions.

Yet, as Iris Murdoch has suggested, this idea neglects something of considerable importance, for we also make moral assessments of the way people think. (Recall Lillian Smith's remark that "the South grew . . . defensive and dishonest in its thinking.") Such moral assessments are not terribly common. It is not often that we remark on the fact that someone is guilty of self-deception or willful ignorance or is steeped in sentimentality or is complacent or insincere or thinks in terms of stereotypes or is sunk in prejudice or bigotry. Many people take little notice of such things, and fewer still can talk about them articulately. Those who do pay attention to such matters, and comment usefully on the moral quality of people's thinking, are generally social critics, novelists, essayists, and those who read and learn from such authors. The reason for this seems fairly obvious: The moral character of someone's thinking, especially one's own, is not easily discerned and is most difficult to talk about in a revealing and useful way.[1] George Eliot can write novels displaying the complex dynamics of the ways in which people persuade themselves of what they want to believe. And Humphry Cobb, in his novel *Paths of Glory,* can display the ways in which people attempt to justify to themselves deeds for which no cogent justification can be given. But displaying such matters with clarity takes a special talent, and many people fail to discern what these novelists have seen. It is no wonder, therefore, that moral assessments of this kind are not very prominent in our lives, so that most philosophers overlook them and mistakenly think of morality as being concerned only with actions.

"Morality Consists of Moral Principles"

This idea is so much taken for granted by philosophers that it seems almost inconceivable that the idea could be fundamentally wrong. And yet the interesting fact is that nowhere in our actual thinking and discourse about moral matters are these alleged principles to be seen. I may protest someone's actions by saying, "You are being unfair to him," but I do *not* say, nor do I think to myself, "One ought not to be unfair" (or "One ought to be fair"). Again, I may say apologetically, "I shouldn't have said that to him; it was cruel," but I would *not* say or think, "Cruelty is wrong" or "One should not be cruel." And yet what are called "moral principles" are these things we neither say nor think: "One ought to be fair," "It's wrong to be cruel," etc. So these alleged principles are nowhere in evidence. But if that is so, and if philosophers are nevertheless convinced that there are such principles, it must be that they think they have good grounds for *inferring* their existence. They must believe, for example, that when I protest someone's conduct, saying, "But that's dishonest," there are good grounds for inferring that I subscribe to the principle "Dishonesty is wrong" (or "One ought to be honest"). What could such grounds be? And are they good grounds?

Perhaps the most tempting source of this idea is found in cases of the following sort. Suppose that someone putting a horse up for sale disguises its lameness in order to command a better price. Knowing about this, I say to him, "But that's dishonest!" He in turn replies, "So it's dishonest. So what? People have cheated *me* plenty of times!" Obviously, he is not to be dissuaded. Now a philosopher, thinking about such a case, may want to say, "To dissuade a person from doing something dishonest, it is not enough to point out to him merely the dishonesty of his deed; it is necessary to prove to him that one *ought not* to be dishonest, that dishonesty is *wrong*."

It is here, in this piece of philosophical reasoning, that we find the words "One ought not to be dishonest" and "Dishonesty is wrong." And the philosopher who thinks this thought will also, quite naturally, think that those of us who shun dishonesty do so because we *believe* something, namely, that "dishonesty is wrong." Here, then, is the locus of the philosophers' inference. They see that some people have no scruples about cheating, stealing, lying, etc., while other people scrupulously avoid such conduct. And to explain this difference to themselves, these philosophers say that scrupulous people believe that "Cheating is wrong," that "One ought not to steal," and that "Lying is bad," whereas unscrupulous people do not believe (or accept) these principles.

Such an account is tempting, but is it correct? I can find no reason to think that it is. Consider again the person who replies to criticism by saying, "So it's dishonest. So what?" Is it plausible to represent him as someone who does not *believe* something? Isn't he, instead, someone who simply does not *care* how he treats others so long as he gets what he wants?

How are we to settle this question? We can begin by considering how we might best describe such a person. Depending on how far he is prepared to go, he could be described variously as selfish or mean or hard-hearted or ruthless. Very likely he is bitter or cynical, someone who has so often been disappointed or failed by others that he now can think only of himself. Isn't it this, and not his lacking some belief, that accounts for his willingness to be dishonest? (Think here of the character Hud, in the movie of that name.) It is not as though he were concerned to do right by others and had simply failed, somehow, to realize that "one ought not to be dishonest."

This is why I can find nothing plausible in the philosophers' idea that what distinguishes this person from others is that they believe something and he does not, namely, that "One ought to be honest." Let us suppose that a philosopher were to produce for him a philosophical "proof" with the conclusion "One ought not to be dishonest." Let us also suppose that he can find no flaw in this proof. Will he, on account of this, abandon his dishonest ways? Surely not! But *why* would he be unmoved by the philosopher's "proof"? The answer, surely, is that he just doesn't care. Contrary to the philosopher's picture, he differs from the honest person, not intellectually, but in his attitudes.

The philosopher's way, then, of inferring the existence of moral principles is defective. When I refuse to participate in some dishonest scheme, it is not because I *believe* something about being dishonest, namely, that it's wrong; rather, I understand how the dishonest scheme will harm others, and I am not a mean, uncaring, or ruthless person. And when I protest to someone that his proposed actions are dishonest, I am hoping to latch onto some shred of decency in him, some bit of concern for others. I may even try to awaken such concern in him by vividly describing the misery he will cause others. But if this fails, there is nothing more I can do. It is preposterous to think that in such a case it would be useful to provide him with a philosophical argument whose conclusion is "One ought not to be dishonest." But if that is so, is it really plausible to suggest that those of us who, for the most part, conduct our affairs honestly do so because we intellectually accept the alleged principle "Dishonesty is wrong"?

The Primary Moral Terms Are "Right," "Wrong," "Good," "Bad," and "Ought"

Firth, in a passage quoted earlier, says that moral standards are "those of good and bad, right and wrong." J. D. Mabbott, in *An Introduction to Ethics,* declares that "the key words in morals are 'good,' 'right,' 'and ought.' "[2] Although this is a widely shared view, most thinkers fail to be as explicit about it as Firth and Mabbott. Worse yet, they fail to acknowledge that they are not thinking of the ordinary use of these words. By the "ordinary use" I mean the following. We very often say (or think) that someone (often oneself) *ought* to do such and such (or that it would be *wrong* not to do so), and we ask ourselves what would be the *right* thing to do in these circumstances, and we commend people by saying, "It was *good* of you to do that for her." These are perfectly ordinary uses of the words in question. But this is not the use people have in mind when they philosophize on the present subject. Rather, they are thinking that these are the words that play the key role in "moral principles," such as "One *ought* to be honest," "Lying is *bad*," and "Stealing is *wrong*." There is a crucial difference between this philosophical use and our ordinary use of these words, a difference I shall now try to make clear.

In typical cases in which we say that it would be wrong (or right) to do such-and-such, we can follow up such a remark by adding, "It would be dishonest" or "It's the only fair thing to do" or "That would be cruel." Suppose, for example, that I have been intending to sell a horse, which has recently gone lame. Being in need of the sum the horse would bring if sound, I considering administering an analgesic so that the horse will not limp. A friend, knowing of my plan, says to me, "That's not right, John. It's dishonest. Perhaps its lameness isn't temporary; it may have some permanent injury." Here my friend's comment on the wrongness of my proposed conduct is not left unsupported. His saying, "That's not right," is not the *last* word on the subject; it is backed up by further observations about the dishonesty of my intended conduct.

Now compare this with the philosophical use of the word *wrong*. When a philosopher formulates a so-called "moral principle" by saying, "Dishonesty is wrong," he makes the word *wrong* the last word on the subject and thereby places it in an untenable position, for now there is nothing to back it up, that is, if someone were to ask "What's wrong with being dishonest?" there is no *morally* relevant answer the philosopher can give.[3]

Consider another example. We are rebuking a university student and say to him: "Fred! Stop lying and *listen* to me. What you did was *wrong*. You forced yourself on the girl. You *raped* her! Now you've got to face up to that." We do *not* say to him: "It's not right to rape a woman."

A final example. Suppose that during a political discussion I have harangued someone and tried to make him look ridiculous. Next day, having reflected on my obnoxious conduct, I apologize, saying, "It was wrong of me to carry on in that fashion; I was being unfair to you and not trying at all to understand your position." Here again when I remark that my conduct was wrong, this is not the last word on the subject; it is an introductory remark, followed up by my admission that my conduct was unfair. By contrast, when a philosopher says, "It is wrong to be unfair" (or "One ought to be fair"), he puts the word *wrong* (or *ought*) in an untenable position, for he invites the question "Why is it wrong to be unfair?" But now he cannot say, "Because it is unfair," for that would come to "It is unfair to be unfair," which makes no sense at all.

The truth is that if we had to single out any words as being the primary moral terms, it would make more sense to pick out such words as *fair, unfair, dishonest, cruel, deceitful, cheat, steal, lie, torment, rape,* and other such descriptive moral terms. This, as we saw in chapter 15, is a point made by Iris Murdoch. But what she says needs some modifications. First of all, she places too much emphasis on these single moral terms, for we often give morally relevant explanations without these words. (For example, a parent might say to a son, "You told Uncle Henry you would help move his furniture, and he was counting on that. Now it's too late for him to find someone else. So he'll end up moving it himself. And you *know* he has a bad heart.") Second, Murdoch goes too far when she says that "the primary general words [such as *right* and *good*] could be dispensed with entirely and all moral work could be done by the secondary specialized words [such as *fair* and *cruel*]." If we were to dispense with the "primary general words," how could we say, "I thought I was doing the right thing when I . . ."? And how could we ask such questions as: "What's the right thing to do in this situation?" or "Would it be terribly wrong of me to . . ."? We are not always prepared to substitute a more specific wording ("Would it be *fair* to . . . ?") for the more general.

The proper way to put Murdoch's point would be to say that the words *right, wrong, good, bad,* and *ought* play a relatively subordinate role in our actual moral discourse. They are words that require the backing of other terms or explanations, a backing that can generally be given. When it cannot be, when someone is pushed to the point of saying, "Well, it's just *wrong*, that's all I can say," we think of him as being inarticulate or suspect him of trying to defend an indefensible position, for instance, of opposing something he finds threatening or frightening and hasn't thought about in a sensible way, such as sex between gay partners.

Could we imagine an entire society in which moral discourse regularly comes to a halt with people saying, "It's just wrong, that's all!" or "You ought to . . . , and that's the end of the matter"? If so, it would be a society in which the words *ought* and *wrong* really are the primary moral terms. But how will we have to envision these people? They do many things because they feel obliged to, but they can say nothing to explain the obligation, to make it understandable even to themselves.[4] And they shun many things because they think them wrong, but they cannot explain the wrongness of such conduct, that is, it is not that it's unfair or cruel or the like. So how do they come to think that doing certain things is wrong and that doing certain other things is obligatory? What is their background? I can only think of them as having been indoctrinated in some way, perhaps as members of a cult. But in that case they are simply stooges and not people conducting themselves morally.

What we find, then, is that if we *try* to envision the words *ought* and *wrong* being our primary moral terms, that is, as carrying all the weight in moral discourse, we end up with something that may not be moral discourse at all and is certainly different from moral discourse as we know it. We can also see why philosophers, once they have declared that such words as *ought* and *wrong* are the primary moral terms, fall to arguing about whether morality isn't merely arbitrary and subjective. (I will pursue this further in chapter 18.) But if my diagnosis is correct, there is no reason why we should enter into such arguments.

"Moral Principles Are 'External' to the Individual"

Firth, in a passage quoted above, says that moral principles "are regarded as not emanating from the person giving the judgement, but from outside him; they are external, non-personal in their origin." Of the four ideas comprising what I've called "the common conception of morality," this is, for our purposes, by far the most important. Its importance resides in the fact that it is central to the relativist's Fully Developed Argument against moral absolutism. Herskovits, as we have seen, maintains that relativism is "an epistemology that derives from a recognition of the force of enculturative conditioning in shaping thought and behavior."[5] This is the crux of the relativists' argument because it provides their grounds for saying to the absolutist: "You have no good reason to think that your moral principles are true; you only imagine that they're true because they were so firmly impressed upon you by the culture in which you were raised. Had you been raised in some other culture, you would imagine that quite different principles are true."

What would remain of moral relativism if it had to abandon this argument? Nothing, really. Someone might, perhaps, still make the bare assertion that moral principles, to be properly formulated, require a relativizing clause. But if relativists had to abandon the foregoing argument, with its account of how morality is learned, they could no longer give any reason for accepting a relativistic account of morality. This is why, as I said above, the relativist's idea that morality is the product of enculturative conditioning is the most important of the four ideas comprising the common conception of morality. If we could persuade relativists to abandon this idea about moral learning, the other ideas could, for present purposes, be left largely unchallenged. For this reason I will devote special attention to the idea that we acquire morality by a conditioning process. In this chapter I will make some elementary observations about this idea and will then discuss it more fully in the following two chapters.

If we are to assess this idea about morality, we are faced with a problem more fundamental than discovering whether it is true or false. For we must first ask ourselves whether we know what it *means*. At the beginning of the chapter I remarked that this idea seems to imply that the role of the individual in morality is limited to that of following rules (or applying principles) which he had no hand in fashioning. But if we interpret this to mean what it most naturally suggests, the result is rather disconcerting, for it turns out to be not merely false but obviously false. For it takes only a moment's reflection to realize that we seldom speak of following a principle *unless* we have made it for ourselves, as when we say, "I have made it my principle never to borrow money from friends." So if the idea in question is interpreted to mean that we never make such principles for ourselves, it is plainly false. I cannot, however, believe that those who propose this idea intend to say anything so obviously untrue. It is more likely that they have something quite different in mind when they say that morality originates outside the individual. So let us look for another interpretation.

Recall here that Firth, having said that relativists and absolutists agree that moral principles are "external, non-personal in their origin," goes on to say that they hold entirely different views as to what that origin is. Absolutist, he says, most commonly hold that "the source of all morality is God." Now someone who holds this view is likely *also* to hold that the individual's role in morality is limited to that of following principles (or commandments) which he had no hand in fashioning—which is the claim we are seeking to interpret. So it seems clear enough what this claim means in the case of absolutism—or this version of it. But what does the claim mean in the case of relativism?

In the hands of the relativist, the claim that moral principles are "external, non-personal in their origin" involves at least the idea that we acquire our morality from our culture in a nonrational way. So let us ask: What is there in our lives that could rightly be described in this way?

One thing that comes to mind is the way in which we acquire certain attitudes that prevail in our society, such as that some occupations are appropriate only for men and others for women, that extramarital sex is immoral, that a girl deserves death if she dishonors her family by becoming pregnant out of wedlock, and so on. Most of us grow up with at least some attitudes of this sort, and we clearly did not invent them for ourselves. They were around long before we were born, and we learned them from people around us, mostly from our elders. Someone who thought that such attitudes are the stuff of morality might very well want to say, with Firth, that moral principles "are external, non-personal in their origin."

If relativists could be interpreted as equating morality with pervasive attitudes of the sort just mentioned, we could at least understand what they say about morality and "enculturative conditioning." But that wouldn't mean that relativists are right about this. For we have already found good reasons for rejecting this view of morality: Socially dictated attitudes and practices are *not* the stuff of morality; they are themselves among the things we subject to moral scrutiny. The fact that someone has been brought up with certain attitudes and practices need not render him or her incapable of reflecting on these and finding fault with them. (Think of Knife Chief, for example.) As was remarked in the preceding chapter, it is a serious moral deficiency in a person to be unable to reflect on and reexamine attitudes and practices that he or she was brought up to accept unquestioningly.

In making this point I am not introducing some invention of my own. Most of us could easily illustrate this point with familiar examples. Until recently, a pervasive attitude in our culture was that regardless of a woman's talents, interests, and aspirations her place was in the home, and yet many people now realize that this is a stultifying and demeaning attitude deserving rejection. In the same way, many people in our culture grow up with the attitude that homosexuality is reprehensible and yet later cast off this attitude upon discovering that a valued friend or respected acquaintance is homosexual. And most of us know of people who grew up with racist attitudes but who, in later life, came to recognize those attitudes as vile and disgraceful.

So although it may be appropriate to use Herskovits's term "enculturative conditioning" to describe the way we acquire the prevailing attitudes of our culture, relativists are certainly making a huge mistake if they think that we acquire morality—or become moral persons—by such a process. Is this mistake, then, at the heart of moral relativism? Is this what the relativists' claim about morality and enculturative conditioning amounts to? If so, their Fully Developed Argument rests on a mistake, and we can now take our leave of the whole subject, for there remains nothing to be discussed.

It may be the case that some relativists have made the mistake of equating morality and culturally induced attitudes, but I do not feel comfortable dismissing all relativists in this way. For some of them may insist that morality consists of principles and that these are *not* to be confused with attitudes. Such relativists, however, still owe us—and themselves—an explanation of what it *means* to say that morality is a product of cultural conditioning. For they must both explain this claim and show it to be true if they are to keep alive their Fully Developed Argument.

Their explanation, I suppose, could begin with their saying that although morality is to be distinguished from attitudes like those mentioned above, morality is nevertheless *acquired* in the way we acquire such attitudes, so that the role of the individual in morality is limited to that of following the principles or precepts that are imposed upon him or her by the ambient culture. This explanation, it seems to me, is clear enough to give us something we can put to the test. We can think about how morality is—or might be—acquired and whether the individual is merely a passive recipient in that process. This is the inquiry I will take up in the next two chapters.

Enculturative Conditioning

How might someone get the idea that morality assigns to the individual a very minimal role, namely, that of following rules (or applying principles) which are imposed upon us from without? That is the question I should like to answer. It is disturbing to think that morality is nothing but the product of "enculturative conditioning" so that our capacity for moral thought is constrained by a cultural straightjacket. Yet there is something in this idea—something I find difficult to describe—which makes me think it is not completely misguided.

In order to locate this elusive "something," I will begin by pointing out that it is possible to find cultures that fit rather well the common conception of morality. In his book *Personal Character and Cultural Milieu*, Douglas Haring gives the following sketch of the "outstanding aspects of Japanese conduct and personal character" in Japan before World War II:

(1) Psychologically and culturally the Japanese people are unusually homogeneous. They act and think much more alike than do Occidental peoples. The avowed aim of Japan's prewar Ministry of Education was to produce subjects of the Emperor so much alike as to be interchangeable for national purposes. . . .
(2) The Japanese conform almost eagerly to numberless exact rules of conduct and exhibit bewilderment when required to act alone or in situations not anticipated in the codes. . . .
(3) The major sanctions of conformity to Japanese codes of conduct are ridicule and shame. Early in life every child learns that the slightest breach of proper conduct may expose his family to ridicule, and that a lapse from propriety may leave him unsupported in the face of the ridicule of the world and the wrath of his own family. . . .
(8) The word *makoto* . . . is charged with emotional significance in Japan. . . . In Japanese eyes *makoto*, utter devotion to codes of conduct, is one of the highest virtues.[1]

How does all this come about? Haring presents part of the explanation in the following account of Japanese education:

> The aims of all education culminate in a single theme: the sanctity of the Emperor. Not for a moment in his school career may a Japanese forget that the purpose of life is to serve the Emperor. His history books—and above all, his "morality" courses—insure that every Japanese thinks of himself as a loyal subject. Whatever his social class he is a subject, never a citizen. . . .
>
> Shinto doctrines are impressed upon the young in their books by participation in rituals at school, and by group worship at Government Shinto shrines. These cult activities are compulsory. . . .
>
> The middle schools, junior colleges, and universities conform to similar standards. There is no relaxation of the duties of Emperor worship in the higher institutions. . . .
>
> The educational system has achieved two major ends. . . . [First,] by the nature of the language and the system of writing with Chinese ideographs, the masses of the people cannot hope to acquire foreign ideas except as the officials permit their publication in Japanese. . . . Secondly, the relatively small number of persons who achieve higher education are rendered irrevocably Japanese in the formative years of childhood. By the time they encounter foreign ideas in the colleges, they have formed emotional habits which guarantee immunity against beliefs that might threaten their patriotic devotion.[2]

Haring goes on to give a number of illustrations of the inability of the prewar Japanese to think for themselves. Here is one:

> The streetcar conductor also knows his place. He carries a book of rules. Therein are printed all possible questions that passengers might ask, together with correct replies. His speech is confined to these prescribed sentences, and "whatsoever is more than these cometh of evil." . . . [O]riginality transcends the conductor's imagination.[3]

I cannot vouch for the accuracy of Haring's description of the prewar Japanese, but I have no reason to think that it is not for the most part true—or true, at least, for a large part of that population.

Even from Haring's highly abbreviated account it is possible to see that the life of the prewar Japanese fits pretty well the philosophical picture that represents morality as a set of rules or principles imposed upon the individual and that assigns to the individual little, if any, capacity for moral insight and innovation. In the life of prewar Japan, as in that picture, the individual, when it comes to codes of conduct, is a kind of puppet. This is why Haring's account is of philosophical interest. It provides us with an example that could be *appropriately* described by saying: In *this* instance a code of conduct is acquired, as Herskovits says, by a process of "enculturative conditioning."

Yet the case of the prewar Japanese is, obviously, a rather special one. They seem to have been so much in the grip of their indoctrination that they were incapable of reconsidering and altering their moral beliefs. But not everyone is like this. Think of Knife Chief. As we saw in chapter 4, he came to think of human sacrifice very differently from other members of his tribe. He came to regard such sacrifices as a "cruel exhibition of power, exercised upon unfortunate and defenseless individuals whom they were bound to protect." Think also of our own case. Our lives have not been prescribed for us in the minutest detail, and unlike the prewar Japanese we—or at least most of us—are not utterly bewildered when faced with morally novel situations. I will say more about this in the next chapter, but it should already be apparent that an account of morality that rather aptly describes the prewar Japanese will not be an accurate description of us or of what morality amounts to in our lives.[4]

This raises an interesting question about the word *morality*. If an anthropologist were studying the culture of prewar Japan and reported finding the sort of thing Haring reports, would he say that he was describing their *morality*? We can be sure that Herskovits would say this, for the sort of thing Haring reports fits Herskovits's account of "morality" as neatly as anything could. But what would others say? It is noteworthy that Haring, in the passages quoted above, uses the phrases "rules of conduct" and "codes of conduct," but he does not use the word *morality* except in one instance when he places it in inverted commas, sometimes called "scare quotes." He does so, evidently, because he is not entirely comfortable using our word *morality* for describing the prewar Japanese. What might be the source of his discomfort? Is there something about what we understand morality to be that is missing from what Haring found?

Consider in this regard what Arthur Murphy says about morality, beginning with his remarks about moral training.

> The categories in whose terms [moral] thinking is done and the language in which [those categories] have a practically significant use are not those of behavioral conditioning but of moral understanding, of practical action, agent and justifying or normatively cogent reasons. Until we have learned to view our own conduct and that of others in this light nothing moral has been learned and the training given is not moral training. A man whose behavior was appropriately conditioned might behave all his life as he had been brought up to behave and still be a moral moron. . . .
>
> No doubt what passes for "moral" training is often given and understood [as social conditioning]. But this is not the way in which a man learns to become, and to conduct himself as, a moral agent. Those who learned no more than [to act as they were commanded to] would rightly be regarded not as men we could respect as persons but, morally, as cases of arrested development. . . . For men thus trained what would be the sense or use of [morally] justifying reasons? They would need only to remember their instructions and in fear and trembling or with a glow of conformist satisfaction or just as a matter of course, of social habit and routine, to do as they had long ago been told. They would obey the traditional maxims of their community without hesitation or discussion.

What, with respect to the morality of the action, would there be to discuss? . . . [They] were brought up *not* to think. To suppose that it is in such "bringing up" as this that we learn the meaning and the use of moral reasons would be patently absurd.[5]

Murphy, obviously, is rejecting Herskovits's idea that morality is acquired by means of conditioning. His alternative account begins with a comment on the sort of community within which moral training could take place:

A society that offers effective [moral] training . . . must practice what it preaches. . . . And if the training is to be moral, this practice must be that of a community in which a going concern for right action is an effective factor in the way of life in which the learner is called upon responsibly to share. . . . Admonitory speech has a useful part in such training, and rewards and punishments may support it, but unless the practice itself supports it in a different way, by example and not punishment and precept merely, only the timid or the gullible will in the long run be imposed on by it. . . .

Of course, the content of such training, as formulated in familiar maxims, will be the accepted moral precepts of the group in which the training is given. . . . If everything in a moral situation were arguable or questionable at once there could be no significant questioning or argument. And until the learner has acquired this working basis of understanding, until he knows in some cases what good reasons are, he will have nothing to reason with or about when he is called on in his own person to distinguish between actions that are right and wrong. . . . But while this is the beginning of moral wisdom it cannot in principle, or in hard cases, be the end. . . . The learner thus equipped [with an understanding of rudimentary moral reasons] is launched on a voyage of discovery that can carry him a long way from his starting point. For the process of the use of reasons is a self-corrective process. The customary acceptances with which it begins are the grounds for action each of us has learned to respect in the local communities in which he was brought up. . . . In many situations they are good enough. If they were not, the group that taught him what it is to be a responsible agent would not itself be a moral community. But in changing conditions and in the larger situation with which he and his group . . . have to deal, they are sometimes not good enough. There are issues that cannot on their local and parochial terms be adequately met and [there are] other people's reasons to be weighed that are not those he learned in childhood to respect. And if he has not merely been "brought up" but has grown up, he must come to understand and use the better reasons here acquired. . . . Moral learning is not for children merely; we must go on learning all our lives if the requirements of our moral situation are rightly to be met. The point of moral training is to supply a starting point and to develop the concern and capacity with which we can thus go on. . . .

Do we ever get this kind of training? Indeed we do—not in admonitory verbal slaps and sweetmeats, though for the very young and for those who never do grow up such admonitions have a social use, but in living and working with those who in their own person embody this kind of excellence and, by precept and example, can bring out the best in us. It is in this way and in the light of their achievement that we come to understand what makes good reasons "good" and how, in their terms, to distinguish between right and wrong as we share with them in the concerns and responsibilities of a way of life in which such goodness has a practical sense and use.[6]

What Murphy says here about the difference between moral training and social conditioning seems very reasonable. And it may have been considerations such as these that led Haring to place the word *morality* within scare quotes. He may have thought that the word's suitability for describing what he found in prewar Japan is at least questionable because it differs so greatly from what we understand morality to be.[7]

We can now pose our question about the word *morality* in terms of the following three alternatives. Herskovits would see nothing problematic about using the word *morality* to describe what Haring found in prewar Japan. He would think that using the word in that way is the *standard* use of the word. Murphy, on the other hand, might have taken the opposite position: He might have refused to use the word *morality* in such a case, insisting that anyone using the word as Herskovits does is *misusing* it. And then we have Haring, who uses the word but puts it in scare quotes. Now which is the most sensible of these alternatives?

The first alternative is plainly wrong. For the reasons given by Murphy, using the word to describe the prewar Japanese is *not* unproblematic. And it is certainly not its *standard* use. Herskovits can think otherwise only because he has embraced a theory which tells him that *everyone* is like the prewar Japanese in being incapable of reconsidering and altering their moral beliefs. But the fact that we can find cases like that of Knife Chief shows that Herskovits is wrong about this. So his use of the word *morality* is *not* unproblematic, and we can throw out the first of the aforementioned alternatives.

What about the second alternative, the idea that it is a *misuse* of the word to say: "Haring has given a description of the *morality* of the prewar Japanese?" Someone might say: That's a misuse of the word because the training—the *indoctrination*—they received did not supply them with the capacity for moral growth. Murphy might have viewed the matter in this way.[8] But would we really want to say: "Haring's study of prewar Japan reveals it to have been a culture with a code of conduct but no *morality*"? To justify this we would have to show that the word *morality* has a hard and fast definition that excludes what Haring discovered in prewar Japan. Where are we to find such a definition? I have not the slightest idea. For this reason I am inclined to say that there is simply no such thing as the *essence* of morality, which is the same in all times and places. So we can throw out the second of the aforementioned alternatives. The use of the word can be stretched to include the prewar Japanese. Even so, a Boasian point seems in order here: We must be wary of deploying transculturally a term such as *morality,* for in doing so we may mask important differences.

We come down, then, to the third of the aforementioned alternatives: placing the word *morality,* as Haring did, within scare quotes. If he did this in order to acknowledge the very significant differences he found between the culture of prewar Japan and what morality amounts to in our lives, then his is certainly the most sensible of the three alternatives.

Perhaps we should say that the culture of prewar Japan presents us with a *borderline case* of morality. If we put the matter in this way, we can allow that the sort of moral development that Murphy emphasizes is a very *important* part of morality and at the same time allow that there is no hard and fast definition of the word *morality* that excludes the prewar Japanese. In any case, if we are going to continue using this term for describing practices outside our own culture, let us be prepared to notice differences.

I have already pointed out that there are noteworthy differences between us and what Haring found in prewar Japan. But are there similarities as well? I suspect that there are. I also suspect that if we take proper notice of these similarities we may find the answer to the question with which I began this chapter: How might someone get the idea that morality assigns to the individual a very minimal role, namely, that of following rules (or applying principles) which he had no hand in fashioning?

I am suggesting here that the answer to that question is this: (i) What passes for morality in our culture contains features that make it *somewhat* similar to the culture of prewar Japan. (ii) Some thinkers, having noticed these features, give them prominence and even exaggerate them—so much so, in fact, that they overlook important differences, and then (iii) having both neglected the differences and exaggerated the similarities, they end up imagining that an account of morality that rather aptly describes the prewar Japanese (i.e., an account that depicts morality in terms of cultural conditioning) must also be an apt description of us, of what morality amounts to in our lives. If I am right about this, the relativists' picture of morality has *some* basis in fact—in certain features of our culture that relativists exaggerate, so that it is more like a caricature than an utterly false representation. In the next chapter I will offer support for this suggestion by drawing out and identifying those features of our culture which have, I suspect, been seized upon and exaggerated in the relativists' picture of morality.

18

Islandia and Despond

In order to identify those features of our culture that relativists have seized upon and exaggerated in their picture of morality, I will sketch two imaginary cultures, which I shall call "Islandia" and "Despond."[1] Both sketches will be made up chiefly of features borrowed from our own culture, or from the lives of certain members of our culture, but only in my second culture, Despond, do we find anything that fits the relativist's picture of morality.

I must emphasize that my purpose here is philosophical, not sociological. I have not aimed at presenting a complete picture of Islandia and Despond, and I have proposed no explanation of how they came to be as they are. (Did Islandians, perhaps, learn some hard lessons from their own sad history? Do we see in Despond the remnants of a religion gone sour?) In sketching these cultures, I have confined myself to such details as are relevant to my larger purpose, which is twofold: first, to bring out differences in the ways people think and reason by giving sharply different accounts of the ways in which the members of Islandia and Despond think and reason and, second, to use these sharply different accounts as a means of suggesting how someone might get from our culture the idea that the sort of thing Haring found in prewar Japan is the very essence of morality, that is, that morality assigns a very minimal role to the individual and requires little or no thought.

Islandia

If we were to meet the Islandians, we would discover that they are, on the whole, impressively insightful, thoughtful, and articulate in their comments on and discussions of moral issues. So much so that many of them would strike us as men and women of remarkable wisdom. I am not suggesting that they all exhibit these qualities to the same degree. But it is rare to find an Islandian whose thinking is burdened by clichés and stereotypes, who is guilty of self-deception or willful ignorance, who indulges in exaggeration or distortion in discussion, or who is so smug, arrogant, or insecure that he cannot listen carefully and thoughtfully to those who offer an opposing view. Most of the citizens are impressively sincere, imaginative, discerning, and self-critical. Moreover, the Islandians who would strike us as being remarkably wise are greatly respected in this culture. There is no status to be achieved among the Islandians by mere prowess, by stardom in athletics, by amassing great wealth, by glamour, or by achieving high office. And they have no body of literature that resembles our pulp Westerns, in which characters are portrayed as virtuous or villainous merely by their deeds. The Islandians prefer literature that is psychologically more subtle, studies of self-deception, hypocrisy, bigotry, prejudice, insincerity, complacency, obtuseness, smugness, callousness, and so on. And much of their literature is concerned with people who struggle against moral failings of this kind.[2]

Although I say that we would find Islandians to be impressively wise, we would not discover this easily. For they are somewhat reticent in matters of morality. They are not given to moralizing and are not quick to condemn. In fact, they might strike us as being extremely cautious in this regard. This is owing, not so much to their charity, as it is to the fact that they do not think it is always easy to know what a person should do. It is hard enough, they say, to think about one's own conduct and oftentimes next to impossible to be sure what others should do. (They sometimes caution themselves with the words "Judge not.") For this very reason, however, when they do speak about moral matters, their remarks tend to be impressively thoughtful.

The children of Islandia are encouraged, at home and in school, to think carefully about and to describe in relevant detail a variety of situations calling for discerning judgment or difficult decisions. They are discouraged from hastily judging other people and urged to try understanding the thoughts and feelings of others, even of bitter, cynical, and self-centered people. (This skill is facilitated by their writing stories in which character development is paramount.) As a result of their meditations on such matters, they become adept at correcting their own biases, identifying blind-spots in their own understanding, and recognizing their tendencies toward defensiveness and perversity.[3] Islandians also learn by this means to use reason and gentle humor to expose the absurdity of someone's rationalizations or self-deceptions. And they learn that when discussing a matter with unreasonable, perverse, or fanatical people, they must proceed very differently from the way one discusses matters with people who are earnest, candid, and open-minded—that with persons of the former sort persuasion is often useless, so that one can do no more than lead them on, in the hope that the absurdity of their position will, in time, become inescapable even to them. Islandians also realize that neurotic defenses are often too rigid to be overcome by any rational means. And having realized that a possible obstacle to reaching agreement with someone may be his or her lack of imagination, they develop subtle ways of reaching those people, such as telling stories and parables to

expand their imagination and insight. In short, they are intellectually re-
sourceful and articulate in ways that many of us are not.

I do not mean that Islandians are all of equal competence in thinking
about and discussing moral matters. Some are more acute, insightful, imaginative, and articulate than others, but they do not, except for the most
obtuse among them, resort to saying something like: "It's just wrong, that's
all I can say!" or "You just ought to, that's all!" If they find themselves in
disagreement with someone and getting nowhere, they typically conclude
either that they have been unsuccessful in exhibiting the character or motivation of the action in question or that they have failed to see what the other
person was driving at. At other times, when two of them fail to bridge the
gap in either direction, they conclude, not that one of them is obtuse, but
that neither of them knows how to think clearly about the matter under
discussion. Their discussions of moral matters are seldom thwarted by eva-
sion, impatience, or defensiveness. They are, for the most part, sincere and
thoughtful people.

One area of their lives in which these qualities are evident is in their
political discussions and campaigns for elective office. Islandians are not
divided by deep prejudices, and among their politicians there are no dema-
gogues, or at least none that gain a following. While some of them are
inclined, from time to time, to develop rigid ideological theories on social
and political matters, wiser men and women endeavor to expose the nar-
rowness and rigidity of such thinking and do so with patience and gentle
humor rather than acrimonious debate and personal attack. Insofar as Islandians can be said to have national heroes, these are people revered for
their good sense and ingenuity in dealing with national problems and in
keeping Islandia at peace with other nations. In Islandia war is not glorified,
and there are no monuments to military figures.

Something needs to be said about the material side of Islandian life. Like
certain of our own subcultures, such as the Amish and the Shakers, Islandians have chosen to live relatively simple lives. Much could be said here
about their reasons for this choice (Islandian authors have written volumes
on the subject), but I will confine myself to a few comments. First, their
choice was grounded, not in holy writ, but in both practical and moral
considerations. Among the latter was their recognition that people are easily
corrupted by acquisitiveness. It tends to become an insatiable appetite, and
this in turn tends to crowd from one's mind a variety of important considerations. The pursuit of wealth can blind a person to his or her neglect or
mistreatment of family and friends; it can even turn one against those less
fortunate than oneself, as epitomized in Dickens's character Scrooge. And if
one pursues wealth for the sake of greater consumption, one may ignore the
fact that unrestrained consumption can destroy the quality of life, by way
of pollution, for example, and the destruction of the landscape.[4]

The Islandians' decision to live rather simply has many ramifications. For
example, anything that smacks of conspicuous consumption becomes an
object of humor. Also, commercial advertising is used only to inform, never

to create demand for a product. One result is that fads and fashions are almost nonexistent, and few Islandians pursue wealth in order to acquire luxuries. Also, there is little disparity of wealth among the Islandians, and poverty is largely unknown. Because most Islandian businesses are owned by the employees themselves, the salaries and bonuses earned by executives do not greatly exceed the wages of other employees.[5]

It is perhaps important to add that behind all of the foregoing is the Islandians' great concern with raising happy, healthy, well-educated, and emotionally secure children. This is fostered in many ways in Islandia: by child-rearing classes, by teachers trained to recognize children who need special help with emotional problems, and by the readily availability of such help. Also, children are neither exposed to violence in the public media nor given war toys to play with. Although intramural sports are popular in the schools, sports are treated strictly as games. (At the collegiate level there is no recruiting of athletes, and coaches are unsalaried volunteers.) Many students elect, instead of team sports, such activities as hiking, skiing, mountain climbing, and canoeing. Illiteracy is unheard of in Islandia, and teenagers are encouraged to join discussion groups, which specialize in such subjects as science fiction, current events, and poetry. All students are required to have a solid grounding in the sciences, one result of which is that Islandians are not prone to embrace absurd theories about natural phenomena or human nature. (They have no tendency to believe in, for example, psychic phenomena.) The children of Islandia, therefore, grow up in an environment that is supportive of their emotional needs and that discourages magical thinking.

I began this chapter by saying that my purpose here is philosophical, not sociological, and it may seem that I have strayed from this intention. I believe, however, that some knowledge of their social setting is necessary for appreciating the manner in which Islandians think about and discuss moral matters. It is important to know, for example, that they do not see injustice all about them, that racism is not pervasive in their society, and that they can count on civility from one another. They reside in what Arthur Murphy would call a "moral community."

What, then, are we to make of the fact that none of us grew up in a place like Islandia? The answer, pretty clearly, is that this is not a matter of all or nothing. Most of us grew up in a community in which there were some—if only a few—people like my Islandians or people who closely resembled them in at least some respects, and in which some—if only a few—of the features of Islandian society were present. But if our community resembles Islandia only in part and to some degree, what is the rest of it like? For that we can turn to Despond, which I will describe in such a way as to give prominence to these other features of our society.

Despond

Here we find a situation somewhat like that of prewar Japan. The people of Despond are not encouraged to think honestly and carefully about moral matters. Although their dictionaries contain such words as *hypocrisy, self-deception, willful ignorance, bigotry, callousness, insincerity,* and the like, people lack a ready command of these words. They seldom turn up in either their literature or their conversation.

Their moral literature is predominately concerned with property rights, physical heroism, national honor, and sexual temptation, the villains being thieves, cheats, murderers, seducers, sexual "deviants," and traitors. Their moral exemplars, on the other hand, are those who sternly oppose vice, who resist temptation, who uphold their country's honor, or defend it in wartime, even at great cost to themselves. Self-sacrifice and self-denial are highly esteemed, and in their children's literature there are plenty of books that eulogize the humble, forbearing poor who cheerfully endure their station in life. Everyone in Despond is exposed to such literature and absorbs it, for the most part, uncritically.

I said that the Islandians have no body of literature that resembles our pulp Westerns. Quite the opposite is true of Despond, where the most popular fiction displays good and evil in the manner Anthony Storr describes as follows:

> Many of us harbour a secret wish to be transported back to the world of the nursery, where black is black and white is white; where the forces of good finally triumph over the forces of evil; where the righteous are taken up into heaven whilst the wicked perish in the lake of fire. A good deal of the less sophisticated fiction panders to our primitive taste for dividing the world into heroes and villains. Conan Doyle's invention of Sherlock Holmes and Professor Moriarity is an apt illustration. His protagonists are polar opposites; and Holmes's description of Moriarity fuels our paranoid phantasies:
>
>> He is the Napoleon of crime, Watson. He is the organizer of half that is evil and of nearly all that is undetected in this great city. . . . He has a brain of the first order. He sits motionless, like a spider in the centre of its web, but that web has a thousand radiations, and he knows well every quiver of each of them. He does little himself. He only plans. But his agents are numerous and splendidly organized.
>
> Enjoyable as this is, we have to admit that its appeal is to an unregenerate child in ourselves who delights in such simplicities.[6]

Such simplicity is prized by Despondians because they are ill equipped to think about, and are thus bewildered by, matters of moral complexity. They also find it deeply satisfying to vilify those who differ from them. This tendency has various consequences for their culture, racism being one of them. The others I will leave to the reader's imagination.

Unlike the Islandians, Despondians are not reticent in matters of morality. They feel sure that they know what everyone should do and are quick to condemn those who do otherwise. Those whom they think of as wise are pompous moralizers rather than sensitive, insightful thinkers. Far from being thoughtful and imaginative, they deliver themselves of speeches laced with platitudes and clichés. They are largely incapable of laughing at themselves and seldom, if ever, engage in self-examination. Any intimations of their own hypocrisy are quickly stifled. They are given to self-righteousness, and their deficiencies are disguised—even from themselves, it seems—by smugness or arrogance.[7]

I do not mean that the people of Despond are perfectly alike in the characteristics I have described, and we will presently consider how some members of this culture deviate. But what I have described thus far is a dominant theme of this culture.

Another aspect of moral upbringing in Despond is that everyone learns a great many dos and don'ts that have no very evident point.[8] Duty is a dominant moral category here, and obedience is sternly enforced. As a result, most of these people would recognize something of themselves in the following lines from the autobiography of Rudolf Hess, commandant of the Nazi extermination camp at Auschwitz:

> I had been brought up by my parents to be respectful and obedient toward all grown-up people, and especially the elderly, regardless of their social status. I was taught that my highest duty was to help those in need. It was constantly impressed upon me in forceful terms that I must obey promptly the wishes and commands of my parents, teachers, and priests, and indeed of all grown-up people, including servants, and that nothing must distract me from this duty. Whatever they said was always right.
>
> These basic principles on which I was brought up became part of my flesh and blood. I can still clearly remember how my father, who on account of his fervent Catholicism was a determined opponent of the Reich government and its policy, never ceased to remind his friends that, however strong one's opposition might be, the laws and decrees of the state had to be obeyed unconditionally.
>
> From my earliest youth I was brought up with a strong awareness of duty. In my parents' house it was insisted that every task be exactly and conscientiously carried out. Each member of the family had his own special duties to perform. My father took particular care to see that I obeyed all his instructions and wishes with the greatest meticulousness. I remember to this day how he hauled me out of bed one night, because I had left the saddle cloth lying in the garden instead of hanging it up in the barn to dry, as he had told me to do.[9]

One of Hess's more striking remarks here is: "I was taught that my highest duty was to help those in need." He does not say at all that he was brought up to *care* about people in need, to empathize with them. What Hess's remarks suggest is a degenerate form of Christianity: the story of the Good Samaritan colored by the legalism of the Old Testament and stories of a wrathful deity. One is reminded of Kant, who said that "those passages of Scripture which command us to love our neighbor and even our enemy" must be understood in a special way, "for love as an inclination cannot be commanded." What is commanded, then, is "beneficence from duty, when no inclination impels it." This, said Kant, is "practical love," and "it resides . . . not in tender sympathy."[10] The world of Hess's childhood may have included some of this "beneficence from duty," but it was woefully lacking in empathy. This omission may help to explain how, as an adult, he was capable of serving as the commandant of a Nazi extermination camp.

In any case, this is very much how matters stand with the people of Despond. They have little understanding of what they are doing, but they feel obligated to do it anyway. Any of them might describe their upbringing as Hess described his: "I had been brought up by my parents to be respectful and obedient toward all grown-up people. . . . Whatever they said was always right." On account of this demand for blind obedience, one might say that the Despondians conception of morality is modeled on that of military discipline. (A line from Tennyson comes to mind: "Theirs not to reason why / Theirs but to do and die.") In Despond a code of conduct has been handed down from one generation to the next, and perfect conformity is demanded of everyone. In this respect they closely resemble the prewar Japanese.

Most Despondians not only conform but do so unquestioningly. There are, however, exceptions. For among the people of Despond there are some who are repelled by the deadening effect of all this talk of duty and obligation. They feel, somewhat vaguely, that there is something amiss in their lives, in their culture. These disaffected individuals would readily agree, therefore, with the attitude expressed in the following verses by Arthur Hugh Clough, an English poet who became popular in the late Victorian period:

Duty—that's to say complying
With whate'ver's expected here;
Upon etiquette relying,
Unto usage nought denying,
With the form conforming duly,
Senseless what it meaneth truly,

Duty—'tis to take on trust
What things are good, and right, and just;
And whether they be or be not,
Try not, test not, feel not, see not. . . .

'Tis the stern and prompt suppressing,
As an obvious deadly sin,
All the questing and the guessing
Of the soul's own soul within:
'Tis the coward's acquiescence
In a destiny's behest,
To a shade by terror made,
Sacrificing, aye, the essence
Of all that's truest, noblest, best:
'Tis the blind non-recognition
Either of goodness, truth, or beauty,
Except by precept and submission;
Moral blank and moral void,
Life at very birth destroyed,

Atrophy, exinanition!
Duty!—
Yea, by duty's prime condition,
Pure nonentity of duty![11]

This attitude, as I said, is shared by a small minority of Despondians. And what does it lead to? A few of these disaffected individuals become expatriates and seek out a healthier society elsewhere in the world. Most, however, remain and are thus faced with coming to terms, somehow, with the culture from which they feel alienated. Some do so by becoming cynical nonconformists and taking pleasure from the consternation they elicit. A few simply turn a deaf ear to all moral suasion and take up criminal pursuits. Others, having less adventurous inclinations, become intellectuals and develop philosophies of the nihilistic or existentialist variety.

It goes without saying that moral philosophy flourishes in Despond. And naturally one of the questions their philosophers become obsessed with is: "Why should I be moral?" The reason for this, as outsiders can see, is that they understand the word *moral* to mean (as perhaps it mostly does in Despond) "adherence to duty" or something close to that.[12] So the philosophical question "Why should I be moral?" poses a problem for them because, although much of what passes for duties is lacking in any sense for them, many of them regard nihilism as an unacceptable alternative: It opens the door to murder, rape, theft, and so on. Caught in this dilemma, then, they argue endlessly about why one should be moral, never recognizing the nature of their quandary.[13]

Another aspect of their moral philosophy is that their philosophers are always talking about moral rules or principles, as though these were somehow the guidelines of action. Of course, they never quite succeed in explaining what a moral rule or principle is, but they also never manage to see what is queer about this notion, for in fact their lives do, in certain respects, look as though they are living by rules—as if, like boys at summer camp, they need someone to set limits and prescribe duties. (In other words, they are very much like the prewar Japanese Haring describes.) The kinds of things these philosophers call "rules" or "principles" are such things as "One ought to keep one's promises," "One ought not to tell lies," "It is wrong to steal," and so on. Like our philosophers (see Firth, chapter 15), they argue about where these rules come from, and various theories are developed to explain this puzzling matter. Some say that moral rules come from God, others argue that these are self-evident and necessary truths, while still others insist that these are not truths at all but only expressions of the feelings of approval and disapproval toward certain actions. Other philosophers, who have read some anthropology, insist that moral principles are merely the arbitrary rules that a society has laid down for the conduct of its members and are thus like rules of the road.

Another feature of their philosophizing arises from the fact that some of their philosophers are dissatisfied with the sort of lives generally regarded by Despondians as morally exemplary. So they devise various theories (hedonism, utilitarianism, and others) which purport to set different limits to conduct. The typical attitude of these theorists toward the morality they hope to displace is that expressed by the philosopher Charles Sanders Peirce when he spoke of morality as follows:

> We all know what morality is: it is behaving as you were brought up to behave; that is, to think you ought to be punished for not behaving. But to believe in thinking as you were brought up to think defines *conservatism*. It needs no reasoning to perceive that morality is conservatism. But conservatism again means, as you will surely agree, not trusting to one's reasoning powers. To be a moral man is to obey the traditional maxims of your community without hesitation or discussion. Hence, [philosophical] ethics, which is reasoning out an explanation of morality, is—I will not say immoral [for] that would be going too far—composed of the very substance of immorality.[14]

Such is the general state of dissatisfaction with morality among the dissident intellectuals of Despond, and their resulting confusion deserves our sympathy.

Among the people of Islandia, of course, no such confusion could occur. For one thing, the question "Why should I be moral?" would never arise, as it does for the philosophers of Despond, because Islandians would have no word with the associations that "moral" and "morality" have in Despond. Also, since it would never seem to them that they were living according to a set of rules, like boys at summer camp, they would find no plausibility in the idea of "moral rules" or "principles." And, finally, it is inconceivable that Islandians would be intellectually drawn to nihilism.

To understand why Islandia and Despond differ as regards this last point, we must recall why the alienated members of Despond find nihilism tempting, if not fully acceptable. The explanation must begin with the fact that in Despond "morality" is thought of as consisting, at bottom, of rules or principles. Moreover, many of the requirements and prohibitions have no sense for the people of Despond themselves. This being so, Despondians can easily come to think that "moral principles" have a peculiar and dubious status. For these people, then, the status of morality *itself* can seem dubious, which is to say that all of morality is in danger of being called into question at once. Hence their readiness to consider nihilism. (They would feel a kinship with Sartre, who said that if God does not exist, then everything is permitted.)[15]

Islandians, by contrast, have no inclination to think of themselves as living by a set of rules, that is, as having a "morality" whose foundations have some peculiar and dubious status. There is nothing in their own culture, therefore, that would make them think that nihilism is even intelligible. While they may from time to time reexamine a particular social arrangement or form of conduct, the wholesale rejection of morality would be unthinkable. An Islandian who seriously asked, "Why shouldn't I lie and cheat and steal?" would rightly be regarded, not as a philosopher posing a question that deserves an answer, but as a psychopath from whom society needs protection.

We can now consider the relevance of all this to moral relativism. In the last several chapters we have been considering that picture of morality shared by both relativists and absolutists. It represents morality as being "external, non-personal in origin," and in the relativists' version of this we are said to acquire morality by a process of "enculturative conditioning," that is, in a causal, nonrational way. This idea would have some merit if relativists meant to be describing a borderline case of morality like that of the prewar Japanese. This was not, of course, their intention. They meant to be describing morality as found in *any* culture. This is what their Fully Developed Argument requires, for its aim is to show that morality *wherever it is found* is relative. Our own culture, however, differs significantly from that of prewar Japan. Our lives, unlike theirs, have not been prescribed for us in the minutest detail, and unlike the prewar Japanese we—or at least most of us—have some capacity for moral insight and innovation. So the relativists' picture is not an accurate depiction of us, of what morality amounts to in our lives. We must, therefore, reject that picture, especially the claim that we acquire morality by a process of enculturative conditioning. But since that claim is the crux of their Fully Developed Argument, that argument now collapses, which means that there is no longer any reason to adopt a relativistic view of morality.

At the beginning of the preceding chapter I raised this question: Why have so many of our philosophers and anthropologists shared the view of morality described by Firth? Why, that is, do they think of morality as assigning to the individual a very minimal role, namely, that of following rules (or applying principles) which he or she has had no hand in fashioning? I have now suggested an answer to this question by sketching Islandia and Despond. I constructed these two cultures chiefly by borrowing features of our own,[16] and I did so for the following reason. The fact that there are certain features of our culture—or of the lives of *some* members of our culture—from which I could construct Islandia shows that it is inaccurate to say, in a completely general way, that in our lives morality is "external, non-personal in origin." But although inaccurate, it is not *entirely* wrong. For I was able to borrow from certain other features of our culture the material for constructing Despond, which to some degree resembles the culture of the prewar Japanese.

It is this resemblance, I am suggesting, that has led philosophers and anthropologists to describe us as though we are like the prewar Japanese—as though with us, too, morality is "external, non-personal in origin." This description of us is neither wholly accurate nor wholly inaccurate. It is a sort of caricature.

Perhaps we should have expected our investigation to arrive at such a conclusion. For philosophical ideas are seldom complete falsehoods. More

often they are distortions, exaggerations, or one-sided descriptions of something that cannot be easily—which is to say, simply—depicted. And morality—especially the forms it takes in a culture with a history as complex as
ours—is certainly something that cannot be easily described. It consists of
such a bewildering variety of elements that I almost want to say that it's too
messy to be described at all. Relativists have produced a caricature by picking out one or two of these elements and declaring them to be the essence
of morality. But there *is* no essence here. Life is not as simple—not in our
culture, anyway—as those philosophical accounts suggest. While some
among us are quite accurately depicted by the relativists' account of "enculturative conditioning," others are not. There are even a few who do not
fit that account at all, for even in our culture there are individuals who, with
maturity, shed those elements of which Despond is constructed.

At this point someone may protest that even my Islandians can be portrayed relativistically and that therefore I have not succeeded in ruling out
moral relativism. This objection might be stated as follows:

> Thinking is carried on by means of concepts, so a person's thinking is
> circumscribed, limited, by whatever concepts he happens to have. And this
> is as true of moral thinking as of any other. But two cultures might have
> different moral concepts, in which case their moral thinking would differ.
> For example, the Islandians, as you have portrayed them, are an intro-
> spective, self-critical people and accordingly have many moral concepts
> used to assessed a person's thinking, such as "prejudice," "evasion," "self-
> deception," "willful ignorance," etc. But another culture—let us call it
> "Antagonia"—might employ different concepts. Antagonians might be a
> boisterous, swaggering, and bellicose people, and central to their way of
> thinking are such concepts as "courage," "valor," "fortitude," "loyalty,"
> "duty," and "honor." They regard Islandians as faint-hearted, weak, and
> timid. Also, conduct that Islandians would regard as domineering and
> aggressive Antagonians regard as manly and virile. They go in for blood
> sports, and big game hunting is a favorite pastime of their wealthier mem-
> bers. They are also a lusty people, and with no fear of censure they con-
> duct themselves in ways Islandians would regard as obnoxious sexual ha-
> rassment. Furthermore, if Islandians were to engage Antagonians in
> discussion, they would find that they could produce no rational consid-
> erations that would convince them to give up their view of life and the
> concepts that go with it. They could not persuade them to adopt Islandian
> ways of thinking. The reverse is also true: Antagonians would find that
> they could not persuade Islandians to come around to their way of think-
> ing. This is because each culture is locked into its own set of concepts.
> And on account of this we could say that Islandians and Antagonians have
> different moralities, neither of which can be rationally justified. But this
> is all that is needed for formulating a new version of the relativists' Fully
> Developed Argument. It would run as follows: "You may think that you
> have the appropriate set of moral concepts, but another culture might
> think the same of its (quite different) set of concepts, and since neither set
> can be rationally justified, you must admit that your moral concepts have

no privileged status. Therefore, you cannot use your concepts to pass judgment on members of other cultures. If you are going to make moral assessments of their conduct, you must do so by means of their concepts."

Someone might be impressed by this defense of relativism, but it is not as reasonable as it may appear.

First, I will observe that it is simply not true that a person's thinking is circumscribed by the concepts he or she happens to have at a given time. Scientists, for example, are not locked into a set of concepts. They not only discard old concepts ("phlogiston," "caloric," "the luminiferous ether," etc.) but are constantly devising new ones. This is not unique to the sciences. People are constantly inventing new concepts, and in fact we wouldn't have the language we presently have if this were not so. So the chief premise of the foregoing argument is untrue. I will return to this point presently.

The new argument claims that "we could say that Islandians and Antagonians have different moralities, neither of which can be rationally justified." The only grounds given for this claim is that the Islandians can find no rational means of persuading the Antagonians to give up their way of life and its associated concepts. But this does not support the claim in question, for we could just as well infer that the Antagonians won't listen to reason. Perhaps they are like slaveholders in the American South who refused to concede that there was anything wrong with enslaving Africans and exploiting their labor to enrich themselves. Callousness and perversity are seldom acknowledged by those who exhibit these qualities. So the mere refusal of the Antagonians to alter their thinking is no reason to say that they have a different morality. The argument attempts to show that if the Islandians cannot persuade another culture to see things their way, they will have to regard their own ways of thinking, and the moral concepts involved, as being arbitrary and unjustifiable. But on the slavery issue, abolitionists did not come to think this way when they found they couldn't persuade slaveholders to abandon slavery.

Second, the foregoing defense of relativism is very much like Westermarck's argument in that it simply asserts that the Islandians can produce no rational considerations that would convince the Antagonians to give up their view of life and the concepts that go with it. I said above that one could infer from this failure that the Antagonians simply won't listen to reason. But we could infer instead that the Islandians were not patient enough or were not very imaginative in their attempt to change the Antagonians' thinking. A proponent of the argument must reject this inference, but on what grounds could he do so? I mean, if we are supposing that the Antagonians do not simply refuse to take the matter seriously, how will we know that they and the Islandians, when they discuss their differences, have addressed all the morally relevant considerations and have done so with complete candor? Can we credit ourselves with knowing what all of those considerations might be and with being ourselves free of every sort of prejudice, every sort of self-deception and perversity, so that we could judge this matter? I don't think we can always do so. So we are not in a position to say that the Antagonians remain unmoved despite being presented with *every* possible rational consideration and *every* means of removing prejudices, etc. We cannot, therefore, conclude what the foregoing argument would have us conclude, namely, that the Islandians' failure to persuade shows that relativists can rightly declare that moral concepts are arbitrary.

Finally, the foregoing defense of relativism depends, as I said above, on depicting the Islandians (and everyone else) as being locked into a particular set—"their own" set—of concepts, and that this renders them incapable of examining and fairly (or objectively) assessing another culture's way of thinking.[17] But Islandians are no more "locked into" a set of concepts than we are, and we, from time to time, both drop old ideas or concepts and adopt or devise new ones. For example, we no longer employ the concept of miscegenation for moral criticism, and the terms "male chauvinism" and "sexual harassment" have recently become part of the active vocabulary of most adults in our society. So the foregoing defense of relativism rests on a faulty assumption. I do not mean that no one's judgment is ever adversely affected by the concepts he makes particular use of. (As Iris Murdoch remarks, "Certain ways of describing people can be corrupting and wrong. A smart set of concepts may be a most efficient instrument of corruption."[18]) But while it may be that people tend to think about things, whether moral or otherwise, in the terms most familiar to them, many people—and certainly the Islandians—are capable of realizing, on appropriate occasions, that they may need to think about certain things in a new way.

There is a tendency to think that if you wanted to convince someone to abandon a way of life and its associated concepts, you would need to devise some sort of esoteric argument, the sort that intellectuals, including philosophers, have tried to provide. (Anything other than such an argument would be a nonrational form of persuasion, like brainwashing, and so could not be regarded as *justifying* whatever change it might bring about in someone's thinking.) But this idea is surely misguided. Consider an example I mentioned in chapter 14: a culture which gives up polygamy because the women succeed in making it clear that it is unfair to them, that it is an important element in a pervasive pattern of male chauvinism. Such a change in thinking would not come about over night. On the contrary, such change is typically a slow and incremental process. But it is what occurs *in* such a process that can, when thoughtfully carried out, justify our ways of thinking and the associated concepts. Recall how the modern feminist movement developed. It began, in the 1960s and 1970s, with a period of "consciousness raising" among women, after which men were led—against varying degrees of resistance—to recognize the ways in which social, legal, and commercial arrangements systematically favored men. They were led, gradually, to see that common expectations and myths about women simply ignore their abilities, talents, interests, and ambitions. Some men, of course, persisted in the old ways of thinking, for they were loath to surrender their advantages. But those who managed to acknowledge what they were being shown really did see what was wrong in the old arrangements. They also came to see that women can be capable physicians, brilliant lawyers, shrewd business people, able military personnel, and so on. And they found that society was not damaged when women entered occupations formerly reserved for men.

Coming to see such things was a genuine achievement; the change that came about was not just a *change* but a change *for the better*. Yet at no time in this process did men change their minds on account of an esoteric argument that only intellectuals could follow. And we could say the same of the civil rights movement of the 1960s and 1970s. Although we still have far to go in overcoming racism in America, those who discarded the old myths and stereotypes came to see how badly African-Americans had been treated since the Civil War. But this did not come about by way of esoteric argumentation.

I said above that there is a temptation to think that anything other than an esoteric argument would, if it changed people's minds, be a nonrational form of persuasion and so could not be regarded as *justifying* the change. But would it be plausible to say that people's minds were changed by non-rational processes in the two cases I have just mentioned? Surely not! So there are no grounds for maintaining the relativistic view that the changes that came about in these cases cannot rightly be said to be changes for the better—unless we are prepared to qualify this relativistically and say merely that they were for the better *in our culture*.

Let us think about one more example. Can we not suppose that the Islandians were, at one time, just like the Antagonians and that gradually they came to realize that the lives they were leading and the ways they were thinking were, in various respects, unsatisfactory? Surely we can, for they may have become the people I have described as the result of learning some hard lessons from their own sad history. We can suppose, then, that their culture became the Islandia I have described very gradually, over an extended period of time. How might such a transformation have come about? In small increments, one would think. And one would expect that literature played an important part in this—and not only novels and short stories but poems that have the moral force of the great antiwar poems and plays with a moral impact like *The Death of a Salesman*. They may also have had their great orators who, like Martin Luther King, Jr., called them to accounts. Perhaps, too, there were insightful essayists whose writings could jolt and enlighten people, as did John Howard Griffin's *Black Like Me*.[19] But more impelling than any of these may have been the feelings of disgust some of them experienced when, on rare occasions, they stepped back from the routine of their lives and saw how thoughtless and insensitive they tended to be and how *careless* they were with matters that might be viewed more seriously.

My point, once again, is that if the Islandians had undergone a change of thinking on account of such things as I have just mentioned it would not be plausible to say: "They weren't being rational when they underwent that change." And yet the philosopher's model of rational justification played no role in the process I have described.

So the new version of the relativists' argument rests on a misconception. It purports to show that our ways of thinking about moral matters, and the concepts involved, are merely arbitrary unless we can justify them in a quite particular way, by an esoteric, philosophical argument. But this is surely a myth about what rational justification (or reasoned persuasion) is actually like in this area of our lives. There is a temptation to think that we must try to justify morality by appealing to something *outside* morality. (We saw an example of this in chapter 2: James Q. Wilson's attempt to refute the moral skeptic, including the moral relativist, by arguing that scientific facts can justify moral principles.) But the test of whether we are being rational if we accede to a particular form of persuasion is not how closely that form resembles some philosophical model of rationality. Nor do we decide whether a particular form of persuasion is rational by seeing whether it changes the mind of a psychopath. We can all agree that it would be futile to try changing a psychopath's thinking about moral matters by means of an ordinary moral appeal, the sort we address to one another. And we can all agree that such an appeal will be thought irrelevant if presented to a Despondian philosopher who worries that all of morality will be called into question at once unless we supply an abstract argument to prove that moral principles are true. We can agree because both of these are tautologies. But having conceded these two tautologies, we are in no way committed to allowing that we are not engaged in a *rational* enterprise, are not giving genuinely *good* reasons, when we seek to change people's ways of thinking by means that do not resemble the philosopher's model of rational argument. What John Howard Griffin attempted to do with his book *Black Like Me,* namely, to change the thinking of people who have racist tendencies, cannot rightly be compared to brainwashing or some other nonrational means of influencing minds. Undoubtedly, there are many racists whose mind would not be changed by reading Griffin's book, but if a philosopher were to say that that book does not, therefore, constitute a rational means of persuasion, that would merely show how artificial is the philosopher's ideal of rationality.

A Final Look at the
Relativist's Argument

It is time to balance our accounts. Thus far we have been pretty hard on defenders of moral relativism, and it may appear as though there is nothing at all to be said on their behalf. But it would not be fair to end this discussion without giving them credit for something.

To see what credit may be due them, let us recall the remarks by Congressman Dannemeyer that I quoted in the Introduction. The congressman declared that moral relativism and the Judeo-Christian ethic are "two philosophies in conflict." Plainly, he is what relativists would call "a moral absolutist," for he proclaims not only that the Judeo-Christian ethic comes from God—by which he no doubt meant to suggest that this "ethic" is indisputable—but also that it is composed of standards meant to "govern people in any society." Relativists, of course, would be delighted to find Dannemeyer stating moral absolutism in this way, for it plays directly into their hands. It does so because relativists can now point to other religions whose adherents claim with equal fervor that theirs is the one true religion and that Mr. Dannemeyer is subject to the commandments and prohibitions of *their* religion. (Shi'ite Muslims, for example, regard Christians and their culture as "the Great Satan.") And having called attention to these other religions, relativists will declare:

> You think that there are universal moral truths, namely, those taught by your own religion. And yet you are in exactly the same position as the people of other cultures who imagine that *they* know that their principles (which conflict with yours) are true. But since you regard their "knowledge" as illusory, you must admit that they could say the same of you, for your certitude has the same source as theirs, that is, you, like they, learned your morality from your own culture. Perhaps you will say that your religion comes directly from God, but they, of course, will make the same claim for their religion. You must agree, then, that your Judeo-

Christian principles hold no privileged position and that you have no right to impose them on other people.

This, as we saw in chapter 1, is the sort of argument put forth by Herskovits, and so far as I can see there is no cogent reply available to a moral absolutist like Mr. Dannemeyer.

We might put the matter as follows. Disregard for the moment everything we have taken note of in the preceding chapters about the nature of morality and suppose, for the sake of argument, that "morality" is nothing other than what is taught by the various religions. (This isn't an absurd supposition. As we saw in chapter 15 Raymond Firth, commenting on what people believe to be the source of moral standards, said that "the commonest answer, probably, in the history of Western society is that the source of all morality is God.") If we begin from this supposition, and if we give due attention to the fact that there are numerous religions, each with its own set of "moral" prescriptions, what must we conclude?

Before answering this question let us consider a particular instance. Mormons at one time practiced polygamy and were for this reason despised and persecuted by members of America's mainstream religious community. In search of a safe haven, the Mormons fled from state to state, settling briefly in Illinois. There, in 1844, the founder of that sect, Joseph Smith, who had forty-nine wives, was killed by an angry mob. Brigham Young then led the group further west to the Utah Territory. Young, who ultimately married twenty-seven women, named polygamy a tenet of the church in 1852, an act that further exacerbated tensions with the dominant Christian community. Shortly after the Civil War, President Grant delegated authority to the territorial governor to stamp out Mormon polygamy. Hundreds of Mormons were arrested, among them George Reynolds, who eventually figured in the U.S. Supreme Court case which decided the issue.[1] The high court, declaring that "polygamy has always been odious among the Northern and Western Nations of Europe," ruled against the Mormons. It said that while the First Amendment gave them the right to believe in plural marriage, the government has full authority to regulate religiously motivated actions. Eventually, in 1890, the Mormon church, in order to remove the remaining obstacle to the admission of the Utah Territory to statehood, issued an executive order banning polygamy. That is to say, it banned the practice of polygamy but did not declare that plural marriages, including those of Joseph Smith and Brigham Young, are immoral. The relevant point being that neither the Mormons nor the mainstream religious community abandoned their moral convictions.

The question I am posing, then, is this: If we suppose that morality consists of nothing other than convictions of the sort illustrated by this example, that is, if we take this as the model by which we are to understand morality, what must we conclude? Must we not conclude that moral relativism is true?

It depends, of course, on who "we" are. Religious believers will not conclude that relativism is true, for each of them—of whatever faith—will go on proclaiming that his or hers is the only true religion.[2] But if our aim were to study the world's cultures *without bias,* we would think (given the aforementioned supposition) that, in our survey of the worldwide scene, we had discovered the following: (i) there are several different moralities, and (ii) although the adherents of each claim to have the truth on their side, they have no objective grounds for believing this, which means that they are obliged to admit that they are in the same position as the others in regard to morality. Each can say that they *believe* that such and such is wrong and that so and so is their duty, but they cannot rightly claim to *know* this. As we saw in chapter 1, (i) and (ii) constitute the premises on which the relativist rests his case. Thus, given our present supposition about morality, we, as unbiased students of culture, would have to conclude that moral relativism is true.

What does this show us? It shows us at least that those who insist that their own religion (or the God in whom they believe) is the one and only source of (true) moral standards are in no position to denounce moral relativism, for the religious character of their claim plays directly into the hands of the relativists' argument. So although religious believers are not going to agree that moral relativism is true, they must, if they are honest, agree that to a neutral observer it must appear that, if the religious account of morality is correct, moral relativism is true.[3]

This, it seems to me, is what some defenders of moral relativism—Herskovits, for example—may have recognized, and they deserve credit for having done so. Where they go wrong is in taking too narrow a view of what morality is. This is why the argument with which I have just credited moral relativists is not, when all is said and done, a sound argument. To make it work, we have to suppose either that morality consists of nothing other than the teachings of various religions or that, in its nonreligious forms, morality is the sort of thing Haring found in prewar Japan—something acquired by a process of enculturative conditioning. But this is a misrepresentation of morality. So although relativists may be in a stronger position than moral absolutists when these two parties do battle, this does not mean that moral relativism is true.

What about Westermarck, whose views differ from Herskovits's? Since he explicitly sets aside religiously grounded morality and concerns himself with (in his words) "the moral consciousness when left to itself," we cannot extend to him the qualified credit I have just extended to Herskovits. The crux of his argument is his claim that there occur unresolvable disagreements over moral matters even when both parties to a dispute agree on all the facts. In earlier chapters we have found reasons to challenge Westermarck's view of morality, but let us here reflect just on his account of moral disagreements. The existence of unresolvable disputes proves, according to Westermarck, that the contending parties are caught up in what he calls "a clash of principles." Had he been asked why such clashes cannot be resolved, he would no doubt have answered: "Because moral principles are the bedrock of moral reasoning"—meaning that when a moral disagreement reaches this level, there is no use giving the matter further thought and one must fall into silent resignation.

Is this what moral disagreements actually look like? Perhaps in some cases they do. But they needn't. When Islandians find themselves in disagreement over some moral issue, their ways of proceeding do not give even the appearance that they are standing pat on unarguable principles. In some instances one party will seek to open the eyes of the other to some aspect of the matter that he or she has been insensitive to or willfully ignorant of. In other instances both parties may agree that they do not know how to think about the matter at hand and that further reflection is needed. We might sum up the matter by saying that when in Islandia moral disagreements occur and the contending parties fail to reach unanimity, they do not think they have reached the end of the road but instead take a tentative attitude toward the matter in question. This is because Islandians do not think that anyone can be certified as being free of every sort of prejudice, every sort of insensitivity, every sort of self-deception and perversity. (For the same reason no one in Islandia is regarded as a moral expert, as having all the answers, so that others must defer to his or her judgment.) So the way they deal with moral disagreements does not support Westermarck's claim that such disagreements, in the last analysis, come down to a "clash of principles."

Another point can be made here about the relativists' view of morality. Their view of moral disagreements (whether between cultures or individuals) leads them to conclude that moral principles are, ultimately, arbitrary. This means that in every case in which we declare some course of action to be morally wrong we could just as well condone it. But what does this mean? At the very least it means that a reversal of our judgments would not mean that we had become monsters. This might seem plausible in some cases, but it surely has no plausibility at all in regard to such matters as slavery, torture, rape, and a great many other things. Could my Islandians just as well condone as condemn rape or torture? I mean, could we, with equal plausibility, depict them either way? Surely not! For if they began to condone such things, they would no longer be the people I described. There are many matters regarding which it would be absurd to think of Islandians in the manner suggested by the relativists' view.

The relativists' picture of morality, then, must be rejected. There is no reason at all to regard it as being complete or as being an accurate picture as far as it goes. Moreover, when we look back from our present perspective at those paradoxes we took note of in chapter 4, we can see that each of them provides an additional reason for rejecting moral relativism.

One of those paradoxes was that moral relativism is a complete and obvious failure if it is regarded as being what it ought to be, namely, a *description* of morality. In chapter 4 I set aside this objection on the grounds that moral relativists think of themselves, not as giving a description of (our present) moral principles, but as telling us how moral principles ought to be formulated if we are going to formulate them in accordance with what anthropologists have discovered, that is, that they ought to contain a relativizing clause. We have now seen, however, that what anthropologists have regarded as the relevant discoveries are not discoveries at all; they are philosophical misconceptions. And now that we've established this we can say (as we could not in chapter 4) that moral relativism is fatally flawed *because* it fails as a description of morality.

This has a bearing on a dispute about philosophical method that I mentioned in chapter 2 (see note 5). As I remarked there, philosophers have disagreed as to whether it is or is not a legitimate method to test a philosophical claim against our language as it presently stands. Those who reject this method claim that our language needs—or may need—reforming because those who devised it knew very little about the world and, as a result, encumbered our concepts with various misconceptions, which science can expose.[4] In the present case the claim is that discoveries made by anthropologists demonstrate that a relativizing clause *should* be added to our present moral judgments. What we have found, however, is that anthropologists have made no such discoveries and have therefore given us no reason to think that in this instance our language, that is, the "logical form" of our moral judgments, needs reforming. Should we conclude, then, that a philosopher is within his rights when, like Bernard Williams (see chapter 2) he dismisses a philosophical claim because it conflicts with our present linguistic practices? The answer must be Yes and No. A philosopher will look pretty silly if, like Williams, he dismisses out of hand a philosophical idea for which there is said to be scientific evidence. What is required, clearly, is an investigation of the sort I have undertaken in this book, an investigation into whether the alleged empirical discoveries are what they appear to be. If it turns out, as in the present case, that what is offered as scientific evidence is instead a philosophical misconception, there will be no reason why the philosophical issue should not be decided by an appeal to what we actually say. My own view, based on considerable experience with cases in which philosophers claim that some scientific finding shows that our language needs reforming, is that such claims always involve some philosophical misconception. But I know of no general argument that would demonstrate the truth of this conclusion, and in the absence of such an argument our only recourse is to proceed case by case to show that science has provided nothing relevant to the solution of a philosophical problem.

Our Relation to Other Cultures

The principle concern of moral relativists has been to dissuade the peoples of the world from thinking themselves superior to others where they do not see eye-to-eye on moral matters. What now becomes of that concern if, as I have argued, relativism must be abandoned? Does my argument have the consequence of giving encouragement to moral busybodies who think they know best how everyone should conduct theirs lives? No, for although my position does away with the relativist's all-purpose argument against moral busybodies, there is nothing in it that opens the door to indiscriminate interference in the lives of other peoples. What makes my position different from the relativist's is that it recognizes that the question whether we ought to interfere with the practices of another culture is not a philosophical question but a practical, moral one and is to be answered, therefore, not in a general and abstract way, but in the light of the details of each particular case. This can best be explained by considering a variety of cases and showing how different are the considerations relevant to each.

The first sort of case I want to consider is that which, as I conjectured earlier, relativists themselves have been chiefly concerned with, namely, cases in which, on first encounter, it appears that a real evil is being perpetrated but once a better understanding is gained of the people themselves and their true motivations, it is seen that they are not the cruel or heartless people we at first supposed. These are the cases to which Boas's insight is relevant. When it comes to the question of interference, it turns out that these cases divide into several kinds.

Of these Boasian cases, the most easily dealt with are those that fall into the pattern of the Eskimos' practice of leaving their old people to freeze to death. An outsider, upon hearing of this practice, might think that the Eskimos murder their old people and that something should be done to stop this. However, when the practice is fully understood, it turns out that the Eskimos are *not* murdering their old people and that there is no reason for outside intervention. There is also another factor involved, namely, that the people affected by this practice, the elderly Eskimos, were willing participants. This factor is not, however, found in all of the cases that lend themselves to Boasian insights.

A case in which nonwilling parties were involved is that of the head-hunting Dyaks, although this case, too, lends itself to Boasian treatment. Upon hearing that the Dyaks kill innocent victims, including women and children, we may think, as Hobhouse puts it, that these are a "fiendish" people, the very worst sort of people imaginable. Yet upon understanding the motivation for these killings and seeing also that the Dyaks are not a blood-thirsty crew, we recognize that it is somewhat misleading to call them "murderers." Yet this Boasian insight leaves us with the practical moral question: Ought we, if possible, to do something to prevent the further taking of heads? For in this case, unlike the preceding one, those affected are not willing participants: The victims do not willingly offer up their lives.

There is no easy answer to this question, for a variety of factors need to be considered. First of all, in what situation is intervention being contemplated? Are we in any position in Borneo, the home of the Dyaks, to provide some sort of physical protection, short of armed intervention, for the potential victims of head-hunters? If so, such protection might be warranted by the lives we could thereby save. If such protection were unfeasible, however, so that potential victims could be saved only by threatening and carrying out reprisals for head-hunting, then we would have a very different moral problem on our hands. For it is a well-known fact that disruption of the lives of primitive peoples by outside intervention often results in such thorough demoralization that entire tribes decline and eventually disappear. It would therefore be necessary to think carefully about the effect of active intervention.

If we were not in a position to offer physical protection to potential victims of Dyak headhunting, there are ways other than military intervention that might bring about change. An educational campaign might in time lead the Dyaks to decide for themselves that one does not acquire strength from magical properties of an enemy's skull. This would be a different sort of deterrent to headhunting and might be worthwhile, even if it is less assured of results. Again, the suitability of such a program would depend very much on details about which one cannot generalize and which cannot be decided by abstract philosophical argument.

Our propensity to misunderstand other cultures and the perils of our intruding in them are reason enough for agreeing with Arthur Murphy when he writes: "To make moral judgments at large about the Universe, or the ancient Greeks (*should* Antigone have buried her brother?) or the folkways of the Samoans, is for the most part simply not our business."[1] In trying to think about our own lives, he adds, "there is enough, and more to keep us busy." But while this is, as Murphy says, true "for the most part," there arise from time to time situations that, although outside our cultural domain, inevitably engage our moral concern. How are we to think about these?

There are, for example, those "honor killings" carried out by rural Arabs when a daughter or sister becomes pregnant out of wedlock. According to reports, there are non-Arabs, mainly Europeans, already intervening to save the lives of these women by clandestinely ferrying them out of their countries and providing for them elsewhere in the world. Those who engage in these rescue operations are not in need of some Boasian insight into the thinking of Arabs intent on killing a daughter or sister. Undoubtedly they already know that these Arabs feel that the family honor can be restored only by the women's deaths. Are these Europeans misguided, then, when they intervene to save lives?

An important factor here, obviously, is that in this case the women whose lives are threatened are not willing participants; they don't want to be killed. Also, their rescuers are not intervening in the parents' lives by threatening or incarcerating them. They are simply aiding women to escape who are already determined to do so. While this may have the effect of leaving the women's families feeling dishonored, it does not disrupt the life of the whole community in such a way as to bring about demoralization and cultural extinction. There seems, then, to be no good reason to deplore the rescue efforts of these non-Arabs.

Similar considerations apply to those women from African and Middle Eastern cultures who apply for asylum in the United States on the grounds that at home they would be forced to undergo genital mutilation. Recently the Clinton administration has filed a brief with the Board of Immigration Appeals in which it is argued that asylum should be granted those women who, if returned, would face the more extreme forms of female circumcision. I think we can assume that if a great many of these women apply for and are granted asylum in various western countries, those cultures that now practice genital mutilation will abandon the practice rather than endure the exodus of their young women. If so, we will have interfered with a traditional practice of other cultures, but for the reasons mentioned in regard to "honor killings" there seem to be no good reasons for us not to do so.

A rather different case is that of the rape of Sicilian women by rejected suitors who would force them into marriage. Although we deplore this conduct, it is not at all clear how an outsider could help the potential victims. Perhaps if the Sicilian women were themselves prepared to flee their country, as are the Arab women threatened with honor killings, they too could be assisted. But there is no indication that in this case the women contemplated flight. To have any effect in this case, then, we would have to intrude where uninvited by anyone, and it seems impossible to find justification for such an intrusion. It is not even clear how we could bring it off if we wanted to, but that is not the most relevant consideration. What looms largest in a case of this sort is that every culture has its own inequities, cruelties, and so on, so that an intervention by anyone of them into the affairs of another would not only involve considerable hypocrisy but would, in addition, set an unfortunate precedent. (Should we intervene in Islamic countries to assist those women who would prefer to wear Western dress instead of the mandatory black chador? Should other countries attempt to force the United States to abandon the death penalty or professional boxing?) There are, indeed, exceptions, but it is generally far more sensible to let cultures right their own wrongs, as in fact happened in this instance: Franca Viola won her lawsuit, and the man who raped her was sentenced to eleven years in prison. I assume that this precedent-setting case pretty well did away with the practice. But the decision whether to keep hands off the doings of another culture must always take into account the magnitude of the wrong that needs righting and the means available for righting it.

Consider, for instance, the case of South Africa's policy of apartheid, which is now in the process of being abolished. Not only were the wrongs in this case of very considerable magnitude, with millions of people being harshly oppressed, but the policy was institutionalized in law and rigorously enforced by the government, so that there was little likelihood that change would come about without some sort of external pressure. And in this case a variety of economic sanctions—pertaining to loans, investments, and trading privileges—were available for exerting such pressure.

In this connection it is relevant to consider certain developments at the 1993 United Nations Conference on Human Rights, developments having to do with a nation's so-called "right of development." The conference, held in Vienna, was dominated by claims that international denunciations of human rights abuses are improper because they fail to respect the religious and cultural traditions of the alleged abusers. The claim that each nation has a "right of development" that should take precedence over the rights of its citizens amounts to the claim that liberal democracies should not impose economic sanctions upon nations in which denial of the right of free speech and the imprisonment of political opponents are part of its cultural heritage.

The idea that each nation has such a right is traceable to the 1986 "African Charter on Human and Peoples' Rights," to which most African governments are signatories. The charter provides that "all peoples have the right to their economic, social and cultural development." At the UN conference in Vienna, other nations, many of them Asian, argued for such a right. This position, if adopted by the UN, would mean that a nation's "right of development" had been violated if it were penalized for its human rights abuses by the imposition of economic sanctions. As one commentator, Aryeh Neier, has observed, the idea that the "right of development" takes precedence over individual rights is "extremely dangerous," for it leads directly to such things as slavery in Mauritania and the detention of political prisoners in Chinese labor reform camps. This "effort to expand the definition of rights," says Neier, is really nothing but a disguised attempt at "enhancing state authority and protecting that authority against external interference."[2]

Moral relativists would, of course, have to declare that Neier is guilty of ethnocentrism, on the grounds that only thus could he object to each nation's "right of development." As was observed in chapter 4, in 1947 the executive board of the American Anthropological Association submitted to the United Nations Commission on Human Rights a statement urging that the UN adopt moral relativism in formulating its "Declaration of the Rights of Man." More specifically, these anthropologists invoked moral relativism as grounds for insisting that the proposed UN Declaration "be applicable to all human beings, and not be a statement of rights conceived only in terms of the values prevalent in the countries of Western Europe and America." The UN Declaration, they said, should be "a statement of the rights of men to live in terms of their own traditions."[3] The relativists' position, then, is essentially the same as that of those nations (China, Malaysia, and others) which, nearly fifty years later at the 1993 UN Conference in Vienna, argued for the adoption of a "right of development" for each nation. This, then, is one reason for inquiring into the relativists' claim that there are scientific grounds for adopting such a position. For so long as this claim to scientific respectability goes unchallenged, it may appear to some that it is necessary to extend to all nations the so-called "right of development." And doing so would mean, in practice, that our own country should make no linkage of its foreign policy with human rights issues, as was done during the administration of President Carter.

At the same time we must avoid the opposite mistake, that of thinking we can lay down principles that must be followed everywhere, regardless of a people's history, customs, environment, and the like. As Murphy has rightly observed, what a sound moral philosophy can do is, not "to offer in advance a philosophical blueprint of the 'world order,' . . . [but] to help us to see the problem [of living with other cultures] . . . in a proper *light;* to understand what kind of problem it is, what considerations would be relevant to a solution, and what a right or justifiable solution would be, if we could get it. It can teach us," he adds,

> something of the moral temper and practical habit of mind in which men of good will can seek such solutions in common, and know how to live with them when they have found them. Universal wisdom is not available to us in our professional capacity as philosophers—there is simply too much that we do not know, or whose practical import we lack the experience to measure. . . . But if we are true to the example of Socrates, and we know what it is like to *seek* wisdom here, . . . it may be that we can explain this reasoning at least far enough to make others sensitive to its claims upon us.[4]

Franz Boas, as I have tried to show, contributed greatly to our appreciation of the problem by showing how easily we can misinterpret conduct that occurs in a culture other than our own and how this can be remedied. It is greatly to be regretted, therefore, that his contribution was itself misconstrued and transformed into a philosophical doctrine whose aim is to make us recuse ourselves whenever events in another culture stir us to moral protestations.

What our inquiry has established is that there are no grounds, scientific or otherwise, for adopting moral relativism. In addition, as we have seen in this chapter, when the relativist's simplistic, all-purpose argument for tolerance of other cultures is set aside, what we find is a great variety of cases that can be sensibly thought about only by taking them one by one and giving due attention to the details of each. These are, as I said, practical moral problems, and attempts to solve them by means of sweeping philosophical generalizations lead to grotesque results. The doctrine of moral relativism is a good example of the way in which philosophical generalizations obscure morally important differences, and the fact that this doctrine could find favor among the intellectuals of our own culture shows how much we still resemble Despond. In Islandia moral relativism would be regarded as a grotesque substitute for moral thinking.

Appendices

Appendix A

William Clifford, professor of mathematics at University College, London, at the end of the nineteenth century, began his essay "The Ethics of Belief,"[1] with the following two examples:

> A shipowner was about to send to sea an immigrant-ship. He knew that she was old, and not over-well built at the first; that she had seen many seas and climes, and often had needed repairs. Doubts had been suggested to him that possibly she was not seaworthy. These doubts preyed upon his mind, and made him unhappy; he thought that perhaps he ought to have her thoroughly overhauled and refitted, even though this should put him to great expense. Before the ship sailed, however, he succeeded in overcoming these melancholy reflections. He said to himself that she had gone safely through so many voyages and weathered so many storms that it was idle to suppose that she would not come safely home from this trip also. He would put his trust in Providence, which could hardly fail to protect all these unhappy families that were leaving their fatherland to seek for better times elsewhere. He would dismiss from his mind all ungenerous suspicions about the honesty of builders and contractors. In such ways he acquired a sincere and comfortable conviction that his vessel was thoroughly safe and seaworthy; he watched her departure with a light heart, and benevolent wishes for the success of the exiles in their strange new home that was to be; and got his insurance-money when she went down in mid-ocean and told no tales.
>
> What shall we say of him? Surely this, that he was verily guilty of the death of those men. It is admitted that he did sincerely believe in the soundness of his ship; but the sincerity of his conviction can in no wise help him, because *he had no right to believe on such evidence as was before him*. He had acquired his belief not by honestly earning it in patient

investigation, but by stifling his doubts. And although in the end he may have felt so sure about it that he could not think otherwise, yet inasmuch as he had knowingly and willingly worked himself into that frame of mind, he must be held responsible for it.

Let us alter the case a little, and suppose that the ship was not unsound after all; that she made her voyage safely, and many others after it. Will that diminish the guilt of her owner? Not one jot. When an action is once done, it is right or wrong forever; no accidental failure of its good or evil fruits can possibly alter that. The man would not have been innocent; he would only have been not found out. The question of right or wrong [in such cases] has to do with the origin of his belief, not the matter of it; not what it was, but how he got it; not whether it turned out to be true or false, but whether he had a right to believe on such evidence as was before him.

There was once an island in which some of the inhabitants professed a religion teaching neither the doctrine of original sin nor that of eternal punishment. A suspicion got abroad that the professors of this religion had made use of unfair means to get their doctrines taught to children. They were accused of wresting the laws of their country in such a way as to remove children from the care of their natural and legal guardians; and even of stealing them away and keeping them concealed from their friends and relations. A certain number of men formed themselves into a society for the purpose of agitating the public about this matter. They published grave accusations against individual citizens of the highest position and character, and did all in their power to injure these citizens in the exercise of their professions. So great was the noise they made, that a Commission was appointed to investigate the facts; but after the Commission had carefully inquired into all the evidence that could be got, it appeared that the accused were innocent. Not only had they been accused on insufficient evidence, but the evidence of their innocence was such as the agitators might easily have obtained, if they had attempted a fair inquiry. After these disclosures the inhabitants of that country looked upon the members of the agitating society, not only as persons whose judgment was to be distrusted, but also as no longer to be counted honourable men. For although they had sincerely and conscientiously believed in the charges they had made, yet *they had no right to believe on such evidence as was before them.* Their sincere convictions, instead of being honestly earned by patient inquiring, were stolen by listening to the voice of prejudice and passion.

Let us vary this case also, and suppose, other things remaining as before, that a still more accurate investigation proved the accused to have been really guilty. Would this make any difference in the guilt of the accusers? Clearly not; the question is not whether their belief was true or false, but whether they entertained it on the wrong grounds. They would no doubt say, "Now you see that we were right after all; next time perhaps you will believe us." And they might be believed, but they would not thereby become honourable men. . . . Every one of them, if he chose to examine himself *in foro conscientiae,* would know that he had acquired and nourished a belief when he had no right to believe on such evidence as was before him; and therein he would know that he had done a wrong thing.

Appendix B

Intellectual dishonesty occurs in more than one form. In the sciences such dishonesty occurs when data is deliberately falsified. This is not an especially unique form of moral failing, for it is akin to telling (and perpetuating) a lie. A rather different sort of intellectual dishonesty occurs in those fields in which there are no clear and agreed-upon criteria for the truth of what some thinker proposes or undertakes to defend. Literary theory is one such area. My own field, philosophy, is another. The following remarks by Bertrand Russell call attention to some of the temptations and pitfalls to which philosophers are subject. To become a philosopher, said Russell,

> a certain peculiar mental discipline is required. There must be present, first of all, the desire to know philosophical truth, and this desire must be sufficiently strong to survive through years when there seems no hope of finding any satisfaction. The desire to know philosophical truth is very rare—in its purity, it is not often found even among philosophers. It is obscured sometimes—particularly after long periods of fruitless search— by the desire to *think* we know. Some plausible opinion presents itself, and by turning our attention away from the objections to it, or merely by not making great efforts to find objections to it, we may obtain the comfort of believing it, although, if we had resisted the wish for comfort, we should have come to see that the opinion was false. Again the desire for unadulterated truth is often obscured, in professional philosophers, by love of system: the one little fact which will not come inside the philosophical edifice has to be pushed and tortured until it seems to consent. Yet the one little fact is more likely to be important for the future than the system with which it is inconsistent. . . . Love of system, therefore, and the system maker's vanity which becomes associated with it, are among the snares that students of philosophy must guard against.
>
> The desire to establish this or that result, or generally to discover evidence for agreeable results, of whatever kind, has of course been the chief obstacle to honest philosophizing. So strangely perverted do men become by [their] unrecognized passions, that a determination in advance to arrive at this or that conclusion is generally regarded as a mark of virtue, and those whose studies lead to an opposite conclusion are thought to be wicked. No doubt it is commoner to wish to arrive at an agreeable result than to wish to arrive at a true result. But only those in whom the desire to arrive at a *true* result is paramount can hope to serve any good purpose by the study of philosophy.[2]

Notes

Introduction

1. "Scopes and Beyond: Antievolutionism and American Culture," in *Scientists Confront Creationism*, ed. Laurie Godfrey (Norton: New York, 1983), p. 27.

2. *Congressional Record*, H-5634, July 26, 1990.

Chapter 1

1. This point needs some discussion, because at least one philosopher has contradicted what I say. Peter Gardner, in his essay "Ethical Absolutism and Education," in *Ethics*, ed. A. Phillips Griffiths, Royal Institute of Philosophy Supplement 35 (Cambridge University Press, 1993), maintains that "some absolutists may not feel at all confident that they know what is right or wrong or even how to achieve such knowledge" (pp. 83–84). Gardner goes on to say that absolutists include "those who believe there is a universally valid criterion [of morality], but who confess to not having found it and who admit that *they* may never do so, as well as some who may believe that no one ever will [find it]" (p. 86). Absolutists, he adds, "need not appear as if they have discovered the Holy Grail of morality," for although "committed to its *existence*, [they may] have doubts about their or anyone's chance of discovering it" (p. 86).

There are three things to be said about this account of absolutism. (1) Gardner arrives at his account, not by reviewing the way in which disputes have arisen between relativists and absolutists, but rather as an abstract exercise designed to show that someone *could* subscribe to absolutism while disavowing the attitude of moral superiority that has often (but unfairly, according to Gardner) been attributed to absolutists. (2) In order to adopt Gardner's view, an absolutist would have to think that, since we are always completely in the dark about the morality of our actions, morality can never play a role in our lives, in how we conduct ourselves. This is such an absurd view of what morality is that I cannot imagine anyone being tempted to adopt it. (3) No absolutist—Gardner aside—has ever adopted this view.

2. Alfred Kroeber, *Anthropology*, (New York: Harcourt Brace, 1948), p. 266. Throughout this book I use the word *culture,* and anthropologists may think that I use it too loosely. My reason for not being more fastidious about this is the same as Kroeber's reason for using, in the above-quoted passage, the terms "in-group" and "out-group." The reason is that, in an examination of moral relativism, it does not greatly matter how we pick out the groups in question, so long as they are groups to which people in some sense belong, so that we have an "us" and a "them." Beyond that we may depend on our good sense in picking out examples—in not treating a football team, for instance, as a culture. In a recent discussion of this topic Michele Moody-Adams has maintained that moral relativism of the sort I am concerned with presupposes a mythology about cultures being both self-contained monads and perfectly homogeneous as regards the way various things are valued by their members. (She calls this "the doctrine of cultural integration.") She insists that this is an oversimple way of viewing the social world (*Fieldwork in Familiar Places* [Cambridge, Mass.: Harvard University Press, 1997], esp. pp. 43–54). But if she is right about the social world, I do not see why this should matter to a moral relativist. He can say:

> Although most cultures have been influenced somewhat by contact with one or more others, and although every culture has its nonconformists, still human groups exhibit predominant patterns—such as polygamy, human sacrifice, etc.—that distinguish them from one another, and their members exhibit a *high degree* of conformity, and for the purposes of moral relativism, it is a complex of these predominant patterns to which a majority of members conform that we identify as a culture.

It seems to me that this would be an adequate response to Moody-Adams, but what puzzles me about her argument is this: Does she think that if the doctrine of cultural integration were true, then moral relativism would also be true—or have a chance of being true? If she does think this, then I believe she is wrong. But if she does *not* think this, why does she make so much of the point?

3. Kroeber, *Anthropology*, p. 266.

4. Melville Herskovits, *Man and His Works* (New York: Knopf, 1960), p. 63.

5. Alfred Kroeber and Clyde Kluckhohn, *Culture, A Critical Review of Concepts and Definitions*, Papers of the Peabody Museum, Harvard University, XLVII (1952), no. 1, p. 174.

6. Edward Westermarck, *The Origin and Development of the Moral Ideas*, vol. 2 (London, 1906), p. 742.

7. *Christoph von Fürer-Haimendorf, Morals and Merit* (London, 1967), p. 1.

8. Ibid., p. 2.

9. Melville Herskovits, *Cultural Relativism: Perspectives in Cultural Pluralism*, ed. Francis Herskovits (Random House: New York, 1972), p. 14.

10. "Some Further Comments on Cultural Relativism," *American Anthropologist*, vol. 60 (April 1958), p. 270. William Graham Sumner states a version of this argument as follows: "Every attempt to win an outside standpoint from which to reduce the whole to an absolute philosophy of truth and right, based

on an unalterable principle, is a delusion." *Folk-ways* (Boston: Ginn, 1934), sec. 232.

11. Melville Herskovits, "Tender- and Tough-minded Anthropology and the Study of Values in Culture," *Southwestern Journal of Anthropology*, vol. 7 (1951), p. 24.

12. Michele Moody-Adams says that "it is not clear why accepting the fact of enculturation . . . must commit one to any relativist conclusions" (*Fieldwork*, p. 56), even though on an earlier page (p. 23) she has quoted Herskovits as saying that enculturation produces patterns of conduct that are simply "automatic" and patterns of thought and belief that are often "below the level of consciousness." Herskovits, quite clearly, was thinking that something we have learned to say and believe as the result of a conditioning process is something that we do not believe on account of its perceived *truth,* and in this respect the way morality is acquired is similar to the methods (repetition, sleep deprivation, ridicule, etc.) that are used to inculcate the tenets of a cult into its new recruits, that is, the inductees come to say—and to say with conviction—things that they have no reason to believe.

13. "Statement on Human Rights," *American Anthropologist*, n.s. vol. 49 (October-December 1947), p. 542. My authority for attributing this to Herskovits is David Bidney, "The Concept of Value in Modern Anthropology" in *Anthropology Today*, ed. A. L. Kroeber (Chicago: University of Chicago Press, 1953), p. 693.

Chapter 2

1. If relativists have been mistakenly branded as moral skeptics, the reason for this would seem to be that they argue, as we saw in the preceding chapter, that those who hold that moral principles are universal are forced to embrace moral skepticism. But the fact that they argue in this manner does not show that relativists are themselves skeptics. Rather, their position is that moral skepticism is implied by the absolutists' *false* view of moral principles. Absolutists do not agree that their view of moral principles is false, but they will have to agree that those who hold the relativists' position do *not* think that moral principles are unknowable. Absolutists, of course, may say: Since we hold that moral principles can apply to people who don't share them, and since relativists hold that principles of *that* sort are unknowable, relativism can only strike *us* as a skeptic's view of morality. Even so, unless absolutists can show that their kind of principles *are* knowable, they must agree that their view, unlike relativism, provides no grounds for rejecting moral skepticism.

2. William Graham Sumner, *Folkways* (Boston: Ginn, 1934), Sec. 439.

3. Bernard Williams, *Ethics and the Limits of Philosophy* (Cambridge, Mass.: Harvard University Press, 1985), pp. 158–59.

4. Melville Herskovits, "Tender- and Tough-minded Anthropology and the Study of Values in Culture," *Southwestern Journal of Anthropology*, vol. 7 (1951), p. 23.

5. Perhaps Herskovits would think that this case is analogous to the following. People are typically taught that the boiling point of water is 212° F. (or 100° C.) and thus do not learn—not initially, anyway—that the boiling point of a liquid varies according to altitude. Most people, therefore, do not realize that

the *correct* statement about the boiling point of a liquid would include a relativizing clause, for example, "*At sea level* the boiling point of water is 212° F." If we were to point this out to someone who is uninformed as to this matter, we would not be making explicit something that had been (as Williams puts it) "hidden" in our language. We would be explaining how one *ought* to formulate statements about boiling points if we want to formulate them in accordance with scientific knowledge. How, if at all, could Williams respond to a relativist who explained his position in terms of this analogy? I take up this question in chapter 4 (see the discussion that concludes section 7). This, incidentally, is a good example of a long-standing dispute regarding claims made by philosophizing scientists, especially social scientists. When the latter make a claim, such as "Morality is relative," which can be shown to conflict with our language as it stands, many philosophers react as Williams does in the passage quoted above: They insist that the supposed scientific claim, just because it conflicts with our language, is neither scientific nor true. Not all philosophers agree; some say that our language needs reforming because those who devised it knew very little about the world and, as a result, encumbered our concepts with various misconceptions, which science can correct. In later chapters (see especially the final paragraphs of chapter 19), we will see how this debate plays out in the case of moral relativism. The outcome, obviously, will depend on whether, in the end, we can agree with anthropologists who claim that moral relativism is supported by empirical data gathered in studying various cultures. If it turns out that what have *appeared* to be discoveries are themselves misconceptions, there will be no grounds for claiming that our moral language needs a relativistic overhaul.

6. Elvin Hatch, *Culture and Morality: The Relativity of Values in Anthropology* (New York: Columbia University Press, 1983), p. 8. Emphasis added.

7. This is a common mistake. Robert Bierstedt makes it when he says that, faced with moral relativism, one will want to ask whether there are any "universal norms, that is norms that prevail in every society. . . . Are there any actions that are commended alike in all societies or condemned alike in all? Are there, in short, any absolute norms?" After considering and rejecting several candidates, Bierstedt answers this question by saying that "in the present state of our knowledge [it is] apparently impossible to find a universal taboo, that is, the prohibition of a single act in all circumstances at all times in all societies. As far as our knowledge goes, the norms are always relative to a particular culture and a particular set of circumstances. They are never absolute." *The Social Order* (New York, 1957), pp. 163–64.

8. James Q. Wilson, *The Moral Sense* (New York: The Free Press, 1993.

9. Ibid., pp. viii-ix.

10. Ibid., p. 10.

11. Ibid., p. viii.

12. Ibid., p. xii.

13. Ibid., p. 238.

14. Ibid., p. 240. Emphasis added.

15. Ibid., p. 239.

16. Ibid., p. 240.

17. See Ibid., p. 225.

18. Alan Ryan, "Reasons of the Heart," *The New York Review of Books*, vol. XL, no. 15, p. 52.

19. "Who Can tell Right from Wrong?" *The New York Review of Books,* July 17, 1986, p. 52. Emphasis added.

Chapter 3

1. Elvin Hatch, *Culture and Morality: The Relativity of Values in Anthropology* (New York: Columbia University Press, 1983), p. 64.

2. Ibid., p. 67.

3. Ibid., p. 66.

4. This sort of criticism has been made by, for example, Peter Gardner in "Ethical Absolutism and Education" (in *Ethics,* ed. A. Phillips Griffiths, Royal Institute of Philosophy Supplement 35 [Cambridge University Press, 1993]). At one point he writes that those who oppose moral absolutism "may themselves be absolutists," and he goes on to say: "We could . . . claim that those who are committed to freedom and tolerance as important social . . . principles are likely to be absolutists as well" (p. 90). Several pages later, having noted that absolutists may "think that the norms and values of some other culture are wrong" and may also "be prepared to criticize those same cultures," Gardner remarks that those holding a relativistic view "may wish to oppose these thoughts and activities on the grounds that such absolutists would be doing something . . . *morally reprehensible,* though given their own [relativistic] thesis it is difficult to see how [they] could consistently advance such criticisms. As when they recommend tolerance, [they] may often be inclined to challenge their own [relativistic] thesis" (pp. 92–93, emphasis added). This is the moralistic interpretation of relativism.

5. The word *intolerant* is not always used to mean "bigoted." Think of the situation in which a woman says to her husband, "I wish you weren't so intolerant of the grandchildren. I know they're noisy and rambunctious, but they're having such fun, and it is Christmas, you know." We are not concerned with cases of this sort, in which being intolerant amounts merely to expressing annoyance or vexation.

6. See, for example, Paul H. Schmidt, "Some Criticisms of Cultural Relativism," *The Journal of Philosophy,* vol. 52 (1955), pp. 783–84.

7. *Culture and Morality,* pp. 66-68.

8. The Spanish philosopher George Santayana once wrote: "I cannot help thinking that a consciousness of the relativity of values, if it became prevalent, would tend to render people more truly social than would a belief [in absolute] values," for in that case people would not regard those who differ from them "as if they were morally vile." *Winds of Doctrine* (New York: Charles Scribner's Sons, 1926), p. 151. Is Santayana here merely venturing an opinion as to a matter of fact, or is he suggesting that moral relativism warrants a moral denunciation of people who foster disharmony by regarding others as "morally vile"? If the latter, he is vulnerable to the charge of inconsistency.

9. Melville Herskovits, *Man and His Works* (New York: Knopf, 1960), p. 76.

10. Ibid., p. 78.

11. David Bidney, "The Concept of Value in Modern Anthropology" in *Anthropology Today,* ed. A. L. Kroeber (Chicago: University of Chicago Press, 1953), p. 693.

12. The point I am making here rests on a variety of well-known facts. For instance, the First Amendment of the Constitution of the United States, prohibits governmental establishment of religion; it also declares in Article VI that there shall be no "religious test" of a person's fitness to hold public office. The kind of tolerance implied in this is a cornerstone of our democratic way of life. As John Rawls has remarked,

> The historical origin of political liberalism . . . is the Reformation and its aftermath, with the long controversies over religious toleration in the six-teenth and seventeenth centuries. Something like the modern understanding of liberty of conscience and freedom of thought began then. . . .
>
> [P]olitical liberalism assumes the fact of reasonable pluralism as a plu-ralism of comprehensive doctrines, including both religious and nonreli-gious doctrines. . . . Indeed, the success of liberal constitutionalism came as a discovery of a new social possibility: the possibility of a reasonably harmonious and stable pluralist society. Before the successful and peaceful practice of toleration in societies with liberal institutions there was no way of knowing of that possibility. It is more natural to believe, as the centuries-long practice of intolerance appeared to confirm, that social unity and concord requires agreement on a general and comprehensive religious, philosophical, or moral doctrine. Intolerance was accepted as a condition of social order and stability. The weakening of that belief helps to clear the way for liberal institutions. (*Political Liberalism* [New York: Columbia University Press, 1993], pp. xxiv–xxv)

13. *Culture and Morality*, p. 65.
14. Ibid., p. 144.
15. Alfred Kroeber, *Anthropology*, (New York: Harcourt, Brace, 1948), p. 266.
16. Herskovits, *Man and His Works*, p. 80.
17. "Tender- and Tough-Minded Anthropology," p. 25.
18. Alfred Kroeber, "Values as a Subject of Natural Science Inquiry," in *The Nature of Culture* (Chicago: University of Chicago Press, 1952), p. 137.

Chapter 4

1. T. Ellis, *Polynesian Researches*, vol. 2, p. 25; quoted by John Lubbock, *The Origin of Civilization and The Primitive Condition of Man* (New York; Appleton, 1873), pp. 257–58.
2. Quoted in Ernest S. Dodge, *Beyond the Capes* (Boston: Little, Brown, 1971), pp. 216, 217.
3. Ruth Benedict, "Anthropology and the Abnormal," *The Journal of General Psychology*, vol. 10 (1934), reprinted in *Personal Character and Cultural Milieu*, ed. Douglas Haring (Syracuse, N.Y.: Syracuse University Press, 1956), p. 195.
4. Robert Redfield, *The Primitive World and Its Transformation*, (Ithaca, N.Y.: Cornell University Press, 1953), pp. 131, 132. Redfield is quoting three sources: Reuben Gold Thwaites, *Early Western Travels, 1748–1846*, vol. 15 (Cleveland, Ohio: Arthur H. Clark and Co., 1905), pp. 151–54; Jedediah Morse, *A Report to the Secretary of War of the United States on Indian Affairs* (New

Haven, Conn.: S. Converse, 1822), pp. 247, 248; and John T. Irving, *Indian Sketches* (London: John Murray, 1835), pp. 136–44.

5. Notice that the word *wrong* does not occur in the actual report, quoted by Redfield. It tells us that Knife Chief regarded these human sacrifices as a "cruel exhibition of power, exercised upon unfortunate and defenseless individuals whom they were bound to protect." I have allowed myself to use the word *wrong* here because that is the word that a relativist or an absolutist would use in such a place. As we will see in a later chapter, using such words as *wrong, right, good,* and *bad* in the indiscriminate way these theorists do is a source of some confusion.

6. Melville Herskovits, "Tender- and Tough-minded Anthropology and the Study of Values in Culture," *Southwestern Journal of Anthropology*, vol. 7 (1951), pp. 30, 31.

7. "Statement on Human Rights," *American Anthropologist*, n.s. vol. 49 (October-December 1947), pp. 539, 543.

8. "Tender- and Tough-Minded Anthropology," p. 23.

9. Melville Herskovits, *Man and His Works* (New York: Knopf, 1960), p. 78.

10. Ruth Benedict, *Patterns of Culture* (New York: New American Library, 1957), p. 278.

11. *The Primitive World and Its Transformation*, p. 145.

12. Frank Hartung, "Cultural Relativity and Moral Judgment," *Philosophy of Science*, vol. 21 (1954), p. 122.

13. Henry B. Veach, *Rational* Man (Bloomington, Ind.: Indiana University Press, 1962), pp. 37, 38.

14. Norman Mailer, "The White Negro: Superficial Reflections on the Hipster," *Dissent* (Summer, 1957), pp. 289, 290.

15. James Q. Wilson, *The Moral Sense* (New York: The Free Press, 1993), pp. 8–10.

16. Melville Herskovits, "Some Further Comments on Cultural Relativism," *American Anthropologist*, vol. 60 (April 1958), p. 270.

17. Quoted in Helmut Kuhn, *Freedom Forgotten and Remembered* (Chapel Hill: University of North Carolina Press, 1943), pp. 17, 18.

18. One philosopher, Philippa Foot, comes at least very close to this view when she says (see below chapter 18, note 13) that she feels an "uneasiness about morality" and adds that "there is some element of fiction and strain in what we say about right and wrong."

19. Herskovits, *Man and His Works*, p. 77.

20. Ibid., p. 655.

21. John Howard Griffin, *Black Like Me* (New York: New American Library, 1962), p. 100.

22. Ibid., p. 101, note.

Chapter 5

1. Franz Boas, "Human Faculty as Determined by Race," *Proceedings of the American Associations for the Advancement of Science*, vol. 43 (1894), pp. 318-19.

2. "The Aims of Ethnology," reprinted in Boas, *Race, Language and Culture* (New York: The Free Press, 1940), p. 626.

3. Eugen Fischer, "Die Rassenmerkmale des Menschen als Domestikationserscheinungen," *Zeitschrift für Morphologie und Anthropologie* (1914), p. 512.

4. E. B. Tylor, "The Religion of Savages," *Fortnightly Review*, vol. 6 (1866), p. 86.

5. Tylor develops this view in *Primitive Culture*, 2 vols. (London, 1891).

Chapter 6

1. E. B. Tylor, *Primitive Culture,* vol. 1 (London, 1891), p. 15.

2. Ibid., p. 68.

3. "Decorative Designs of Alaskan Needlecases: A Study in the History of Conventional Designs, Based on Materials in the U.S. National Museum," in Boas, *Race, Language and Culture* (New York: The Free Press, 1940), pp. 588–89. See also: "The Methods of Ethnology" in ibid., pp. 282–83.

4. "The Methods of Ethnology," in *Race, Language and Culture*, p. 283.

5. "The Limitations of the Comparative Method of Anthropology," reprinted in *Race, Language and Culture*, pp. 273.

6. Ibid., p. 274. See also Boas, *The Mind of Primitive Man* (New York: The Free Press, 1963), chap. 10.

7. Ibid., p. 275.

8. "The Origin of Totemism," in *Race, Language and Culture*, p. 317.

9. *The Mind of Primitive Man*, p. 171.

10. "Review of Graebner, 'Methode Der Ethnologie,' " in *Race, Language and Culture*, p. 299.

Chapter 7

1. "Review of Graebner, 'Methode Der Ethnologie' " in Boas, *Race, Language and Culture* (New York: The Free Press, 1940), p. 296.

2. Boas, "Recent Anthropology," *Science*, vol. 98 (1943), p. 314.

3. Ibid.

4. Ibid., p. 336.

5. A. Irving Hallowell, *Culture and Experience* (Philadelphia, Penn., 1955), p. 103.

6. "The Idea of the Future Life among Primitive Tribes" in *Race, Language and Culture*, p. 597.

7. "Recent Anthropology," p. 314.

8. "The Kwakiutl of Vancouver Island," *Publications of the Jesup North Pacific Expedition*, vol. 5, pt. 2, p. 309.

9. "The Mind of Primitive Man," *Journal of American Folklore*, Vol. 14 (1901), p. 1.

10. "The Aims of Ethnology," reprinted in Boas, *Race, Language and Culture*, p. 636.

11. E. B. Tylor, *Primitive Culture* (London: J. Murray, 1891), 2 vols., p. 31.

12. Ibid., pp. 30–31.

13. Robert Redfield, *Human Nature and the Study of Society, The Papers of Robert Redfield*, ed. Margaret P. Redfield (Chicago, 1962), p. 441.

14. Boas, *The Mind of Primitive Man* (New York: The Free Press, 1963), p. 203.

15. Edward Westermarck, *Ethical Relativity* (New York: Harcourt, 1932), pp. 184–85.

16. *The Mind of Primitive Man*, p. 203.

17. Ibid. p. 10.

18. David Bidney, "The Concept of Value in Modern Anthropology," in *Anthropology Today*, ed. A. L. Kroeber (Chicago: University of Chicago Press, 1953), p. 687.

19. Elvin Hatch, *Culture and Morality: The Relativity of Values in Anthropology* (New York: Columbia University Press, 1983), p. 38.

20. *Language, Race and Culture*, p. 277.

21. Ibid., p. 276.

22. Ibid., p. 283.

23. Notice the sort of evidence sometimes cited to prove that Boas was a relativist. Herskovits offered the proof that Boas, in *The Mind of Primitive Man*, wrote that "it is certainly conceivable that there may be other civilizations, based perhaps on different traditions and on a different equilibrium of emotion and reason, which are no less valuable than ours." But this is *not* a statement of moral relativism. It is, in fact, inconsistent with that doctrine, because in order to think that one civilization is "no less valuable than" another, that is, that the two are of *equal* value, one would have to think that there is a neutral way comparing the two. And yet on the same page Herskovits explains that relativism involves the idea that "objective indices of cultural inferiority and superiority cannot be established" (Melville Herskovits, "Tender- and Tough-minded Anthropology and the Study of Values in Culture," *Southwestern Journal of Anthropology*, vol. 7 [1951], p. 22). But obviously, if there can be no such indices, then it won't make sense to say what Boas is quoted as saying. The passage from *The Mind of Primitive Man* comes from pages 202–3 of the 1963 edition I have cited throughout. (Herskovits quotes from the first edition.) Anyone who reads the paragraph in which the passage occurs will see that Boas is expounding, rather ineptly, an ethical argument. It begins with his citing as an example of "progress" the fact that there has been a "gradual broadening of the feeling of fellowship during the advance of civilization," so that whereas fellowship was formerly extended only to members of the hoard or tribe, it is now extended to an entire nation. But this nationalism, regrettably, "seems to be the limit of the ethical concept of fellowship of man which we have reached at the present time." The fact that we haven't extended the concept of fellowship to all mankind is explained by Boas as follows:

> The ethical point of view which makes it justifiable at the present time to increase the well-being of one nation at the cost of another, the tendency to value our own form of civilization as higher—not as dearer to our hearts—than that of the whole rest of mankind, are the same [tendencies] as those which prompt the actions of primitive man, who considers every stranger as an enemy, and who is not satisfied until the enemy is killed. (p. 201–2)

But progress needn't stop with nationalism, Boas maintains, because history has shown that "the fewer the number of traditional elements that enter into our reasoning . . . the more logical will be our conclusions" (p. 201).

24. Franz Boas, "Human Faculty as Determined by Race," *Proceedings of the American Associations for the Advancement of Science*, vol. 43 (1894), p. 319.

25. Boas, "An Anthropologist's Credo," *The Nation*, vol. 147 (1938), p. 202. Since this statement of his did not appear in a professional journal, it may have escaped the attention of anthropologists.

Chapter 8

1. Robert Redfield, *Human Nature and the Study of Society, The Papers of Robert Redfield*, ed. Margaret P. Redfield (Chicago, 1962), pp. 458–59.

2. "I am persuaded," said Redfield, "that cultural relativism is in for some difficult times. Anthropologists are likely to find the doctrine a hard one to maintain. . . . It was easy to look with equal benevolence upon all sorts of value systems so long as the values were those of unimportant little people remote from our own concerns. But the equal benevolence is harder to maintain when one is asked to anthropologize the Nazis." Robert Redfield, *The Primitive World and Its Transformation*, (Ithaca, N.Y.: Cornell University Press, 1953), p. 145.

3. Alfred Kroeber, "Values as a Subject of Natural Science Inquiry," in *The Nature of Culture* (Chicago: University of Chicago Press, 1952), p. 137.

4. Some anthropologists have tried to wiggle out of the difficulty by explicitly equating cultural relativism with Boas's method, hoping thereby to escape the charge that anthropologists have advocated or fostered moral nihilism. For example, we find Micaela di Leonardo, an anthropologist, defending relativism against attacks from political conservatives, such as Dinesh D'Souza, and doing so by contending that "cultural relativism . . . [is] the attempt to envision other cultures from within their own cognitive frameworks." The charge of nihilism, then, is a malicious lie: "But claiming that 'cultural relativism tells us there are no ultimate moral principles' is a canard. All that most of the practitioners of my benighted discipline have ever advocated is the attempt, from the bedrock of one's own enculturation, to empathize with the moral logics of others" ("Patterns of Culture Wars," *The Nation*, April 8, 1996, pp. 25-29).

She extends this interpretation even to Herskovits, saying: "Melville Herskovits could be considered the discipline's ur-cultural relativist. . . . But he explicitly confined this orientation to fieldwork, rejecting the [kind of] 'moral relativism' his attackers accused him of espousing" (ibid., p. 28). She means: Herskovits rejected the view that there are no ultimate moral principles. She is obviously wrong, but it's clear how she arrived at this. Having chosen to combat the charge by political conservatives that Boas and Herskovits were moral nihilists, she had to come to the defense of her discipline by saying either that anthropologists have never been relativists or that relativism is perfectly innocuous. Both alternatives are false, but the first is so obviously false that she sought a way to render the second one acceptable. And her way of doing so was to equate relativism with Boas's method. But while Boas's method is perfectly innocuous, it is in no way relativistic. Plainly, anthropologists cannot successfully do battle with political conservatives by distorting the history of their own discipline. The alternative would be to acknowledge relativism for what it is and to abandon it in favor of Boas's method. This, as I will argue in part III, need not involve going over to moral absolutism.

Chapter 9

1. It is also important to realize that we needn't say that there are *not* different moralities. For it is not yet clear whether the phrase "different moralities" has a meaning apart from the relativist's view of morality.

2. See Michele Moody-Adams, *Fieldwork in Familiar Places* (Cambridge, Mass.: Harvard University Press, 1997), chap. 2, esp. pp. 85–105. Moody-Adams maintains that "the best explanation for the persistence of slavery in [ancient Greece and similar societies] will appeal to some form of affected ignorance. In this instance it is reasonable to posit that people who benefit from a social practice can effectively ignore those features of the practice—such as the rational complaints of those most severely harmed by it—that might prove morally unsettling" (p. 105).

3. I have been considering what people may have thought *prior* to becoming relativists. But it is fair to ask: What do anthropologists, *after* embracing relativism, think of type A cases? Those who understand what moral relativism commits them to realize that it bars them from being morally critical of *any* sort of conduct so long as it is culturally sanctioned. Herskovits understood this very well. He bravely bit the bullet and said that being a relativist "is not easy" because it requires the anthropologist "to adjust his reactions to grasp, in terms of the values of the people he is studying, customs as repugnant to his personal experience as infanticide, head-hunting, . . . and the like" (Melville Herskovits, *Man and His Works* [New York: Knopf, 1960], pp. 80-81). What did Herskovits intend that his phrase "and the like" should include? Being a relativist, he can only have meant that it should include *all* type A cases, including Nazi atrocities. (That is why being a relativist "is not easy.") But notice that although someone who has already embraced relativism is committed to this relativistic view of type A cases, he cannot demand that this view be shared by those of us who have not yet embraced relativism and are searching for the evidence that, according to relativists, should convince us to adopt the relativistic view of morality. It would be a mistake, then, for a relativist to oppose my rejection of type A cases and to justify this by saying: "In order to discover the evidence for moral relativism, you must not dismiss type A cases on the grounds that, when it condones *that* sort of conduct, a culture is condoning, not morality, but immorality, for it is only by withholding judgment in *these* cases that one can discover that there are different moralities." This would amount to saying that one must already be a relativist in order to discover the evidence for relativism, which would mean that relativists have arrived at their doctrine by arguing in a circle. So while it is true that moral relativism commits its adherents to regarding type A cases in a particular way, that is, relativistically, it is a mistake to think that those of us who are not yet relativists must do so as well.

4. Care must be taken in stating this point. It would be a mistake to say: 'What *they* are doing would be bragging if *we* did it.' For *what* they are doing is something *other than* bragging, so that if we did *that* it would *not* be bragging. It would also be a mistake to think: 'They are *doing* what we do when we brag, but it's not to be *called* "bragging" when they do it.'

5. In chapter 3 it was observed that ethnocentrism is not to be regarded as a moral failing and a sign of bad character. Bigotry, by contrast, is a moral failing, a sign of bad character. Xenophobia is, too, when it isn't merely fear of foreigners but rabid hatred of or contempt for foreigners.

Chapter 10

1. Peter Freuchen, *Book of the Eskimos* (New York: Fawcett, 1961), pp. 41–42.

2. Raymond Firth, *Elements of Social Organization* (London, 1951), pp. 190–92.

3. Bronislaw Malinowski, "Introduction," in Ian Hogbin, *Law and Order in Polynesia* (Hamden, Conn.: The Shoestring Press, 1961), pp. xxxviii–xxxix.

4. Ruth Benedict, "Anthropology and the Abnormal," *The Journal of General Psychology*, vol. 10 (1934), reprinted in *Personal Character and Cultural Milieu*, ed. Douglas Haring (Syracuse, N.Y.: Syracuse University Press, 1956).

5. See, in addition to the article cited, Benedict's *Patterns of Culture* (New York: New American Library, 1957), pp. 235 and 249–55.

6. "Anthropology and the Abnormal," p. 190.

7. Ibid., p. 192.

8. Ibid. pp. 188–89.

9. *The Neurotic Personality of Our Time* (New York: W. W. Norton and Co., 1964), p. 25.

10. Ibid., p. 20.

11. Ibid.

12. Ibid., p. 24.

13. "Anthropology and the Abnormal," p. 194.

Chapter 11

1. Edward Westermarck, *Ethical Relativity* (New York: Harcourt, 1932), p. 184.

2. Ibid., p. 185.

3. L. T. Hobhouse, *Morals in Evolution: A Study in Comparative Ethics* (New York, 1915), p. 26.

4. The question we have dealt with regarding the morality of their actions is distinct from this question: Since their actions take the lives of people who do not willingly offer up their lives, shouldn't outsiders, where possible, do what they can to discourage or stop the Dyaks' headhunting? In chapter 20 we will take up this latter question.

Chapter 13

1. Edward Westermarck, *The Origin and Development of the Moral Ideas*, vol. II (London, 1906), pp. 745–46.

2. *Ethical Relativity*, (New York: Harcourt, 1932), p. 196.

3. *Origin and Development of Moral Ideas*, pp. 9–10.

4. Westermarck's comments on human sacrifice serve to illustrate the point.

Having surveyed numerous cultures that practice human sacrifice, he reports that this practice is typically grounded in the belief that the gods, for one reason or another, require it as a condition of the tribe's (or an individual's) survival or welfare, as in time of crop failure or widespread illness. He concludes that "human sacrifice is essentially a method of life-insurance—absurd, no doubt, according to our ideas, but not an act of wanton cruelty" (*The Origin and Development of the Moral Ideas*, p. 466). He adds that various peoples who have practiced human sacrifice "have afterwards, at a more advanced stage of civilization, voluntarily given it up. . . . With the growth of enlightenment men would lose faith in this childish method of substitution, and consequently find it not only useless but objectionable" (ibid., p. 468). This, as we have seen, was the case with Knife Chief.

5. *The Origin and Development of the Moral Ideas*, pp. 11–12.

6. *Ethical Relativity*, p. 216.

7. *The Origin and Development of the Moral Ideas*, p. 12.

Chapter 14

1. There is an interesting question that can be posed at this point. An essential step in Westermarck's argument is his claim to know of actual instances in which several people disagree about some moral issue *despite* their having "full insight into the governing facts" of the case. But how, in a given instance, can he assure us that the differing parties do have full insight into the relevant facts? Can we not suppose that Westermarck has a moral blind spot and therefore fails to take into account some relevant aspect of the matter? Suppose, for example, that he were that conventional fellow we described above as being morally obtuse. Would he, then, be a competent judge of whether, as regards a particular moral disagreement, both parties have "a full insight into the governing facts of the case"? Of course not. But then we cannot take *his* word for it that he knows of cases in which the two parties differ in their moral convictions while agreeing on all the relevant facts. (He may know that there are people who, in regard to some moral issue, fail to reach agreement and get into shouting matches. But how is he to know that wiser heads wouldn't find some accommodation?) Westermarck's argument, therefore, is in a bad way. Consider his options. Suppose that he were to assure us that he has no moral blind spots, that he is free of all prejudice, self-deception, etc., and so can recognize in any instance what the relevant facts are. In giving such assurance, he would be claiming a rather unique position for himself and would therefore be conceding the very thing his argument for moral democracy was designed to deny, namely, that people differ in their capacity to think about moral matters. But he would be no better off if he were to allow that he may have moral blind spots and so may fail in a given instance to recognize or acknowledge some relevant fact. If he allows this, he cannot claim to know that there are examples of the sort his argument requires, namely, examples of people whose disagreements reveal their conflicting moral principles rather than their blindness to certain relevant facts. In either case, then, he cannot make his argument for moral democracy and so fails to make his argument for moral relativism.

2. Peter Freuchen, *Book of the Eskimos* (New York: Fawcett, 1961), p. 86.

3. Ibid., pp. 56–57. I have transposed this last paragraph out of the order in which it occurs in the text.

4. In further explanation of this they might contrast us with citizens of The Netherlands, where thinking about sex is far less determined by taboos. In The United States teenage pregnancy has become an epidemic. In The Netherlands, where sex education is both universal and thorough, teenage pregnancy is almost unknown. A teacher there recently reported that he could think of only one case in the past ten years.

Chapter 15

1. Raymond Firth, *Elements of Social Organization* (London, 1951), p. 183.
2. Ibid., p. 186.
3. Ibid.
4. Frank Ramsey, *The Foundations of Mathematics* (London: Routledge & Kegan Paul, 1931), pp. 115–16.
5. *The Sovereignty of Good* (New York: Shocken Books, 1971), p. 29.
6. Ibid., pp. 17–18. At the opposite extreme is the character Percy Grimm in William Faulkner's novel *Light in August.*
7. Ibid.
8. Murdoch writes: "On my view it might be said that . . . the primary general words [such as 'right' and 'good'] could be dispensed with entirely and all moral work could be done by the secondary specialized words [such as 'fair' and 'cruel']" (ibid., p. 42). (William Davie makes much the same point in "A Dogma of Modern Moral Philosophy," *The Southwestern Journal of Philosophy*, vol. 10, no. 2, pp. 21–38.) As regards those "specialized words," Murdoch makes a further point, which begins with her remark that we have a different view "of courage at forty from that which we had at twenty." As we grow in understanding, "a deepening process . . . takes place. There are two senses of 'knowing what a word means', one connected with ordinary language [which all speakers share] and the other very much less so. Knowing a value concept is something to be understood, as it were, in depth, and not in terms of switching on to some given impersonal network [of linguistic rules]" (*The Sovereignty of Good*, p. 29).
9. Murdoch is not entirely alone in calling attention to such matters. William Clifford, in his 1877 essay "The Ethics of Belief," reprinted in William K. Clifford, *Lectures and Essays*, vol. 2, ed. F. Pollock, (London, 1879), discussed willful ignorance. (An excerpt will be found in Appendix A of this volume.) Also Michele Moody-Adams briefly discusses what, following Aquinas, she calls "affected ignorance" (*Fieldwork in Familiar Places* [Cambridge, Mass.: Harvard University Press, 1997], pp. 101–2 and 105). She also makes the claim, in a very general way, that "self-scrutiny" is central to moral inquiry (ibid., p. 140).
10. *Killers of the Dream*, (New York: Doubleday, 1963), pp. 47–53.
11. The word *perception* may seem out of place here. But notice that Lillian Smith says: "Our people were meeting trouble by . . . trying not *to see* . . . things as they really were." Consider also the following. A defector from Tom Metzger's hate group, White Aryan Resistance (WAR), testified in court as follows: While he was under Metzger's influence, he said, an African-American walking ahead of him on the street "looked to me like an ape, like scum." For an autobiographical example of someone who, by struggling to overcome his racist hatred, achieved a more honest moral perception of things, see the chapter

"C. P. Ellis" in Studs Terkel, *American Dreams: Lost and* Found (New York: Ballantine Books, 1980), pp. 221–33.

Chapter 16

1. The sort of thing I have in mind can be illustrated by a passage from Alice Miller's *The Drama of the Gifted Child*, trans. Ruth Ward (Basic Books: New York, 1981):

> I was out for a walk and noticed a young couple a few steps ahead, both tall; they had a little boy with them, about two years old, who was running alongside and whining. (We are accustomed to seeing such situations from the adult point of view, but here I want to describe it as it was experienced by the child.) The two had just bought themselves ice-cream bars on sticks from the kiosk and were licking them with enjoyment. The little boy wanted one, too. His mother said affectionately, "Look, you can have a bite of mine, a whole one is too cold for you." The child did not want just one bite but held out his hand for the whole ice, which his mother took out of his reach again. He cried in despair, and soon exactly the same thing was repeated with his father: "There you are, my pet," said his father affectionately, "you can have a bite of mine." "No, no," cried the child and ran ahead again, trying to distract himself. Soon he came back again and gazed enviously and sadly up at the two grown-ups, who were enjoying their ice creams contentedly and at one. Time and again he held out his little hand for the whole ice-cream bar, but the adult hand with its treasure was withdrawn again.
>
> The more the child cried, the more it amused his parents. It made them laugh a lot and they hoped to humor him along with their laughter, too: "Look, it isn't so important, what a fuss you are making." Once the child sat down on the ground and began to throw little stones over his shoulder in his mother's direction, but then he suddenly got up again and looked around anxiously, making sure that his parents were still there. When his father had completely finished his ice cream, he gave the stick to the child and walked on. The little boy licked the bit of wood expectantly, looked at it, threw it away, wanted to pick it up again but did not do so, and a deep sob of loneliness and disappointment shook his small body. Then he trotted obediently after his parents. (pp. 65–66)

Dr. Miller says that her aim here is "to describe [the situation] as it was experienced by the child," and she does so very effectively. Most of us, of course, do not have this kind of insight into others, whether they be children or adults. This is not so much because we are incapable of such insight as that we do not make the effort. Certainly the parents she describes did not make the effort. Or as Dr. Miller puts it, these were not "unkind or cold parents," but their treatment of the child revealed a "lack of empathy" (p. 66). Her point is that most people are like that. This fact does not, of course, excuse anyone. It is the very insensitivity Dr. Miller portrays that makes her account of the parents so damning. We think that people shouldn't be like that.

2. J. D. Mabbott, *An Introduction to Ethics* (Garden City, N.Y.: Anchor Books, 1969), p. 15.

3. It may be objected that I am neglecting the fact that philosophers have undertaken to *supply* a backing in the form of higher-order principles, such as that people should be treated as ends, not as means, so that our supposed moral principles are saved from being the queer things I have made them out to be. But I find no merit in this objection for the simple reason that the kind of backing offered by philosophers is not something we can reasonably credit the ordinary man or woman with already having in mind. So *if* people who are not philosophers are supposed to be reasoning from the premise "It's wrong to be dishonest" and can, therefore, be asked, "Why is dishonesty wrong?" they will have no ready answer. Perhaps a philosopher will think that this is unimportant, since he can always answer *for* the plain man. But this makes a travesty of our ordinary moral thinking, since it amounts to saying that only philosophers can think cogently or responsibly about moral matters. Someone may object that philosophers can remedy this by instructing the uninitiated in sound moral reasoning. But this would not impress me. Those who are thus "instructed" are unlikely to understand philosophers' higher-order principles, and even if they understood them, they are unlikely to feel confident that these principles actually perform the service for which they are intended. And in any case, they will go right on raising their children just as they themselves were raised, that is, *without* imparting to them the philosophical idea that moral reasoning rests on principles such as "It's wrong to be dishonest" and that these in turn are backed up by some "higher-order" principle, which can be justified on abstract philosophical grounds. The reason for this, of course, is that in the ordinary affairs of life we have no need of the philosophical machinery with which abstract thinkers endow our moral reasoning.

There is another reason, albeit a reason of lesser importance, for not appealing to the theories of philosophers here. Edward Westermarck, in his book *Moral Relativism,* argued that the moral theories advanced by philosophers, although they purport to rest on nonrelative grounds, all *fail* in their effort to achieve a truly universal, nonrelative status. So a defender of moral relativism, if he found someone seriously proposing that relativism is false because utilitarianism (or Kantianism) is true, would double over in laughter. He would reply: "You can't refute moral relativism by invoking a moral theory which, being *itself* the product of a particular culture, is no more an *absolute* truth than any ordinary moral principle, such as that stealing is wrong."

4. See the passage from Leo Tolstoy's essay "On Life," quoted below in note 8 of chapter 18. Tolstoy, describing the members of his own society in nineteenth-century Russia, says that they "accustom themselves more and more to doing things that have no reasonable meaning. . . . And the less they understand the meaning of the things they do, and the more questionable these things are, the more do they attach importance to them and the more solemnly do they perform them. Both the rich and the poor do what is done by others around them and call it "doing their duty."

5. Melville Herskovits, "Tender- and Tough-minded Anthropology and the Study of Values in Culture," *Southwestern Journal of Anthropology,* vol. 7 (1951), p. 24.

Chapter 17

1. "Comment on Japanese Personal Character," in *Personal Character and Cultural Milieu*, ed. Douglas Haring (Syracuse, N.Y.: Syracuse University Press, 1956), pp. 425–26.

2. Ibid., pp. 405–6.

3. Ibid., p. 409.

4. For the benefit of readers who are unfamiliar with philosophical method, I should point out that the manner in which I have proceeded here—showing that a very general philosophical claim is not true by showing that it fits only a very special case—is a valuable part of philosophical method. Ludwig Wittgenstein was the first to employ this method in a systematic fashion. In lectures that he gave in the summer of 1938 he said: "If someone talks bosh, imagine a case in which it is not bosh. The moment you imagine it, you see at once it is not like that in our case" (*Lectures and Conversations on Aesthetics, Psychology and Religious Belief* [Oxford: Blackwell, 1966], p. 34). This is not, however, the end of the matter. One must still go on to discover how someone who "talks bosh" came to do so, for he does not think he *is* "talking bosh." He thinks he is saying something important and has *reasons* for saying what he does. One must, therefore, investigate those supposed reasons.

5. *The Theory of Practical Reason* (Open Court: La Salle, Ill. 1964), pp. 189–90.

6. Ibid., pp. 192–95.

7. One could, I suppose, make out a case for saying that Christianity teaches—not explicitly, but by example—the sort of thing Murphy had in mind when he spoke of going beyond the maxims learned in childhood. I am thinking of scriptural passages in which Jesus sets aside the Mosaic Law. Of interest here are the reasons he gives for doing so—for not keeping the Sabbath, for example. On one such occasion, he and his disciples were stripping ears of corn and eating the kernels as they walked through a field, whereupon some Pharisees rebuked him for doing "what is forbidden on the Sabbath." In response Jesus asked whether they hadn't heard what David and his men had done when they were hungry: They entered the temple and ate consecrated loaves, which only the priests are allowed to eat (Luke VI, i–iv). The point, I suppose, is that while the law is often sufficient, there can also be overriding considerations. On another occasion, when the Pharisees accosted him for healing on the Sabbath, Jesus responded: "What hypocrites you are! Is there a single one of you who does not loose his ox or his donkey from the manger and take it out to water on the Sabbath?" (Luke XIII, xv). On another Sabbath, when he was rebuked for healing a man's arm, he said to his accusers: "I put the question to you: is it permitted to do good or to do evil on the Sabbath, to save life or to destroy it?" (Luke VI, ix). Someone who learns from such examples could be said to have learned (in Murphy's words) that although the maxims we learn in childhood are "the beginning of moral wisdom," they "cannot . . . be the end."

8. This might also seem to be Iris Murdoch's position, for in a passage quoted in chapter 15 she says that "morality is *essentially* concerned with change and progress [in a person's capacity for insight and understanding]." So she might say that the prewar Japanese lacked something essential to morality. It should be noted, however, that Murphy and Murdoch are concerned with different matters. Murphy is saying that although one's moral training begins with,

as he puts it, "the traditional maxims of [one's] community," one does not become fully a moral agent until one can go beyond these. Murdoch's point is that we are all burdened with prejudices or stereotypes, that we tend to indulge in self-deception or willful ignorance, and that we must overcome such things before we can make sound moral judgments about our own conduct or that of others. "In the moral life," says Murdoch, "the enemy is the fat relentless ego" (*The Sovereignty of Good* [New York: Schocken Books, 1971], p. 52), and she is concerned with the struggle to overcome the ways this "enemy" distorts our thinking and our perceptions of ourselves and others.

Chapter 18

1. For suggestive purposes I have borrowed the name of Austin Wright's utopian novel, *Islandia,* for one of my imaginary cultures, although Wright's Islandians are not in all respects the people I mean to be describing here. I should add that my purpose in sketching certain features of Islandia is not that of describing a utopian society. My purpose, rather, is to provide a sharp contrast for my other imaginary culture, Despond, so as to throw into relief what it is about the "morality" of our own culture that has led relativists to describe *us* as if we were like the prewar Japanese and to say that we acquire our morality by a process of "enculturative conditioning."

2. As regards literature, Iris Murdoch writes:

The most essential and fundamental aspect of culture is the study of literature, since this is an education in how to picture and understand human situations. We are men and are moral agents before we are scientists, and the place of science in human life must be discussed in *words*. This is why it is and always will be more important to know about Shakespeare than to know about any scientist. (*The Sovereignty of Good* [New York: Schocken Books, 1971], p. 34)

(Films as well as literature are important in this regard—think of the morally relevant depictions in the film *Twelve Angry Men.*)

3. These meditations are treated as largely private affairs, especially as they apply to oneself. As Iris Murdoch has said, in reference to her own example of the jealous mother-in-law: "One feels impelled to say something like: M's activity is peculiarly *her own*. Its details are the details of *this* personality; and partly for this reason it may well be an activity which can only be performed privately" (ibid., p. 23).

4. In their concern for the *moral* significance of acquisitiveness, Islandians have antecedents in our own history. As Robert Heilbroner has remarked:

In every pre-capitalist society we find acquisitive activity disliked or despised . . . in part as a expression of popular revulsion against money lenders and exploitative local traders; in part perhaps as a deep-rooted protest against the depersonalization of monetary dealings. Nowhere was this distaste more pronounced than within Christianity, where the taking of ordinary interest was declared to be an excommunicable offense as late as the Council of Vienne in 1311, and where three centuries later a disapproving view of wealth-seeking continued to inform Protestant as well as

Catholic religious sentiments even after both churches had made their formal truce with profits and interest." (*The Nature and Logic of Capitalism* [New York: Norton, 1985], p. 109)

Heilbroner goes on to point out that apologists for capitalism, while arguing that unlimited private acquisition leads to an increase in the amount of wealth, have failed to address "the moral significance of acquisition," that is, "the morally destructive impact of the accumulation of wealth *on the gatherer himself.* The legend of Midas speaks volumes here, for Midas's curse has nothing to do with any impoverishment that his passion for gold would impose on others" (ibid., p. 113), that is, acquisitiveness brings on one a "threat of self-destruction."

It has often been pointed out that what seem to Americans to be necessities of life are regarded quite differently by others. Anthony Burgess once remarked: "American individualism, on the face of it an admirable philosophy, wishes to manifest itself in independence of the community. You don't share things in common; you have to have your own things. A family's strength is signalized by its possessions. Herein lies a paradox. For the desire for possessions must eventually mean dependence on possessions. Freedom is slavery. Once let the acquisitive instinct burgeon . . . , and there are ruggedly individual forces only too ready to make it come to full and monstrous blossom. New appetites are created; what to the Europeans are bizarre luxuries become, to the Americans, plain necessities" ("Is America Falling Apart?" *The New York Times Magazine*, November 7, 1971).

5. In the 1920s top executives in the United States were paid roughly thirty times as much as the average wage earner. That is about the difference that exists today (1994) in Japan. In the United States, however, the gap has become enormous: Top executives are now paid, on average, 140 times as much as the typical wage earner. The (legal) minimum wage is today worth only about 40 percent of its buying power in 1955, and some Republican congressmen have proposed to abolish minimum wage regulations altogether.

6. *Feet of Clay: Saints, Sinners, and Madmen* (New York: Free Press, 1996), pp. 166–67.

7. Here is Michael Kelly's description of William Bennett, former official in the Reagan administration, self-appointed moralist, and editor of the best-selling anthology *The Book of Virtues*: "He is, inarguably, an opportunist. He is also something of a bully, . . . who traffics in confrontation and intimidation rather than reasoned discourse. He is rude. . . . He is a Barnumesque sensationalist, a light-fingered popularizer of others' ideas, and an unregenerate middlebrow. He is quick to lose interest, and deeply disinclined toward anything that does not feature himself as the center of the action. He is a self-promoting, self-important sermonizer." Kelly goes on to report: "His writings, and a heavy schedule of speaking engagements that command a stratospheric forty thousand dollars a pop, have transformed Bennett into a leading voice of the force that is driving American politics right now—the national hunger for a moral society" ("The Man of the Minute," *The New Yorker*, July 17, 1995, p. 27). Bennett is a very Despondian character.

8. In his essay "On Life" Leo Tolstoy, reflecting on the culture of his own nineteenth-century Russia, wrote:

Man cannot live without guidance in the choice of his actions, and so he involuntarily submits, not to reason, but to that external guidance of life which has always existed in every human society.

That guidance has no reasonable explanation, but it is what prompts the enormous majority of the actions of men. It is the habit of social life which governs men the more completely the less they understand the meaning of their life. It cannot be definitely expressed since it is composed of the most heterogeneous things and actions differing widely according to time and place. For . . . a military man it is fidelity to the flag and the honour of his uniform, for a man of the world it is the duel, for the mountaineer it is the vendetta; it is a certain sort of education for children; it is a certain arrangement of the house; certain ways of celebrating funerals, births, weddings; it is an infinite number of affairs and actions which fill a man's whole life. It is what is called "propriety," "custom," and—most often—"duty" or even "sacred duty."

And it is to this guidance . . . that the majority of men submit. From childhood a man sees around him people performing these acts with full assurance and outward solemnity, and . . . he not only begins to do the same things himself but tries to ascribe a rational meaning to them. He wishes to believe that the people who do these things know why they do them and what for. And so he tries to convince himself that these actions have a sensible meaning and that the explanation, though not known to him, is clear to other people. But most of those other people . . . are in exactly the same position as himself. They, too, only do these things because they think that others who have an explanation demand that they shall do them. And so, involuntarily deceiving one another, men . . . accustom themselves more and more to doing things that have no reasonable meaning. . . . And the less they understand the meaning of the things they do, and the more questionable these things are, the more do they attach importance to them and the more solemnly do they perform them. Both the rich and the poor do what is done by others around them and call it "doing their duty." (*On Life and Essays on Religion*, trans, Aylmer Maude (London: Oxford University Press, 1950), pp. 32–34.

9. *Commandant of Auschwitz*, (New York, 1959), p. 32.

10. Immanuel Kant, *Foundations of the Metaphysics of Morals*, trans. Lewis White Beck (New York: Bobbs-Merrill, 1959), pp. 15–16.

11. This is one of Clough's Ambarvalia poems, circa 1847.

12. Their conception of morality, or moral worth, is very like that expounded by Kant. Kant says "there are many persons so sympathetically constituted that without any motive of vanity or selfishness they find an inner satisfaction in spreading joy, and rejoice in the contentment of others which they have made possible [by their actions]. But I say that, however amiable it may be, that kind of action has no true moral worth. . . . For the maxim lacks the moral import of an action done not from inclination but from duty" (*Foundations of the Metaphysics of Morals*, p. 14).

13. Mark Twain, suffering from acute dissatisfaction with the Despondian culture in which he lived, nicely satirized the morality of that culture in the episode in which Huck Finn tells a lie in order to save Jim from being captured and returned to slavery (*Huckleberry Finn*, chap. XVI). It is noteworthy that

what Twain intended as a satire is treated by some of our philosophers as revealing something of the true nature of morality as such, namely, that it makes
good sense to ask, "Why should I be moral?" (See, for example, Kai Nielsen,
"Is 'Why should I be moral?' An Absurdity?" *Australian Journal of Philosophy*,
vol. 36 [1958], pp. 25–32, reprinted in *Readings in the Problems of Ethics*, ed.
Rosalind Ekman [New York: Charles Scribner's Sons, 1965], pp. 357–64.) Huck
thinks he has done something bad in lying to save Jim and so is led to ask
himself, "What's the use of you learning to do right?" It should, of course, be
obvious what Twain was doing by putting this question is Huck's mouth: It was
an indictment of the culture depicted in the novel. But Kai Nielsen, in the article
just cited, takes Huck's question to show that one (anyone) can ask in a perfectly
general way, that is, apropos of no *particular* culture, "Why should one be
moral?" What this reveals is that our own philosophers are still enmeshed in
the same style of thinking as that found in Despond. Another example of a
philosopher unwittingly exhibiting the intellectual stresses of our Despondlike
culture is Philippa Foot in her British Academy Lecture of 1970, "Morality and
Art" (*Proceedings of the British Academy*, vol. LVI, pp. 3–16.) She says that
she feels an "uneasiness about morality," and adds that "there is some element
of fiction and strain in what we say about right and wrong" and that these "are
even reflected in the forms of language that we use" (p. 3). Moreover, Mrs. Foot
goes on to call for a "conceptual revision" of morality. What Mrs. Foot has
failed to realize, I think, is that what she thinks of as morality—as the essence
of morality—consists only of those features of our culture from which I have
fashioned my account of Despond. Rather than calling for a "conceptual revision" of morality, she ought to be calling for is a saner society, something akin
to Islandia. That she has failed to realize this is precisely what interests me about
the philosophers of Despond: much of their philosophizing about morality is the
upshot of (i) their living in a morally dysfunctional society, (ii) their failing to
realize this, and (iii) their belief that the essence of morality is what they find in
their own society. This is why they can neither answer nor drop the question
"Why should I be moral?" Their compulsive pottering with that question is part
of their socio-philosophical pathology.

14. *Collected Papers of Charles Sanders Peirce*, eds. Charles Hartshorne and
Paul Weiss (Cambridge, Mass.: Harvard University Press, 1931), vol., I para,
666. Quoted by Arthur Murphy, *The Theory of Practical Reason* (Open Court:
La Salle, Ill. 1964), p. 187.

15. G. E. M. Anscombe has said something relevant to this point. She observes that because "of the dominance of Christianity for many centuries, the
concepts of being bound, permitted, or excused became deeply embedded in our
language." And yet

> to have a *law* conception of ethics is to hold that what is needed for
> conformity to virtue . . . is [that it be] required by divine law. Naturally
> it is not possible to have such a conception [of ethics] unless you believe
> in God as a law-giver. But if such a conception is dominant for many
> centuries and is then given up, it is a natural result that the concepts of
> "obligation," of being bound or required as by law, should remain though
> they had lost their root. . . .
>
> It is as if the notion "criminal" were to remain when criminal law and
> criminal courts had been abolished and forgotten. . . . The situation, if I

am right, was the interesting one of the survival of a concept [i.e., the concept of moral obligation] outside the framework of thought that made it a really intelligible one.

Because of this state of affairs, Anscombe makes the following recommendation: "The concepts of obligation, and duty—*moral* obligation and *moral* duty, that is to say—and [the concept] of what is *morally* right and wrong, and of the *moral* sense of 'ought,' ought to be jettisoned if this is psychologically possible; because they are survivals, or derivatives from survivals, from an earlier conception of ethics which no longer generally survives, and are only harmful without [that conception]" ("Modern Moral Philosophy," reprinted in *Ethics*, eds. Judith J. Thomson and Gerald Dworkin [New York: Harper and Row, 1968], pp. 192–93, 186).

Sartre's saying that everything "is permitted" would be an example of the harm Anscombe most likely had in mind. For Sartre meant that if God does not exist, then there can be no sort of morality.

16. Occasionally one can see these very different features of our culture clashing with one another in the writings of philosophers. See, for example, Cora Diamond, "Anything but Argument," *Philosophical Investigations*, vol. 5, no. 1 (January, 1982), pp. 23–41.

17. This idea in its most general form is known as "linguistic relativism." I have criticized this idea in detail in my essays "Whorf's Linguistic Relativism, I," *Philosophical Investigations*, vol. 1, no. 1, pp. 1–30, and "Whorf's Linguistic Relativism, II," *Philosophical Investigations*, vol. 1, no. 2, pp. 1–37.

18. *The Sovereignty of Good*, pp. 32–33.

19. John Howard Griffin, *Black Like Me* (New York: New American Library, 1962). Griffin, a Caucasian, darkened his skin and traveled through the southern United States in 1959 posing as a black man in order to record and publish his experience with racism. Those who have read the book are likely to recall Griffin's account of the white man's "hate stare," which he first encountered when he tried to buy a bus ticket in New Orleans:

> I walked up to the ticket counter. When the lady ticket-seller saw me, her otherwise attractive face turned sour, violently so. This look was so unexpected and so unprovoked I was taken aback.
>
> "What do you want?" she snapped.
>
> Taking care to pitch my voice to politeness, I asked about the next bus to Hattiesburg.
>
> She answered rudely and glared at me with such loathing I knew I was receiving what the Negroes call "The hate stare." It was my first experience with it. It is far more than the look of disapproval one occasionally gets. This was so exaggeratedly hateful I would have been amused if I had not been so surprised.

After buying a bus ticket—which the ticket-seller threw at him, together with his change, so that he had to stoop and pick it up from the floor—he looked about for an appropriate place to wait for the bus. Then,

> Once again a "hate stare" drew my attention like a magnet. It came from a middle-aged, heavy-set, well-dressed white man. He sat a few yards away, fixing his eyes on me. Nothing can describe the withering horror of this. You feel lost, sick at heart before such unmasked hatred, not so

much because it threatens you as because it shows humans in such an inhuman light. You see a kind of insanity, something so obscene the very obscenity of it (rather than its threat) terrifies you. It was so new I could not take my eyes from the man's face. I felt like saying: "What in God's name are you doing to yourself?" (pp. 52–53)

This was not, Griffin discovered, a rare event:

The hate stare was everywhere practiced, especially by women of the older generation. On Sunday, I made the experiment of dressing well and walking past some of the white churches just as services were over. In each instance, as the women came through the church doors and saw me, the "spiritual bouquets" changed to hostility. The transformation was grotesque. In all of Montgomery only one woman refrained. She did not smile. She merely looked at me and did not change her expression (p. 117).

I am suggesting that if Islandians, in their early, Antagonian phase had been confronted with similarly revealing descriptions of themselves, these might have forced them—or some of them—to critically evaluate their ways of thinking.

Chapter 19

1. Reynolds v. United States, 98 U.S. 145 (1879).

2. In parts of the southern United States, school boards dominated by Christian conservatives have ordered teachers to emphasize that the culture of the United States is superior to all others. This is a rather odd claim inasmuch as the United States is something of a cultural hodgepodge, but that difficulty is to be overcome, apparently, by declaring that this is a Christian nation (or Christian as conservatives understand this). Even so, one may wonder how these board members acquired sufficient knowledge of the world's other cultures, including the most remote, to be sure that their own is superior. The answer, of course, is that they do not claim familiarity with other cultures; it is enough, they think, that theirs is a Christian culture, which trumps being heathen or pagan every time.

3. A separate question arises here. How should people who are religiously committed regard the relation of their own moral views to other people? Plainly, they are not going to abandon their view that, as Congressman Dannemeyer puts it, their religion sets forth standards meant to "govern people in any society." Thus, those who, on religious grounds, oppose the use of contraceptives for preventing pregnancy will continue to think that the use of contraceptives is a sin. Some of these people may also believe it to be their duty to proselytize and win converts to this view of contraception. But if they are citizens of a democracy, rather than a theocracy, they ought, as citizens, to take the position that the government must remain neutral, that it should not interfere with the use of contraceptives by those who see nothing wrong in doing so. And the same goes for other matters, such as abortion: Those who, on religious grounds, would refuse to abort a fetus, ought to insist that those who do not share their religious views should be allowed the choice of abortion. The justification for their taking this position would be that if there is a divine prohibition against abortion and the use of contraceptive devices, this is something be-

lieved, rather than something that anyone can *know*. Even in a democracy, however, there will be religious zealots who deny that the government should remain neutral in such matters. This is what we see happening in the United States today. Christian conservatives complain bitterly about the religious neutrality of the federal government, arguing that it is an atheistic myth that the U.S. Constitution erects a "wall of separation" between government and religion, especially their own religion. Those among them who understand the logic of their position maintain, although not very publicly, that the United States is a theocracy. This is the position taken by the small but enormously influential Christian Reconstructionist movement, founded by Rousas J. Rushdoony. Democracy, according to Rushdoony, is a heresy: Christians are intended by God to take "dominion" over all aspects of society and reign until Jesus Christ returns. All civil law must be based on a fundamentalist reading of the Old Testament legal code, so that blasphemers, atheists, homosexuals, and incorrigible children are to be executed—by stoning, according to some members of the movement. Gary Demar, head of the avowedly Reconstructionist group American Vision, wrote recently in *Biblical World View*: "God does not tolerate rival religions, and neither should we" (quoted in *Church and State*, vol. 49, no. 3 [March 1996], p. 9). As I write there are two bills before Congress to amend the U. S. Constitution in such a way as to allow religion to breach the wall of separation between church and state: the so-called "Religious Equality Amendment" (H.J. Res. 121) and the so-called "Religious Liberties Amendment" (H.J. Res. 127). The sponsors of these bills are not, of course, Hindus, Jews, or Muslims. They are Republican Congressmen Henry Hyde of Illinois and Ernest Istook of Oklahoma. The first of these bills is supported by the National Association of Evangelicals and the Christian Legal Society and the second by the Christian Action Network. Pat Robertson's Christian Coalition says it will support whichever amendment emerges as the leading proposal. If, of course, the United States can be transformed by such constitutional amendments into a theocracy, Christians who oppose abortion can, as good citizens, force all others to comply and can stone homosexuals to death in the public square. But in doing so they will not have refuted moral relativism. On the contrary, they will have made the case for relativism more plausible.

4. Stuart Hampshire, in his essay "The Interpretation of Language: Words and Concepts," (in *British Philosophy in the Mid-Century*, ed. C. A. Mace [London: Allen and Unwin, 1957]) was perhaps the first to state the criticism in just this form. He begins the essay by remarking that "there are many languages, constantly changing and widely different from each other, not only in vocabulary, but also in structure" (p. 267). This leads him to conclude that it would be a "mistake" for philosophers to "try to deduce philosophical conclusions from the description of a few English idioms" (p. 268). Why a mistake? Because, says Hampshire, philosophical conclusions are statements about what there is (or is not) in the world (he instances Gilbert Ryle's denying the existence of acts of will) and because when a philosopher undertakes to reject one of several possible languages or terminologies "on the grounds that its classifications are 'inadequate to the complexity of the facts,' " (p. 276) the philosophical problem "always lies in the choice, and in the grounds for the choice" of one language over another (p. 272). He concludes that although "the mere plotting of the

ordinary use of words . . . is a necessary check upon philosophy, . . . it is not philosophy itself" (p. 279).

Chapter 20

1. Arthur Murphy, *The Theory of Practical Reason* (Open Court: La Salle, Ill. 1964), p. 338.

2. "Watching Rights," *The Nation*, vol. 257, no. 1 (July 5, 1993), p. 7.

3. "Statement on Human Rights," *American Anthropologist*, n.s. vol. 49 (October–December 1947), pp. 539, 543.

4. *The Theory of Practical Reason*, pp. 364–65.

Appendix A

1. Originally published in *Contemporary Review* (January 1877). Reprinted in *Religion from Tolstoy to Camus*, ed. Walter Kaufmann (New York: Harper, 1961).

Appendix B

1. *Our Knowledge of the External World* (London: George Allen and Unwin, 1926), pp. 240–42.

Index